In the House of the Serpent Handler

JULIA C. DUIN

IN THE
HOUSE
OF THE
SERPENT
HANDLER

A Story of Faith
and Fleeting Fame
in the Age
of Social Media

The University of Tennessee Press
Knoxville

24.95

Some of the material in this book originally appeared in articles the author wrote for the *Washington Post, CNN.com,* and the *Wall Street Journal.*

LIBRARY OF CONGRESS CATALOGING-IN-PUBLICATION DATA
Names: Duin, Julia, author.
Title: In the house of the serpent handler:
a story of faith and fleeting fame in the age of social media / Julia C. Duin.
Description: First [edition]. | Knoxville: University of Tennessee Press, 2017. |
Includes bibliographical references and index. |
Identifiers: LCCN 2017004055 (print) | LCCN 2017048213 (ebook) | ISBN 9781621903772 (Kindle)
| ISBN 9781621903765 (pdf) | ISBN 9781621903758 (pbk.)
Subjects: LCSH: Snake cults (Holiness churches)—Appalachian Region, Southern—
History. | Wolford, Mack, d. 2012. | Hamblin, Andrew. | Coots, Jamie, d. 2014.
Classification: LCC BX7990.H6 (ebook) | LCC BX7990.H6 D85 2017 (print) | DDC 289.9—dc23
LC record available at https://lccn.loc.gov/2017004055

To Jamie, Mack, and Seth:
two serpent handlers and a journalist
who left us way too soon

CONTENTS

ILLUSTRATIONS

Liz Hamblin and Her Three Boys Announce
Baby Hamblin Number Six

The Hamblin children

Jacob Gray, Michelle Gray, and Andrew Abrams
at a Homecoming Reception in May 2014

Jonathan Gray, Andrew Hamblin, and Paul Gray at a Homecoming
at the LaFollette, Tennessee, church, May 24, 2014

Tyler Evans Handles Two Copperheads

Michelle Gray, Jullian Evans, and Elizabeth Hamblin

Nathan Evans Handles a Rattlesnake

Veeka Duin Worships during a Service at the Church
of the Lord Jesus in Jolo, West Virginia

Taylor Noe Looks on as Andrew Hamblin Handles
Two Copperheads

Adam and Elizabeth Hensley

Taylor Noe handles fire as Her Husband Places
His Hand on Her Back

ACKNOWLEDGMENTS

I wish to thank the many people who helped me with this project, starting with the serpent handlers who welcomed me into their lives and spent time explaining why they do what they do. Michelle and Madison Gray and Linda Spoon were particularly helpful, along with Jamie and Linda Coots, Jimmy and Pam Morrow and Andrew and Elizabeth Hamblin, all of whom (with their families) spent significant amounts of time allowing me to interview them and pick their brains.

Much appreciation is also due to scholars such as Ralph Hood of the University of Tennessee/Chattanooga, who gave me instructions on how to get to serpent-handling church homecomings, helped me find sources and spent hours explaining to me this century-old custom. Ralph was also part of my master's project committee, along with David Arant and Joe Hayden from the University of Memphis journalism department. All of these men gave me valuable support. Jenna Gray-Hildenbrand of Middle Tennessee State University, with whom I roomed while covering snake handler court hearings, also offered encouragement.

Many thanks to John Morgan, Allison Biggers, Bob Smietana, John-David Hatch and Greg Daniel, who either provided photos, served as sounding boards, or monitored Facebook during times when I could not.

And finally, many, many thanks to the folks at the University of Tennessee Press who believed in this book and took a chance on me.

CHAPTER ONE

CUT OFF FROM THE LAND OF THE LIVING

Mack Wolford began the last day of his life by selecting an olive-colored shirt.

It was his snake shirt. He'd often worn it before venturing out to handle snakes and trying to win people for the Lord. Once a photographer had spotted him in it and used the shirt as a backdrop for a greenish timber rattlesnake that clung to him like a glistening emerald necklace.

On came some dark gray pants, and then Mack, who was also known as Randy, stepped into a guest bedroom to pick out his snakes. The walls of the room were pale yellow, and cases of vipers were everywhere, including a yellow timber rattler he'd handled numerous times. Into the snake box it went, snake boxes being ingenious gift-box-sized contraptions with hinges and handles and Plexiglas tops so you could see which reptile was inside. There were hinges in the middle of the glass that allowed one side to open up like a small door when the handler wanted to take the snake out. Mack had a bunch of snakes—assembled like rows of murderous coiled-up belts—that he proudly showed off on his Facebook page.

He had to be off before the day got so hot that the air would quiver. Mack headed northwest from Bluefield, a town of about ten thousand souls in southern West Virginia just off I-77. The town was not always so humble. A century before, armies of men were busy mining the world's largest and richest deposit of bituminous coal located in the Pocahontas coalfields in the three counties surrounding Bluefield. It was a town that some had compared to New York for its skyline and the bounteous homes of the rich who ran the mines that helped fuel two world wars. Forty million tons of coal came out of the Bluefield region during World War I alone. During World War II, 40 percent of the country's coal supply came from local coal fields. But that was then. Today's Bluefield was rundown and sad. Mack was headed out on Route 52, a meandering road that led through isolated towns like Welch and Iaeger, which also had that boarded-up look from years of neglect and poverty.

It was May 27, 2012, a Sunday. Church that day would be held eighty miles to the west at a picnic shelter.

It was going to be a service with snakes. Mack loved handling all varieties of cottonmouths, copperheads, and canebrake and timber rattlers during worship services. "Handling" meant hoisting a coiled-up reptile in the air with one hand while dancing, shouting, preaching, or some combination of all three. And these were not just any snakes but the venomous, one-bite-and-you're-dead kind. Because if you're going to obey the Bible, that means the *whole* Bible, even the part at the end of the Gospel of Mark that says believers shall handle poisonous snakes and speak in tongues and heal people and drink deadly poison. Not maybe. Not perhaps. But *shall* handle them.

Mack had rented a pavilion at the Panther Wildlife Management Area, which the locals called Panther Park. This being Memorial Day weekend, when folks would be out in the woods picnicking and hiking, the idea was to have a worship band attract some unconverted onlookers. Mack would adroitly wave about a few reptiles hoping to convince everyone by this show of power that they needed to accept Jesus.

"Back in the Bible, it was the miracles that drew people to Christ," he had told one of the many reporters who had made their way to West Virginia to report on the phenomenon of Pentecostal serpent handlers. They'd been practicing their religion in Appalachia for a century, and here it was 2012 and they weren't going away. Mack was one of a new breed of handlers who wanted to take the custom out of its mountain home and make it known to America at large. One way was to visit public places, like the state park to which he was headed. He'd gotten a small crowd last year. If more folks showed up this year, he figured he could start traveling more, maybe show some signs and wonders to the skeptical farther away from home. Today he needed some of the faithful to group themselves about the pavilion so that passersby would check to see what everyone was looking at. He had started beating the bushes a few days earlier on Facebook, encouraging people to show up and joking at those who thought he was crazy as a loon.

Hey, brother, he wrote to Andrew Hamblin, a young serpent handler in Tennessee, *I got us a nice quart jar of Koolaid fixed for the service, brother.*

Andrew, who was all of twenty, was too young to know that poisoned Kool-Aid—or something like it—had killed more than nine hundred people at a cultic Christian commune known as Jonestown in Guyana back in 1979.

Mack continued to toot his own horn.

I am getting primed up, my brothers and sisters, he wrote on May 22, a Tuesday. *I am looking for a great time this Sunday. It is going to be a homecoming like the old days. Good 'ole raised-in-the-holler or mountain-ridge-running, Holy Ghost-filled speaking-in-tongues sign believers.*

He added, *Just letting everyone know we will be having our homecoming service this Sunday around 1:00 at Panther Park. It will be held at the one they call Sandy Bottom [a picnic area]. Everyone welcome; we will be having brothers and sisters from at least 6 states this year.*

On May 23, he had written to a friend, *Praise the Lord and pass the rattlesnakes, brother.* On Friday, May 25, he announced, *To all my brothers and sisters, T minus 40 hours and counting.* The next day, he turned forty-four.

The drive to the park took a while, as one could not speed on those winding roads through the mountains. About twenty people, including Mack's mother, Vicie Haywood, were gathered at the pavilion. Lauren Pond, a twenty-six-year-old photographer, had driven about four hundred miles from Washington, D.C., just to hang out and snap a few shots as part of a long-term project on Appalachia she was working on. Despite the humidity, the men there also had on long-sleeved shirts, obeying an unspoken rule among Appalachian Pentecostals that demanded men keep their arms covered. The women were wearing long skirts and long, unshorn hair, which is how they interpreted a particular biblical passage, 1 Peter 3, telling women not to braid their hair.

The musical band, featuring guitars, keyboard, and drums, swung into action. Mack began to preach on repentance. Vicie, who was wearing a red long-sleeved shirt despite the heat, had her silvery hair done up in a bun.

Her late husband, Mack Ray Wolford, had died at the age of thirty-nine on a Sunday afternoon in October 1983 after a snake bit him on the left arm. The younger Mack, then fifteen, had also watched his father's life grind to a close. But Vicie still believed. She even continued to handle snakes.

Gathered near Mack were some of the younger men to whom he was teaching the arts of serpent handling. One was Donald Dover, a pastor from North Carolina who was intrigued by this "signs following" religion based on the King James Version translation of Mark 16:17–18: "And these signs shall follow them that believe; in my name shall they cast out devils; they shall speak with new tongues; / They shall take up serpents; and if they drink any deadly thing, it shall not hurt them; they shall lay hands on the sick, and they shall recover."

Mack had spent a lot of time on the phone counseling younger pastors like Donald and Andrew and even those his own age who wanted to take up snakes but were frightened of the various state laws against it. Only in West Virginia was it legal to collect and handle poisonous snakes in church. Six other Appalachian states had a patchwork of laws forbidding the practice after snake-handling believers began dying of snakebite in church in the 1940s and 1950s. There were pastors in North Carolina he was visiting, and he was considering a trip to Texas to spread the practice there.

The group worshipped for about half an hour, and snakes were passed about. At one point, Mack even placed his yellow timber rattler on the ground so he could walk on it. Then he sat down. Few people saw the rattler twist around and bite Mack in the thigh.

Mack was not afraid. He'd lived through bites before. His hands were scarred from bites, and what it usually meant is that you were really sick for a few days. He would show people four spots on his right hand where copperheads had sunk their fangs. Snakebites typically attack the nervous system, rendering several fingers or even a whole hand gnarled and useless after the nerve endings have been fried. But these snake handlers did not seek antivenin medication. Their survival was testimony to God's power to heal. And if He didn't do so, then He was calling them home.

And so Mack defiantly continued to handle the rattler for several minutes before handing it off. Several people at the gathering weren't even aware he'd been bitten. But a bite on the thigh can go straight to the femoral artery that leads directly to the heart, and Mack began to falter. Several of the men clustered about and helped him sit down. Mack was sweating heavily and began to vomit. They put him by a garbage can, over which he wearily rested his head on one outstretched arm. By this time, the worshippers had stopped.

Mack made it known he needed to get to the men's room, so two of the men half-carried him there. By the time they returned, he was clearly in dire straits, as he could not walk. Donald hoisted his limp and inert friend in his arms and with the help of a second man carried Mack like a small child to a car. He whispered to Mack that he loved him and left him there to be driven back to Bluefield while he returned to Forest City, about sixty miles west of Charlotte, not knowing if he'd ever see Mack alive again. Everyone knew that Mack did not believe in seeking medical help for his bite, so instead of heading for the Bluefield Regional Medical Center, they caravanned to the home of his mother-in-law in a trailer park just north of town.

Once there, Mack was placed on a brown couch in the living room while friends started to gather at the house. A fan was placed at his feet; even so, Mack was burning hot and he stripped off his shirt. A bucket was placed next to him as he was now vomiting blood. Lauren had followed along and was quietly snapping photos. She caught Vicie, smothered in a hug from someone, her fearful eyes glancing over at her son. Lauren had eaten meals with Mack, had watched his videos about serpent handling, had even spent the night at his home the previous November. This was a friend writhing on the couch. Should she take matters into her own hands and call 911? she wondered. It was clear that no one in the trailer was going to call the medics unless Mack said yes, and he wasn't doing so. Every hour is precious when there's a venomous snakebite. If the stricken person receives antivenin within the first few hours, he can be saved. Or, Lauren asked herself, should she allow Mack to fight his last battle in the way he wished to fight it? He'd watched his father die. He knew the hell the next few hours would bring. He also believed that God could heal him.

A friend sat beside him strumming a guitar. The general mood lightened a bit later when Mack rallied, sipped some water, and attempted to stand. As word spread, more people came by, and the trailer got warmer. Family members removed as much of Mack's clothes as they could and sent someone to buy an extra air conditioner. Everyone was praying, including Vicie, an Appalachian Pietà who sat facing her son, stroking his bare feet.

Meanwhile, Facebook was lighting up, as people holding vigil near Mack were messaging friends in several states. Mack was known everywhere. It was inconceivable that he could pass. *Everyone please say a prayer for 2 brothers in the Lord they need all the prayers they can get. Lord please help,* messaged twenty-one-year-old Kasi Powers, a young woman who attended Andrew Hamblin's church in LaFollette, a town 250 miles west of Bluefield. It was now sometime after 5:00 p.m.

Two people were bitten by snakes that day. Also stricken was twenty-one-year-old Nathan Evans, the great-great-grandson of Barbara and Bob Elkins. The Elkinses were a legendary serpent-handling Pentecostal couple from Jolo, a West Virginia hamlet about eight miles south of the state park. Nathan had been handling a black rattlesnake at a Virginia church near the West Virginia state line. At first, people prayed for him. But when he began throwing up blood, he was taken to Richlands, the nearest city with a hospital, where he was stabilized and then flown to Bristol, a larger city on Interstate 81 on the Tennessee-Virginia state line. Friends drove his wife, Tiffany, to Bristol, where to her horror she discovered the inexperienced staff looking up snakebites on the internet and giving her husband antivenin for a cottonmouth bite.

Hearing of all this, Andrew and two friends—Silas Crawford and Daniel Powers, Kasi's husband—headed to Bristol to be near Nathan, who was going into anaphylactic shock. Then they started getting text messages about Mack. Silas turned to Andrew.

"I feel it in my gut," he said. "One will make it and one won't."

Andrew was feeling wretched. He'd planned to be at Mack's rally that day. He knew Mack would get a little carried away with snakes and would sometimes lie on them. He was hearing from someone at Mack's bedside that Mack had sat on this particular snake, and the reptile had retaliated by biting him on the thigh. There was a video on the internet showing Mack sitting on a poisonous snake, so the possibility wasn't unheard of. But Mack had kept this viper for four years, and lots of people had handled it. Why this snake and why now?

Back in Bluefield, things were getting grim inside the trailer. Mack was clearly fading, his breathing labored as he tossed and turned. About nine hours after he had been bitten, family members finally got Mack to consent for them to call for help. But by the time the paramedics arrived, it was too late. He was officially declared dead a few minutes into Monday morning.

Nathan Evans was in the ICU in Bristol, but he would survive. At midnight Sunday, Kasi messaged again: *Everyone please pray 4 a brother's family.*

He passed away just a little bit ago. My thoughts and prayers go out to the family. And please keep the other brother in your prayers.

Also at midnight, Andrew's wife, Liz, was also sending out messages: *Please say a prayer for a friend of my husband's. He just passed away. Lord come by and help his family.*

A handler named Joshua Southern asked if it was a mutual friend.

No, Randy Wolford, she said.

WHAT, what happen, was his reply.

He got bite in the hip, messaged Liz.

Oh Lord. He has been a good friend and preached many times for me, Southern responded. A few more people chimed in with shocked responses; then Southern—who had apparently been messaging other contacts in the meantime—volunteered that it was Mack's yellow timber rattler that had killed him. *I have handled it several times. It was about 4 1/2 feet,* he wrote. Meanwhile, Lauren, the photographer who had watched the whole thing happen while silently clicking away, couldn't sleep. Finally at 3:30 a.m., she posted: *Rest in peace, Mack. It was a pleasure getting to know you. Thank you for welcoming me into your life and helping me understand the Signs Following faith.*

At 7:28 a.m., Lauren decided to contact a freelance reporter with whom she had worked the previous summer on a lengthy profile of Mack and the serpent-handling movement. The profile appeared in the *Washington Post Magazine* that November.

I'm sorry I haven't responded to your emails in awhile, but I thought you should know, if you haven't heard already, that Mack Wolford died last night from a rattlesnake bite, she wrote. *I'm here in Bluefield and still processing things. I'm somewhat in shock. I feel terrible about the whole thing.*

The message sped four hundred miles east to Hyattsville, a hip Maryland suburb just north of Washington, D.C. I was standing in the aisle of a Home Depot, ordering $1,100 worth of grey boards to rebuild my sagging and rotting porch. It was hot and muggy.

The contractor was loading the boards on a trolley when I glanced at my iPhone. Mack dead? The charming West Virginian we'd covered for that magazine piece on Pentecostal serpent handlers? Mack, who believed so strongly that the Bible ordered Christians to handle snakes that he was going to Texas to preach about it?

And now he would never get there.

CHAPTER TWO

OFF TO
TENNESSEE

● ●

I texted Lauren back.

I was there through the entire thing, she responded. *Very hard to watch, but at least he died with loved ones all around him. I will forever be grateful for his kindness and openness about the faith. I'm not sure when the wake/funeral will be, but I'm going to try to stay for it if I can.*

It was Memorial Day, but a reporter is never off duty. I had worked for twenty-five years for five newspapers, most recently fourteen years as religion editor and assistant national editor at the *Washington Times.* I'd been laid off in 2010, so I was picking up freelance gigs at the *Washington Post,* the *Wall Street Journal,* and the *Economist.* I got back in touch with Lauren via a very bad phone connection. I learned about the yellow timber rattler, how it bit him on the leg, how he stopped breathing just before midnight. It was beyond traumatizing for her to watch it all go down.

I asked her to go over the day once more: what the worship band was like and what happened immediately after Mack was bit. I asked her how he did after the bite. She said he was as good as anyone could expected to be after such a nip, and then her line went dead. Great.

I knew the *Post* would want to jump on this because of the huge piece Lauren and I had done on him only eight months before. I got through to Beth Chang, my editor at the *Post Magazine,* for whom I'd been writing for the past eighteen months. She suggested I do a lengthy blog post. Instructing the contractor to begin working on my porch, I returned home, went upstairs, and began working the phones.

First I called the *Bluefield Daily Telegraph* and got hold of their weekend police guy, Bill Archer, a sixty-two-year-old veteran reporter who joked that his weekend was pretty quiet until I called. He told me that Panther Park was about an hour and forty-five minutes down Route 52 from Bluefield, just west of Iaeger. I'd driven the route the summer before and remembered how hilly and isolated the area was. When we talked again an hour later, he told me the Bluefield Regional Medical Center had confirmed Mack's death in the early hours of May 28, but it was plain that Mack was dead on arrival.

I called Andrew, who was clearly shaken.

"I was supposed to be there but something came up where I couldn't go," he said. "Randy would get overly excited with them. It was that yellow rattler he had for so long. He sat on it and it bit him in the thigh. He's lain on them. He had sat on it before. He had it for four years. It was handled and handled. It was one of those snakes you think it won't bite. It was a good handling snake people feel good with."

Then he told me about Silas Crawford's odd prediction that one person would die and the other would survive. But Andrew was refusing to budge from Mark 16:17–18.

"It devastated me, Miss Julia. It just shook my very foundation," he confessed. "But it is still the Word of God." He added that he'd just gotten a "monster rattler," three southern copperheads, and seven cottonmouths for use in his services.

Meanwhile, Lauren was refusing to release to the *Post* any photos of Mack after he was bitten. She was not amused to learn I was working on a story about his last hours partly gleaned from the information she'd given me. That, she informed me in a message left on my phone, had not been for publication. Moreover, the *Post* would have to use photos from the previous story we'd done on Mack as she was too distraught to give them any newer ones. Maybe in a few weeks, she added.

However, I knew that personal trauma had to be set aside when news happened. Lauren had been the only photojournalist around that day, so she had a goldmine of first-hand information that no one else had. Someone in that position would typically call a news outlet right away and pitch the story as an exclusive. Instead, Lauren had called me. I felt the world needed to know about Mack's willingness to die rather than compromise his faith. I also knew that such a story couldn't wait a few weeks and that it had to hit the news cycle within a day or two—and certainly before the funeral—to get any traction.

Fortunately, Lauren had given me the phone number of Mack's sister, Robin Vanover. Late that Monday night, I felt an inner urge to contact her right then instead of waiting until the next day. I felt like a vulture, but my years as a police reporter had taught me that sources talk best within the first twenty-four hours. After that, they shut down, especially as more media calls pour in.

Robin sounded exhausted. Mack, she told me, was "real excited" about the service and had been preparing for it for some time. I asked her about her brother sitting on the snake, and she indignantly told me he had not sat on it; he had placed the snake on the ground and sat *next* to it. Then the snake bit him.

That sounded odd to me. I'd been following snake handlers for about nine months and had never heard of a handler doing such a thing. They would sit or step on the reptile to show God's mastery over the snakes. I asked her if others in the family handled snakes, and she said only Vicie did.

"At one time or another, we had [all] handled," she said, "but we had backslid." Pentecostals believe that if you're in sin, it's dicey at best to put yourself in mortal danger, as God is not bound to protect those who are estranged from him. I asked another question but she cut off the conversation, saying there were people who needed to talk with her. She promised to call back soon, but after an hour went by and she didn't, I called her several times. She did not answer. Still, the conversation was productive; she confirmed some basic information and had given me some much-needed quotes. Finally near midnight, I sent the story to Beth.

Tuesday morning, I was out on a freelance assignment for the *Wall Street Journal,* so it wasn't until I checked my email that afternoon that I learned the *Post* wanted me to revise the story. Their deadline was 6:00 p.m. At this point, it was close to 3:00. They wanted to run it Wednesday morning in the print version atop the Style section, one of the best spots in the paper. Beth wanted me to wring more details out of Lauren, but Lauren was vague on specifics and said she was thinking of writing her own interpretation of what had happened.

"I didn't see the bite," she told me. "I saw the aftermath." Her dilemma was that the family allowed her to be near where Mack was dying on the premise that she was there as a documentary photographer with the photos coming out months or years later. Her role had not been as a daily news reporter. She was still there in Bluefield. If she released those photos, the family would know where they came from the moment they ran in the *Post* on Wednesday morning. What if they got angry with her and cut off all future access? So she refused to release photos of Mack's last hours for my piece.

I raced through interminable fact-checking, contacting more snake handlers for missing details, calling the ambulance people to find out when Mack was transported, phoning officials at Panther Park as well as other tasks difficult to do when one is several hundred miles away. The story, which went up mid-evening on Tuesday, May 29, with photos from the previous magazine article, went viral. By Wednesday morning, it was trending as the number-one story on the *Post*'s site. I was getting calls from the local news station WTOP, the BBC, and NPR. *USA Today* picked up my story in a blog. So did the Drudge Report. Even my journalist brother, Steve, picked it up for the *Oregonian*. My parents, who live just east of Seattle, were delighted to see my byline in the *Seattle Times*. The phone rang all day. One of the callers was Lauren, who demanded I send some of the interview opportunities her way. But I was done with them by the time she called. Plus, she did not tell me she was writing a story herself for *Style*. I later learned she had wanted to write Wednesday's story, but Beth told her I was already on it. Twenty-four hours after the *Post* put my story up on their site, the article was still number one, with 1,254 comments. It was the biggest story in my entire career.

CNN's Belief Blog asked me to do a story, which got more than 6,500 comments less than twenty-four hours after being posted. On Friday, *Style* ran Lauren's story about the ethical dilemmas facing a photographer forced to watch someone die after he refused medical help. That's where I learned that Mack may have also ingested a highly toxic mix of water and strychnine sometime during the service. Serpent handlers will do this during services to act out the portion of Mark 16 promising that Christians shall not be hurt if they drink poison.

Her striking photos showed Mack just after he was bitten, still clutching the snake; Mack, his eyes half closed, being held up by two men; Mack being carried to his car; Mack face down on a sofa, shirtless, with a vomit bucket beside him and his mother, Vicie, caressing his feet. What must this woman think after losing her husband in 1983 this way—watching him die for ten hours—and then, twenty-nine years later, her oldest son? The Wolford family didn't think much of the shirtless photo. I learned from Beth that they contacted the *Post*, demanding that photo be removed. Apparently Holiness Pentecostal men aren't supposed to go shirtless even if they've died.

Meanwhile I was tracking Andrew and his wife, Liz, through Facebook as their van continually broke down while they drove to the funeral. Liz sent out messages every few minutes detailing their woes. Andrew would be one of the men who preached at Mack's funeral, which was closed to the media, forcing Lauren to wait outside. And over his grave they would handle snakes, just to show the devil who was boss.

The following Tuesday, I was on a plane to Memphis. Union University, a Southern Baptist–affiliated school in Jackson, a small city some eighty miles east of Memphis, had been wooing me to come work for them as a journalism professor. I'd been out of work for two years at this point, so having an institution discover me at the last minute and put me on the fast track for a job in a profession I'd been wanting to enter was sweet indeed. It didn't hurt that my byline had been floating about in some of the country's top papers and websites during the past week. The interviews were a success. Faculty, staff, and students all said they wanted me to come. They sent me a contract by FedEx that I signed on June 8. In twenty-four hours, I cleaned and staged my home, then took off for a ten-day vacation with my seven-year-old daughter while the real estate agent showed off my 101-year-old house. It sold in two weeks.

Clearly, my future was in Tennessee.

CHAPTER THREE

JOLO

Nine months before Mack died, I was quite frightened at the thought of taking my then six-year-old daughter to a church of Pentecostals who worshipped with a rattlesnake in one hand and a Bible in the other. I didn't say much to her grandparents about where we were going. All Veeka knew was that we were racing down I-81 toward the mountains and that Mommy was taking her along on one of her newspaper assignments. I'd started freelancing for the *Post* in the fall of 2011, landing a piece in its Sunday magazine that December. More assignments followed, including one the following June about an outdoor convention of Christian anarchists. That is how I met Lauren, the freelance photographer assigned to the event, as she and I slogged through a soybean field in southeastern Pennsylvania for a few days.

She told me of her fascination with backwoods Appalachia, having hung out with retired coal miners and stayed in their homes. She began documenting the grave-digging going on because of the black lung and cancer that afflicted folks in the southernmost corner of West Virginia. But there was one thing in that region that was totally outside the realm of her experience: snake handling. Some of the West Virginians were Pentecostals who believed the Bible called for Christians, as a sign of faith, to handle poisonous snakes.

She wanted to pitch a magazine piece on these people but needed a writer who knew theology. I was thirty years her senior and had a master's degree in religion with a concentration in theology. The snake handling creeped me out, but my funds were low and the *Post* agreed to pay for a five-day trip for the two of us to the middle of nowhere. On a rainy, misty afternoon just before Labor Day weekend, Veeka and I set out.

Night fell early that evening and we arrived late in Bluefield, the last city of any meaningful size before you hit serious Appalachian territory where the tourists never go. It was a 420-mile schlep west of the Beltway to the southernmost part of West Virginia, where coal once was king. Today's Bluefield had seen better days, and we were driving past gas stations and motels that looked the same as they had decades before. We were on our way to Jolo, an unincorporated hamlet of 1,191 residents that was home to the world's most famous serpent-handing church.

The next day, I stood atop a 2,200-foot-high ridge on the Virginia state line overlooking scenery out of a seventeenth-century Italian landscape painting: sandstone cliffs, steep hillsides cloaked with green against distant horizons of smoky blue ridges. Once I descended into West Virginia on the serpentine curves of Route 83, reality set in. Aside from a few nicely kept residences, the rest were a depressing array of homes with cardboard-covered windows, rows of closed shops, and piles of abandoned belongings alongside the road. Jolo's mines had tapped out forty years ago. What was left were mostly the drugged-out, the unemployed, the retired. Of the country's 2,992 counties, McDowell County had been in the bottom five, in terms of abysmal-life expectancy rates, for years. McDowell was not only the state's poorest county, but for two decades it had been number one in "domestic migration"—a nice way of describing the many people who had left town. This was new territory for me. For years I had skied and hiked about Randolph, Pendleton, and Pocahontas Counties in the state's far prettier and touristy northern half. I'd heard stories about the *other* West Virginia that lay mostly south of I-64: where mountaintop removal was ravaging the landscape, where people lived in shacks. For me, a creature from inside the Beltway, coming here was like being dropped onto another planet.

McDowell County was fifty to sixty miles from several eastern Kentucky counties I'd biked through as a college student. My biking group had enjoyed a problem-free ride through western Virginia, but I'd no sooner entered Harlan County than a man exposed himself to me. A group of men in a pick-up who were following me up one mountain were so menacing that I flagged down an oncoming car and asked them to go for help. And then there was the guy who parked on a country road in the path of my bike and just stood there, waiting to attack or rape me, or both. He did nothing, which at the time I attributed to the Scripture quotation on the back of my shirt that mentioned guardian angels.

More than thirty years later, I hoped I'd see a kinder and friendlier Appalachia. I reached a post office and a grimy Marathon gas station, which seemed to be the only functioning businesses in town, then took a right on Route 635. Two miles up the road appeared the Church of the Lord Jesus, a plain white rectangular building perched on a narrow slip of land on the left side of the road precariously close to a ravine.

The gravel parking lot by the church was tiny. Veeka and I walked into the sanctuary. The Bible verses on the wall included these cheerful admonitions: *For whatsoever a man soweth, that shall he also reap. And be sure your sin will find you out.* Strings of red and white Christmas lights decorated the cross on the front wall of the church. The bright olive-green pews were beneath tiny opaque windows. I learned later that the windows used to be bigger, but vandals would continually break them.

I strolled about, taking notes. On the left wall of the church near the front was a photo gallery of past homecomings. Nearly everyone shown was brandishing handfuls of snakes. One photo showed a woman holding what looked like a Coke bottle filled with kerosene and a burning wick. Then I noticed she was holding the flame to her hand.

"She won't do that unless she's in the Spirit," a man in a striped blue shirt and white cowboy boots informed me. He was Lyndon Salyers, fifty, a local carpenter and gravedigger, who explained that "handling fire" stemmed from Isaiah 43:2, which talks about believers walking through fire and not getting burned.

"It's a faith that's worth dying for," he told me.

And people had died for it there. The Jolo church was founded in 1956 by Bob and Barbara Elkins. He was a coal miner, and she was the mother of six children from a previous marriage that had lasted nineteen years until she couldn't take the wife beating anymore.

Once Bob and Barbara married, they were a magnetic combination. Their church was into "signs following," a scriptural phrase, also from Mark, telling insiders that the congregation is open to the miraculous signs listed in

Mark 16: tongues, healing, snakes, exorcism, and poison. Trouble hit five years later when one of Barbara's daughters, Columbia Hagerman, died of snakebite at the age of twenty-three. Columbia had been handling a yellow timber rattlesnake at church, but after she was bitten, she refused medical help. It took her four days to die. She left behind a nine-year-old daughter, Lydia. As Columbia was divorced and her ex-husband had remarried, the grandparents adopted her child. The resulting uproar led the state house of representatives to approve a law criminalizing snake handling. Bob Elkins marshaled members of his family to appear before members of the legislature in Welch, the county seat, to argue they had a religious right to handle snakes. The law never made it out of the state senate, and thus snake handling remains legal in West Virginia. Several other Appalachian states, such as North Carolina, Virginia, Kentucky, and Tennessee, outlawed it on the grounds that public safety is more important than religious practice.

The couple relocated their church to its present location in the early 1980s. It had been in a much smaller building before then, although its size didn't hinder the crowds of onlookers who packed the place to view the believers' unorthodox religious practices. The state police were around as well, not to monitor the service or arrest anyone but to handle the traffic. Not only were there snakes, but adherents were also drinking poison to prove their faith. Barbara died in 1999, Bob died in 2007, and the two are buried just down the road in a small hillside plot. In 2011, the sign on the church still bore Bob's name as pastor.

The current reverend, however, was the forty-year-old Harvey Payne, a thickly built man with a slight mustache and blond hair. He worked as a timber cutter clearing roads for CNX Gas, a major producer of the plentiful natural gas in the region. He had posted a hand-lettered statement in front of the church near the pulpit: *The pastor and congregation are not responsible for anyone that handles the serpents and gets bit. If you get bit, the church will stand by you and pray with you. And the same goes with drinking the poison.*

Then Mack Wolford walked in, carrying a curious-looking wooden box with a lock on it and a glassed-in top with air holes. Inside was a sandy-colored rattlesnake. Dressed in a green shirt and blue-and-green-striped tie, Mack was a one-man snake-handling Chamber of Commerce, and Lauren had briefed me that he was someone I should concentrate on. He would commute a hundred miles to services at Jolo from Bluefield. His slithery pets—rattlers, water moccasins, and copperheads—were fed rats and mice from the pet store. With bushy eyebrows and a shock of brown hair that sometimes flopped onto his forehead in unruly bangs when he was excited, Mack looked like any one of the thousands of working-class men who inhabited those parts.

We talked, and I asked him who in his family also handles snakes.

"I have a couple of sisters who don't participate," he told me, "so it's just me and my mom. I am trying to keep this alive. Jesus said, 'When the Son of man comes, will he find any faith on Earth?' Anybody can do it that believes it. Jesus said, 'Those signs follow those who believe.' This is a sign to show people that God has the power."

But the snakes still bite, I reminded him, and he showed me four spots on his right hand where copperheads had buried their fangs.

"There's a lot of pain," he informed me. "For the first couple of weeks, you swell up and break out in hives."

"But isn't this tempting God?" I asked him.

"Tempting God is disbelief in God, not belief in Him," he answered.

Then he told me about how, at age fifteen, he saw his dad die of a rattlesnake bite in his left arm, which occurred during a service where people were handling snakes. Mack was now forty-three, but the memory was raw.

"He lived ten and a half hours," he remembered. "When he got bit, he said he wanted to die in the church. Three hours after he was bitten, his kidneys shut down. After a while, your heart stops. I hated to see him go, but he died for what he believed in."

Mack hit the wall after his father died, getting into crime and being arrested for armed robbery and kidnapping when he was eighteen. He spent a year and a half in jail. He was wedded to alcohol, which did in his first marriage. It was also destroying his second when he repented at the age of thirty "and God took the taste for alcohol away from me." He quit his job as a loom technician in a North Carolina cotton factory and since 1999 had been pastoring and evangelizing throughout Appalachia. Sadly for him, none of his children and step-children, he said, went to church, much less followed in his footsteps.

The service started at that point, even though there were only fifteen people present, including five photographers and a few reporters.

"It's a bit thin tonight," one of the leaders admitted, adding that the locals were at a funeral down the road. Cancer rates in this part of the state were sky high, and pastors often found themselves officiating at burials more than baptisms. Six of the male congregants eventually made their way to the front, picked up electric guitars, and blasted away for a good hour of country music before anyone felt anointed by God enough to "go to the box." One of the songs went as follows:

> They call us holy rollers
> Always poking fun
> They need to get the Holy Ghost
> And speak in other tongues.

I suddenly realized—after numbing repetitions of this and other phrases—that someone had just unlocked Mack's box and pulled out the snake, which twisted about as it was passed from man to man. The women clapped, and one tried handling the serpent but quickly handed it back. Harvey Payne posed for the cameras, the reptile twisting away but not biting.

"My life is on the line," he exulted, "all Holy Ghost power!"

Suddenly the snake disappeared back into the box and everyone sat for a sermon from Thomas Addair, a visiting sixty-year-old pastor from nearby Horsepen, Virginia. Dapper and sporting a purple shirt, he spent most of his time telling of his healing from esophageal cancer and exhorting listeners to believe in the miraculous.

"I thank God for strength to be here tonight," he said. "We're the old timers here. Someone's got to keep this thing going. We don't do the signs like we used to."

Lauren had found a hotel we could share, so my daughter and I followed her back up the mountain to our lodgings in Grundy, a forty-five-minute drive just over the Virginia state line. There was nowhere else closer to stay. Other than some Indian reservations I'd been on, I'd never seen a part of the country so devoid of creature comforts. We'd stopped at the gas station to get something to eat, but there were only a few unappetizing snacks. I'd heard of the term "food deserts" but had never driven through one until now. Saturday morning, we returned to Jolo to follow Mack up a mountain to see him hunting snakes. But when I got to the church, there was a team there from a radio show, and they didn't want my daughter on the trip. They were afraid a child's voice would ruin their taping. This was quite unethical, as it was Lauren and I who made the appointment with Mack to do the snake hunt and other journalists weren't supposed to butt in on our story. Or if they tagged along, they had to go along with our conditions. I was about to tell them what they could do with their stupid equipment until I snuck a look at Veeka, who was hot and miserable in her car seat. It was only 10:00 a.m., and the temperatures were soaring into the nineties. I knew she wouldn't last fifteen minutes hiking up some mountain. So we drove back to the hotel and puttered away the afternoon.

At the church that evening, I noticed the crowd had grown. Preaching was Pete Woods, a sixty-six-year-old grandfatherly figure in a black-and-white flannel shirt, who pastored the nondenominational Jesus Church in nearby Bartley. About thirty people go there on a good day. Years ago, 130 attended. "They all moved away," he said. "No jobs. No work." He spent much of his days digging graves for the poor.

"This is a dying county," he told me before the service. "Cancer, heart attacks, diabetes, a lot of overdoses on drugs. I think it's the natural gas wells; they sank our water table and put chemicals in our water." As for his three forty-something kids, "They're out of here. They were raised in church, but none go."

There were thirty-five people in church that night, eight of them photographers or journalists. The parking lot showed license plates from all the surrounding states and Louisiana. The hiss of the rattlers could be heard for several feet. The wooden boxes were buzzing tonight. Again, the music was ear-splitting, and we sang "I've got Jesus on my mind" over and over. People danced in place, including my daughter. I noticed no kids were allowed anywhere near the snake boxes.

Several women were near the front, spinning continuous circles like whirling dervishes. All had long, loose hair that swept well past their waists—no makeup or jewelry, not even a wedding ring. The women were utterly foreign to me and I to them. Although I was wearing a long skirt, my hair was trimmed, I wore tailored clothes, and I was a single mom, which none of them were. I fit in better with the informal scrum of journalists, photographers, videographers, and college professors who hung about these homecomings as chroniclers of this bizarre custom. Jolo was one of the few snake-handling churches that allowed media into its services. I never questioned why, although I think their reasoning was that they wanted to get the word out about the benefits of handling serpents. The foreign outlets especially loved any odd thing Americans did, and good photos of serpent handlers were an automatic placement in the zillions of photography contests out there. One of the men playing the tambourine up front was Professor Ralph Hood from the University of Tennessee at Chattanooga. He is probably the country's foremost expert on snake handlers. All I noticed at the time was his white beard and blue shirt.

Also among the journalists was Seth Williamson, a heavy-set, friendly man who was a columnist for the *Roanoke Times* and a producer for the NPR affiliate in Roanoke. He had heard of my earlier career as the religion editor at the *Times* and told me he admired my work, which appealed to my vanity to no end. He and his girlfriend, Susan Sanders, and I hit it off. Seth thought the music at Jolo was second to none, and a week or so later he wrote a paean to the songsters at Jolo, talking up the amazing performances on organ, guitar, banjo, and keyboards and likening them all to something between the Blues Brothers and Janis Joplin. I headed out the door at 11:00. I'd heard about the nighttime fogs and mists that sometimes hit these mountains, cutting off Jolo from the rest of civilization like some Appalachian Brigadoon, and the road back to Grundy was a precipitous one.

On Sunday some new folks had showed up, among them Joseph Hildebran, a nuclear medicine technologist from Morganton, North Carolina, who had a crew cut and wore wire rims. He wasn't into snake handling, "but I would if the Spirit moved on me," he told me. "There's not a lot of old saints to teach people. And the media has a lot to do with it. Who wants to come to church with your photo being taken all the time?" He said he'd handled fire—that is, denatured alcohol with a tiki torch wick stuck in a Coke bottle—but had never gotten burned.

"It is truly about your faith," he told me. "Pentecostalism as we know it is changing. People are making it more modern. They don't believe like they used to. I miss the old Pentecostalism."

Joseph, who was twenty-four, was the youngest person I'd seen there all weekend. He didn't think these practices were dying out but maybe moving underground.

"In all the states around here, it's illegal," he said. "In North Carolina, you go to jail. In Tennessee, there's a fine. A lot of people may not take up serpents in church, but they may in small home meetings."

I was getting more and more interested in how to find youth who did this sort of risky worship.

"If you want to find a lot of young people into this, eastern Kentucky is where it's at," said Joseph. "The main core Christianity there is Pentecostal, and they've had serpent handling there for years. I was at a huge tent meeting of five hundred people the other night. A tent preacher there said people think snake handlers are crazy, but you see power coming from those churches. People are getting hungry for it. They are ready for something different. We need something that's real where there's power. Maybe there's not as many young people handling serpents, but they are interested in it."

That service was the first time I'd seen the fire handling. Several people had lit the wicks atop Coke bottles, two of them spinning around while holding the flame to their hands. A man in a three-piece suit ripped off his socks and shoes as another worshipper applied the flames to the bottoms of his feet. Not surprisingly, the singing was about "the flame in my soul."

I nabbed the three-piece suit afterwards and examined his hands, which were not burned. He was from eastern Tennessee, and churches near him didn't do such tests of faith, he said, "So when we're offered it, we drive up here." When I asked him his occupation, he told me he was in banking.

Joseph too had handled fire that day. "I've never been burnt," he told me. "This is a way people know that Jesus is still living. It's the Holy Ghost on the inside of you that gives you that fire." When I asked him if he'd ever handled a snake, "The only time I have personally handled a serpent was when I walked out my back door, and there on my back porch was an ugly old copperhead," he said. "I felt I could reach down and pick up that snake. It went limp in my hands." So he threw it off his porch.

"My family thinks I am out of my mind but they love me," he confessed. "And when they need prayer, they call me. People are hungry. They say if you have enough faith to pick up serpents, we'll listen to these guys."

As a religion editor, I'd been covering Pentecostals and charismatics for years. Spiritual power had long since faded from their ranks, and they were continually searching for it like some long-lost chord. Did these serpent handlers know something those church leaders didn't? The service ended at about 4:00 p.m., and then everyone gathered in a grimy back room to eat a potluck supper of fried chicken, potato salad, and sugary desserts. I had to start back home, so I drove the back way through a rainstorm north toward Iaeger, which was eight miles north of Jolo on Route 52. The thunderclouds had moved in low, cutting off views of the tops of the jagged forested peaks that surrounded the area. I raced east along Route 52 toward Bluefield, seeking the closest thing to a freeway out of this wilderness before darkness fell. What looked jewel-like from above felt like a valley in the shadow of death below. The winding road through small hamlets like Northfork, Welch, and Maybeury revealed mostly boarded-up storefronts. The one exception was Bramwell, a small town just north of Bluefield that appeared loaded with Victorian-era homes. A century before, this town had more millionaires per capita than any other U.S. city. Route 52 put me somewhere in Bluefield, where I got lost in the downpour. Finally locating I-77, I headed north for an hour before pulling off at Beckley and calling it a night.

Arriving back in Washington, I immediately began work on the article. As I did some fact checking, I wanted to find out the age of the man in the three-piece suit. Though he was not listed in his hometown, his parents were, and they told me via phone that he was in his early thirties. When I told his mother about seeing her son at the church, I realized she hadn't known he was hanging out with the Pentecostals.

Apparently a small explosion ensued because, a few days later, I was getting frantic calls from both this man and his mother. Apparently he had been lying to them about what he did on weekends.

"My son is not in banking," the mother told me. "He doesn't even have a job. He won't work. He's had all kinds of jobs. He is married, he has a wife, and he has a little daughter. She's a beautiful little girl and it's his second wife and he is still very much married to her. He just left her and my little grandbaby. She's only nineteen months old."

The snake handling culture was dangerous, she added. In her view, its practitioners had mental problems. As for her son, he "certainly wasn't raised in this. He ran away and everything and he got mixed up in this and it's become a mess. I thought he got away from it but apparently he hasn't."

Then I heard from the son.

"I certainly hope you didn't give my parents any information about the church we were at," he pleaded. "Or people's names or phone numbers, addresses, or even the name of the church because you don't understand how they are. People in this area *hate* serpent-handling churches. It's not looked at as an oddity or some peculiar thing; they hate them, they persecute them. I've had to quit jobs, been fired from jobs, and been made fun of every day of my life because of that. My whole family fights me over it. I can't even have a normal relationship with them because of it. So, *please* disregard anything to do with me, and don't have any contact with my family."

Technically, I didn't have to do what he asked. Jolo's homecoming was open to the media, and believers knew that if they showed up there, their photos could be published. I had identified myself to this man as a reporter when we originally talked, and he knew he was on the record. But his name was incidental to the story, and I didn't wish to make his life any more difficult than it already was. So I merely said he was a thirty-four-year-old from Jonesborough, Tennessee.

I also wondered whether such family feuds were the white underbelly of a religious phenomenon that we in the media blithely took notes on and photographed over a long weekend. It was all too strange. There was more to this underbelly, as I learned from Seth and Susan. They'd told me that the name Lydia Hollins, the granddaughter of Bob and Barbara Elkins and the daughter of Columbia Hagerman, sounded familiar to them and that Susan was combing through the Tazewell County, Virginia, court records. Lydia was active in the serpent-handling community, and she'd been interviewed in *The Serpent Handlers: Three Families and Their Faith*, a book by Fred Brown and Jeanne McDonald that I was devouring. Sure enough, Lydia had pled guilty to credit card forgery and identity theft that spring. How odd, I thought. Here's a culture with such an emphasis on outer holiness that didn't transfer to interior ethics.

And then there was the e-mail I got from Susan Sanders on October 9, a Sunday. Seth, who was sixty-two, had been hospitalized with a strangulated hernia on October 5, she said, but he'd had surgery the next day and the prognosis was good. She stayed in the hospital room with him, and in the early hours of Friday morning, she awoke to hear a nurse calling his name. He didn't answer. Seth had died in his sleep.

CHAPTER FOUR

MEETING ANDREW

• •

As the *Post* piece was being edited in the fall of 2011, a senior editor demanded the angle be changed from a look at the dying art of serpent handling to a profile of Mack Wolford. I was beyond annoyed, as I'd already done two drafts and Beth had signed off on it. I tried calling Mack up for more quotes. Like many mountain people and especially pastors, he was short on cash, and so he bought cell phone minutes by the month. He would typically run low before the month ended; hence it was impossible to get him—and many other folks like him—on the line. It wasn't until early October that I located him for a long and thoughtful conversation. He felt he was the Lone Ranger of serpent handling, whose job it was to pass on the custom.

"Back in the Bible, it was the miracles that drew people to Christ," he reminded me. Mack was at the radical edge of Christianity, where life and death met every time you walked into a church and picked up a snake. But that's what drew the crowds and the media; that's what gives a preacher from the middle of nowhere the platform to preach the Gospel to people who would never otherwise listen. In an era of Twitter and Snapchat—which had just been invented the previous year—people's attention spans were being whittled down to almost nothing. It took increasingly radical measures to get anyone to notice the Gospel.

"I know it's real, it is the power of God," he said. "The more knowledge he gives, the more power he gives. If I didn't do it, if I'd never gotten back involved, it'd be the same as denying the power and saying it was not real."

I asked him what was it like to drink strychnine. "All your muscles contract at once," he said. "Your body starts stiffening out. Your lungs are like you can't breathe. Once I was up all night struggling to breathe and move my muscles and repeating Bible verses that say you can drink any deadly thing and it won't hurt you."

Meanwhile, he added, the devil was tormenting him, saying, "You're going to die, you're going to die. You can't go to the hospital. There is not a lot they can do. But that means you're already starting to lose faith." But Mack had soldiered through and won that battle.

We also talked about the Jolo church, where there had been plenty of behind-the-scenes squabbling, mainly over the presence of a handler whom Mack judged to have "backslid."

"Basically, the serpent catches the spirit that person has," he explained. "And a person who does drugs and is not an active person in the church, he should not be catching serpents, and he shouldn't be bringing them to church. That is one of the reasons people get bit. The Bible says the serpent is one of the wisest beasts in the field."

Afraid that a backslidden person could be bitten and end up in hell, Mack had pushed that handler's snake box way under a pew, then offered his own snakes for believers to handle. Harvey Payne didn't take kindly to Mack's interference at his church, and the two men were up until 3:00 a.m. Sunday hashing things out.

"If they get bit and get lost, the blood is on our hands," Mack said he told the pastor. It was known, he told me, that the media showed up in Jolo every Labor Day weekend and that some people came to the homecoming just to get on camera.

"I said, 'Harvey, you had the church closed and I pushed you to open it up. I came down there and slept three nights in my truck so you could have [it open].' I told Harvey there was no anointing that night to handle a serpent, especially not for someone who shows up once a year for the photographs," Mack told me.

Despite Jolo's preeminence among snake-handling churches, he saw little future for it other than as a tourist spot. "If something don't happen or somebody don't take that church, I don't expect it to stay open long," he said. "If it makes it this coming year, it'd be a miracle. I am trying everything in my power to keep it open. I was pretty much raised in this church and part of my history is in the church."

He was setting his sights on other states where snake handling was illegal but interest was much higher. "Here in West Virginia, snake handling's a thing of the past," he mourned. "They've lost interest. People elsewhere, they are hungry for it."

And Mack intended to spend his energies on the latter. "I promised the Lord I'd do everything in my power to keep the faith going," he said. "I spend a lot of time going a lot of places that handle serpents to keep them motivated. I'm trying to get anybody I can get." He'd found some receptive churches in western North Carolina where serpent handling was illegal but the local law enforcement was willing to look the other way.

"The Baptist pastor down there talked to the sheriff, who told them they know it's in the Bible," Wolford enthused. "They said as long as people are not getting snakes thrown on them, we're not going to interfere. I know the Lord had to work *that* out."

I later got in touch with Harvey, but it was a most difficult interview. I had to call his home number several times. He denied there'd been any disagreement between himself and Mack, and the connection wasn't good. My story was published that November in the *Washington Post Magazine*. Lauren then told me about some younger men that Mack was mentoring. One of the most promising was Andrew Hamblin, the twenty-year-old in LaFollette, Tennessee, who had taken a closed-down church and turned it into a serpent-handling congregation. Did I, she wanted to know, wish to drive there for Andrew's New Year's Eve service?

I looked at the map. It was a 530-mile drive—two days there and two days back—and there was a huge chance the weather could go south on us. I was not employed, and the trip would cost hundreds of dollars in lodging, food, and gas. But I managed to find a friend near Knoxville willing to put us up. The last day of 2011 was sunny and warm. I detoured through some gorgeous countryside in northeastern Tennessee to arrive at vista after vista of smoky ridges and blue lakes. Veeka and I ended up at Cumberland Gap National Historical Park at the intersection of Virginia, Tennessee, and Kentucky. The park marked the narrow gap through the Cumberland Mountains that had made it possible for eighteenth-century settlers to bring wagons and their families through the Appalachians. The area was on the western edge of the

Eastern Time Zone, meaning that the sun lingered in the sky for longer than usual that winter day. I drove up to the Pinnacle Overlook, and we followed a trail through the leaves to stupendous views of three states, including a bird's-eye view of the nearby coal town of Middlesboro, Kentucky. The air in the park was sweet and pleasant.

We then drove about thirty miles south to LaFollette, where my daughter and I ended up at a Sonic Drive-In for dinner. This city of eight thousand some thirty-nine miles north of Knoxville looked permanently stuck in the 1950s. I met up with Lauren, who had spent the afternoon with Andrew in Middlesboro borrowing some snakes off his friend Jamie Coots, one of the men profiled in *The Serpent Handlers: Three Families and Their Faith*. I followed Andrew and Lauren up a rutted dirt road to the Andrew's Tabernacle Church of God. Like the Jolo congregation, it was off a back road, but at least it was within six miles of a freeway, in this case I-75. New Year's Eve was a clear, starry night. Inside the church were about thirty-six people, including Andrew's wife, Elizabeth, who was seven and a half months pregnant with Haylin, their first girl and fourth child. Andrew, a boyish-looking young man with brown hair and an easy smile, had a day job as a cashier at the local IGA store and lived off food stamps with his wife and kids in a nearby three-bedroom apartment. He was the first handler I'd met who was using social media to promote his unusual practices. His Facebook page was full of photos of him handling all manner of copperheads, cottonmouths, and various kinds of rattlesnakes, despite Tennessee's ban on possession and transport of the poisonous reptiles.

In front of the church were three boxes of timber rattlers, canebrakes, a northern copperhead, and a cottonmouth. Lots of little kids were running about when the service got underway at 8:00 p.m. The age range of the congregation was much younger than that of Jolo, and at one point a bunch of girls, mostly teenagers, walked in. They wore long skirts and long hair. One was twenty-one-year-old Kasi Powers, who months later would be notifying her friends in cyberspace of Mack's death. She described herself on Facebook as a "holiness country girl," whose interests included "serving the Lord, worshipping the Lord and serpent handling." She had first tried the latter in November, when Andrew had handed her a canebrake rattler.

"I am scared to death of snakes," she told me, "but the Lord really moved on me to handle them." Soon, she talked her twenty-four-year-old husband, Daniel, into doing the same.

That evening, it didn't take long for Andrew to get the snakes out of the box and start slinging them about. In Jolo they waited a good half hour for "the anointing" to fall, but not here. Then an African American snake handler—unusual in those parts—walked into the church, immediately whipped a snake out from a box, and handed it to Andrew, who started stomping to the music while jerking one of the snakes about.

"You might be afraid of the serpents," he announced, "but come up here and we'll lay hands on you." Nearby on the pulpit was a Mason jar of strychnine and water, plus another bottle with a wick in it for the fire handling.

Andrew began to preach. "No matter how many snakes you handle, that won't save you from hell," he proclaimed. The devil, he informed us, can make people handle serpents. He began to preach on Psalm 23, then broke into a song and a dance five minutes later. There was a raw energy here that had not existed in Jolo. Unlike Jolo, where there were so many photographers you could barely see the snakes, this place was undiscovered. Other than a photographer-writer team doing a documentary, there was only Lauren and me. My little girl was enamored of the pastor's four-year-old son, Payton, who was constantly trying to kiss her. I later learned that he was the fruit of Andrew and Elizabeth's "sinning together" when they were fifteen. They married just after she turned eighteen.

The pastor then did some mean banjo picking while others took turns preaching. Andrew had played bass guitar, piano, mandolin, banjo, and Dobro back in his "heathen" days, including a stint with country-bluegrass singer Ricky Skaggs at Dollywood, an amusement park about an hour's drive south. He'd been fifteen then. He'd also played with banjoists Earl Scruggs and Ralph Stanley at Lincoln Memorial University north of LaFollette. Soon Andrew was back at the pulpit simultaneously handling four snakes, and even the teenage girls were getting into the act by handling one. Most disturbing was Elizabeth reaching *into* the box to grab a snake instead of being handed a snake by someone else. Handlers know that bringing a snake out of the box is one of the more dangerous moments, as that is when the snake often bites. Pregnant women had been known to die if they were snake bitten and I was in no mood to watch not just the death of this woman but also her unborn daughter. Fortunately, Elizabeth was not bitten even though she was nearly cuddling one of the rattlers while Andrew whipped another snake around like a belt, draping it over his shoulder like a scarf. Then he and some of the other men chugged down some strychnine, after which Andrew lit a wick and applied the flames to his hands and feet.

All this was happening with the music at impossibly high decibels, and by 11:00 p.m., Veeka was bouncing off the walls. I had a seventy-two-mile drive back to where we were staying the night east of Knoxville, and I was not wild about driving on I-75 after midnight on New Year's Eve. I told Lauren good night and left. As 2011 was turning into 2012, Andrew was holding three poisonous snakes when he was nipped on the index finger by a yellow timber rattlesnake.

He staggered and dropped to his knees. About a dozen members of his church rushed toward the stage, laying hands on his head and praying fervently for his healing. After a few minutes, he got up and continued with the service and made a point of handling the serpent that had bitten him. The next day, Lauren and I arranged to take him out for pizza.

"I felt the anointing of God more than I'd ever felt," he told us. "I look for there to be more serpent-handling churches in this area. I look for it to grow more and more. I look for serpent handling to be finally accepted one day."

Currently they were using snakes that could be found in the local woods, but by Easter, he said hopefully, he planned to have a cobra available. He told us about how he got started in the snake-handling business, how he nearly died at the age of nineteen of one such bite. He had to be airlifted twice to various hospitals in Kentucky because his blood wouldn't clot after the bite from a yellow timber rattler. It was July 2010, and he was in Kentucky preparing some snakes for a service when he felt a check in his spirit about touching one of the yellow rattlesnakes. Shrugging that off, Andrew picked it up, and the reptile bit him on his right ring finger. He was taken to a hospital in nearby Pineville, then flown to another hospital in Lexington. Impetuously, he checked himself out a few days later, believing all was well. He went to church Wednesday at Jamie's and handled a canebrake there. But on Thursday he began vomiting blood. His arm was so stiff that he couldn't move it. He went back to the Pineville hospital, where they found his blood platelet count was zero because the snake venom was hemotoxic; therefore his blood would not clot.

"I was dying. I could feel my soul leaving me," he said. "I was blacking out and people were praying over me." Then a young man touched him on the forehead, and the fading away stopped. But he was internally bleeding to death. "If we don't get you to Lexington in an hour, you'll die," the medics told him, and he was airlifted again to Lexington. A week's stay in the hospital and multiple blood transfusions healed him, and later the doctor offered to fix his stiff finger. "No," Andrew had told him. "That is a reminder of what ignorance will do to you. I felt God telling me to leave the yellow rattler alone. That is when I was snake bit." Some handlers—like Columbia Hagerman—would not have sought medical help at all, but Andrew was not prepared to die at that point. Elizabeth had just had twin boys. There were now three children, his marriage was barely a year old, and this was not the time to leave them.

But a year later—July 2011, he said—he nearly did pull the plug. He was vague on the details, but it was a dark time in his life when he was working as a night watchman. He and Elizabeth were separated; she wanted a divorce and was "backslid" and living with her mother. Plus she had just gotten pregnant with Haylin. He went off into the woods with a gun containing six rounds. But when he pulled the trigger, the weapon misfired. "God had a greater plan," he said. He and Elizabeth reunited in September, and two months later he founded the church. Two months after that, Lauren and I were sitting opposite him in a Pizza Hut.

For a twenty-year-old who had been a professional banjo and guitar player starting at the age of thirteen, had already married and fathered three kids with one more on the way, and survived one suicide attempt, Andrew seemed incredibly well put together. Like Mack, his marketing strategy included publicizing his daredevil spiritual exploits via Facebook. This was clearly a paradigm shift in the serpent-handling culture. Before, such churches were in out-of-the-way hollows where believers could meet in privacy. Andrew was a pioneer in using social media to market these practices, although he wasn't alone. Micah Golden, the black serpent handler who worked alongside him, found out about serpent handling via YouTube. I learned in Jolo that serpent handling had traditionally been passed down through families. But Andrew and Micah were part of a new breed who came to it seemingly out of nowhere. So had Elizabeth. When I asked Andrew about her, he said admiringly, "I've had some awfully mean snakes that she's handled like house cats."

I scrolled down Andrew's Facebook page to that past August. *You were raised better than that!!! IDIOT!! That's tempting God and I do believe the Bible says U should NOT tempt God!!!* wrote a family friend from his hometown of Clairfield.

I might have been raised different. But we all choose our own paths and I love the one I'm on :) was Andrew's smooth reply.

Beneath another photo of the young pastor holding up a handful of snakes, a high school friend remonstrated: *How many times do u have 2 get bit to realize this is crazy!!*

Andrew: *I will die by this and go to the grave believing all of Gods Word.* A few months later in November, there was another Facebook dialogue. Elizabeth and Andrew were just starting their church, and she was defending them both: *Our religon is not foolish. and i would be afraid to speak against on what moves on us 2 do that and thats the holy ghost. and i believe thats blasaphmey and thats one thing god will not forgive u once u have done it. so i would be careful sayin it. and as long as andrew stay in the will of god no harm will come to him.*

When a friend accused her of posting snake-handling photos just to get attention, she snapped back with: *It is in the bible and honey i pray the lord has mercey on ur soul for sayin its not. ur clearley un educated about the bible u need to hit the alter and pray and get ahold of the rite thing before its 2 late. these r our pics. if u dont wont to c them dont look at them.*

The mollified friend then backtracked and said she actually hoped to see Elizabeth, Andrew, and the kids. Elizabeth replied: *Thanks. lol. sorry for bein hateful. its just that we get put down a lot. and weve had peaple say pretty bad stuff to us over it. it just gets hard after awhile to hear peaple say ur wronge all the time. but gods peaple r not sapose to fite. we are to love one another. and we love you.*

I began wondering whether I could get another article out of this. I sought out Ralph Hood, the University of Tennessee psychology professor I'd glimpsed at Jolo, to get some answers. We never got to chat when we both were in West Virginia, but I found him a goldmine of information. We discussed local laws against the practice, and he told me that in Tennessee, it's illegal to handle serpents in a manner that endangers one's self or others.

"The courts say you have religious freedom, but they do rule that if the state has a compelling interest, they can legislate religious practice," he explained. "In Tennessee, they say their compelling interest is to prevent people from becoming widows and orphans. I feel it is a specious argument. As a consenting adult, you are allowed all sorts of high-risk activities. You can hang glide or rock climb or play football. All these activities produce more deaths than snake handling. So the argument that you're protecting people from high-risk activity doesn't work."

Ralph had written two books and many articles on the handlers; he had also amassed a library of six hundred videos of serpent handling.

"The tradition had been declining until recently because the pastors were aged and not attracting new believers," he said. "But now that it's gone digital, that is going to increase its popularity. People are always writing the obituary for this tradition, so as long as there is the King James Bible and serpents, there will be people handling them." In the larger culture, people like Andrew "are considered marginal," he added, "but in the snake-handling culture they have great power. When they feel called and have the anointing, they are like rock stars. They are healing and casting out demons. Andrew handles almost recklessly. I have seen him being cautioned by older handlers, telling him to wait for God's anointing."

During that pizza dinner we had with Andrew on New Year's Day, Lauren showed Andrew a photo of him and Elizabeth standing together, with a snake nearby. The young couple bore a striking resemblance to the famous matriarch-patriarch couple who oversaw revivals and homecomings at the Jolo church for many decades.

"People are already comparing us to Bob and Barbara Elkins," Andrew told us. Clearly, he thought it was time someone picked up their mantle. That got me to thinking. Lauren and I had been accepted to give a presentation on serpent handling at a meeting of the Appalachian Studies Association at Indiana University of Pennsylvania near Pittsburgh. Now I was wondering if I could get even more mileage out of this phenomenon. I did some more research on the topic and then on a whim contacted someone I knew at the *Wall Street Journal*. Yes, he e-mailed me back, he'd like a 1,200-word piece on Andrew to run sometime before Easter.

That assignment gave me the excuse to phone other serpent handers. One of the more interesting individuals was Micah, the African American serpent handler. Appalachia has a black population, but few of them have handled snakes. Micah was twenty-one and had grown up in Cleveland as a Missionary Baptist. He turned Pentecostal at the age of fifteen and became a pastor at age eighteen, then heard of Holiness churches that handled snakes. He went to Jolo soon after I'd visited there and encountered Andrew.

"After I began to read about it in the Bible and seek God and ask Him about it, the Lord led me into serpent handling," he said. "I told God if this is real and if this is for me, let me find these serpent-handling churches, and gradually everything just worked out." He decided to relocate, take a job as a custodian at an elementary school, and marry a local woman.

"When I first moved to Kentucky, I was pretty much the only black guy, and I got threatening emails about this not being my neighborhood," he recalled. "But those were not church people. I used to watch YouTube videos of people handling serpents, and I used to say I'm going to do that someday.

I fell in love with music and their style of doing things, and I never want to leave."

His family was less than taken with his new practice.

"They thought I lost my mind," he told me. "I got snake bitten on my left thumb by a copperhead in August and they threatened to have me committed." After the bite, "I sat down and panicked and blacked out and lost vision for a moment. People got me up and helped me outside. My arm swelled up, and I was in a lot of pain. But I never went to the doctor or took medication. Chances are you will not die from a copperhead, but the pain will make you wish you were dead."

"I knew it was the Word of God and where I was supposed to be," he said, adding that the bite was God's punishment for his disobedience. "I knew I had gotten out of God's will and he had not wanted me to take up that serpent and the Spirit had not moved on me, but I picked it up because I wanted to." As for his new wife Tonya, she "is a serpent handler bred and made. Her uncle was a big-time serpent handler. I know it's the truth and I intend to stay in it."

The other personality was Jamie Coots, the pastor of the Full Gospel Tabernacle in Jesus Name in Middlesboro. He'd been working in coal mining until an accident the previous summer put him on disability. He was a third-generation serpent handler and had lost part of the middle finger of his right hand to a rattler bite. Jamie was an elder in the movement, and I asked him what it was like to handle snakes.

"You feel that anointing and then the Lord speaks to your heart telling you what to do," he explained. "It is a feeling of power, but it is a feeling of peace. You're in your body and you know what you're doing and you can't control it. There is such a power coming over you and you are obedient to the Spirit of God and you compelled to do what He tells you and you know it will be all right. Once you have been a Christian for a while, you know the voice of the Lord."

He first met Andrew in 2008, when his mother and grandmother brought the seventeen-year-old by. Andrew had fasted and prayed about whether serpent handling was for today and had sought Jamie out. A year later, he handled his first snake at age eighteen. Andrew had come from a non-snake-handling background and needed to be trained. Jamie became Andrew's mentor, and Andrew, who grew up without a father, called Jamie "Dad." I asked Jamie if there was any fault with his protégé.

"He has been a little antsy and anxious," Jamie said, "and I've had to get on him in wanting to handle snakes a whole lot. I had to tell him it is not something you have done all the time. Even though it is something we believe in, you don't have to do it every service. I've been handling serpents for twenty-one years. I was nineteen when I started.

"Andrew is a little rough cut, but we've molded him," he added. Jamie's nineteen-year-old son, Cody, who was six months younger than Andrew, also handled, as did Jamie's twenty-year-old daughter, Katrina. She chose an Easter Sunday as her first try at serpent handling. She and her new husband also handled serpents on their wedding day the previous December. I instantly liked Jamie's friendly, welcoming personality. It was so different from the wary attitude I'd run into with some others in his movement.

Like me, Jamie was a bit surprised at the growing youthfulness of the movement. His church had twenty-five members, eight of whom were under thirty. "There are more younger people in it now than what it was when I got married," he said. "I was nineteen, my wife was twenty-nine, and we were the youngest people in our church. There are now probably twenty serpent-handling churches near where I live. There are a *lot* more young people in our churches than when I started. Andrew and Liz are probably two of the very few that just came into without being raised in it."

I slaved away on this piece for part of February but encountered delay after delay after delay. By the end of March, Andrew had turned twenty-one. I reminded the editor that the lead sentence was connected to Easter, which was coming up soon. Sure enough, it ran in the April 7–8 weekend edition, at 828 words, with one quarter of the original piece lopped off.

Still, *37K online page views over the weekend, and you got posted on Drudge this morning, so more to come. Thanks again,* the editor messaged me the following Monday.

For a religion story, 37,000-plus hits was hitting the jackpot. In April 2012, Mack Wolford had less than two months to live. Eight weeks later, I'd be packing for a move to Tennessee. As for Andrew, the world was fast heading toward his door.

CHAPTER FIVE

LAFOLLETTE
AND
MIDDLESBORO

I'd just crossed the state line from Virginia into Tennessee, and it was steaming hot on I-81. It was about 3:18 p.m. on the last day in July, and we'd pulled into a rest area. I figured I had plenty of time to get to LaFollette for an evening with the Hamblins. Then my phone rang. It was Andrew.

"Miss Julia," he began, "I might not be here when you arrive this afternoon." He was leading a revival up in Artemis, a town in Kentucky two hours north of LaFollette, and as things turned out, it had lasted several more days than he'd planned. He was delighted to be single-handedly turning this Pentecostal church into a serpent-handling congregation, so he was taking four copperheads up there that night. He wanted to be on the road by 5:00 at the latest.

I was quite put out. We'd agreed weeks before that I'd show up on my way to Union University, and he'd clear an evening for us to talk. My new home was 350 miles to the west in Jackson, not easy travelling distance to northeast Tennessee. Now it looked like I'd get an hour of his time at the most. I floored it down I-81, continued west on I-40, then north on I-75 to LaFollette. The house of the serpent handler was in the dilapidated Village Apartments at 1308 Loop Road. I arrived there in seventy-five minutes.

We began talking about all the TV crews that had come to his door lately, including CNN and a number of Tennessee stations. My *Journal* article and a long piece in the *Tennessean* (the Nashville daily paper) in early June had put him on the map. I was guessing that other journalists had expected to meet some inbred hayseed who went along with all their stereotypes about the region, only to be surprised at how articulate, determined, and media-friendly this young man was.

A state representative, Dennis Powers, had encouraged him to approach the county commission in nearby Jacksboro about changing state laws on possession of poisonous snakes. Andrew also said the local sheriff, a Baptist, was on his side. "I'm afraid of what God would do to me if I come against you," is how Andrew quoted him.

But all the fame had not translated into earthly riches. He, Elizabeth, and their now four children lived in a three-bedroom HUD-subsidized apartment at the end of a block of brick buildings. Trash was strewn about the parking lot, and a playground in back of one of the buildings was made up of broken swing sets. The folks sitting on their porches cast suspicious looks at me. Andrew and I talked about the "Old Yeller" snake that killed Mack, and he showed me photos of himself, dressed in a tan vest and suit, handling snakes at Mack's gravesite next to the red awning over the casket. When someone dies of snakebite, other handlers show up at the funeral with their snakes as if to say their faith hasn't been shaken a bit. While we talked, Elizabeth—or Liz, as everyone called her—hardly said a word.

After he left, I stayed three hours longer. I wanted to get to know Liz, who was wearing a long skirt, as was expected for a pastor's wife at a Holiness church. Such women also refused to wear wedding bands because they thought a verse in 1 Timothy forbade jewelry of any sort. Nor did they cut their hair, in obedience to a verse in 1 Corinthians 11 that spoke of long hair being the appropriate covering for a woman. I'd heard that Andrew had gotten laid off from the IGA, but Liz threw in an odd extra detail: Andrew *thought* he might be laid off, she told me, so one day he just didn't show up for work. Unemployment benefits were covering their rent and utilities, but they were down to one car, which often broke down. When it worked, Andrew used it, which meant she was trapped at home. He and Jamie had had some kind of falling out as well. Meanwhile, her kids, plus Veeka, were tearing around the place, and Liz and I spent much of our time cleaning up after them again and again. It was clear the home front was not happy. Liz told me that her husband was constantly out fishing or hunting for snakes instead of helping her and that both sets of grandparents were of little to no help in taking care of the kids.

That very morning at 2:56 a.m., Andrew had posted on Facebook: *When you go to good evil is always present.*

At 3:02 a.m., she'd posted: *Well im sorry u think im evil just cause i would like 2 spend more then ten mins a day with u. and would like u to come home at a decent hour and not stay out till 4 and 5 aclock :(*

Obviously I was walking into the middle of an argument. Plus, the couple were being deluged with offers from reality shows. I heard the details about some of them and had explained to Andrew that the $1,000 per episode some were offering was way too low. Both Andrew and she had received hate messages and obscene photos of naked people from strangers on Facebook. Liz told me that such harassment took forever to get off one's wall and that Andrew nearly shut down his account over it.

I stayed until about 8:30, although at one point I left to go pick up dinner at McDonald's for everyone. They seemed to have next to no income, and now she was pregnant with her fifth child. My heart went out to this woman whose husband relished running about with TV crews more than being with his wife. Although well meaning, my visit did little good. About ninety minutes after I left, she posted: *Lord let me hold on 2 u so i dont fall. i wont ur hand in mine rite threw it all. im afraid of this darkness and i cant c the lite at all. so let me hold on 2 u so i wont fall ♥*

The next day, I met with Bob Smietana for lunch in Nashville. I'd alerted the *Tennessean* religion reporter back in January about Andrew being on his front doorstep, and he'd spent part of that spring commuting two hundred miles back and forth to LaFollette researching a story. It had been ready for weeks, but for some reason the higher-ups had sat on it, wanting to wait until June to run it. Then Mack had died and within a week, Bob's story appeared on the front page and reprinted in places like *USA Today*. Bob had been through the fourteen-hour marathon that had been Andrew's homecoming in early May, and he was beyond impressed with what had happened on Saturday night. The folks there had started handling snakes in the parking lot, then had paraded into the church with the serpents as if in some kind of high church processional.

We were both concerned about Andrew having no mentors. "I hope he doesn't flame out," Bob had e-mailed me. It turns out that Andrew had been bitten on Good Friday, but he was only sick for a few hours. During the next few days, I immersed myself in my new life at Union University by day and read Liz's Facebook posts by night. On August 3, she explained to a friend: *Lol we have one of those love hate relation ships. Today is one of those days were we are madly in love.*

The church where Andrew had preached his revival had given the couple a night in Gatlinburg—a resort town about eighty miles away—for some time without the kids. All was well until the evening of August 8, when she wrote: *Dont know what 2 do anymore. . . . Rite now the lord and my kids is all i have. pray for me when u pray.*

A friend messaged her, *What about your Hubby Andrew?*

Im not sayin this in a bad way, Liz responded, *but andrew is never home he is always gone. we need alot of prayer and really needin the lord 2 move for the both of us.*

Then I heard that Jamie Coots's daughter, Trina, was having marriage problems. Even though I'd been in Jackson barely a week, I knew I needed to go to Jamie's "homecoming," that one weekend a year when a church throws a big party for its friends and supporters. People from several states come for these homecomings, just as they showed up at the one in Jolo nearly a year before. Anyone wanting to do any research on this culture must show up at these events. What if, I thought, I try to get some face time with some of the women in this culture? I messaged Kasi on Facebook, asking her if I could drop by her place on the way to Middlesboro.

That Friday morning, I set out for a drive back across the state, forgetting that I lost an hour going into the Eastern Time Zone. It took me eight hours to get to Kasi, her husband, Daniel, and their nearly three-year-old son. Daniel wore jeans and a nondescript dark flannel-like shirt and had sandy-colored hair. Kasi wore dark glasses, a long skirt, and a long-sleeved shirt— perfect Holiness attire. They were clearly not amused that I was two hours late. Of course getting stuck in the Knoxville rush hour during a rainstorm on I-40 didn't help matters any. I tried to call and text Kasi, but she had not bought any new minutes for her phone, so of course she didn't get my message. They were itching to get to a 7:30 service at Andrew's church, which was about a block away. The smell of smoke inside their trailer from their cigarettes was overpowering. Within five minutes, I could feel a headache develop, so I knew this interview would be short. There were two TVs and the wall of their living room was covered with several dozen photos taken by

Lauren of themselves and folks at the church. Both said they were involved in drugs before they heard of Andrew's church. Daniel said he came to see the snake handling.

"I was as lost as a duck in high weeds," he said. "I used to have long hair. I was strung out on drugs." The two responded to an altar call the previous November when Andrew was starting up his church. They were two of his first converts. Daniel was with Andrew when they drove to Bristol the day Mack died to visit Nathan Evans in the hospital. We talked for a while about Mack's death, and Daniel had also heard that Mack had sat on the snake. Apparently people near Mack's deathbed were texting the details about the fatal bite all over Appalachia.

Both were unemployed. Although Daniel liked making hair bands out of copperhead snakeskin, neither he nor Kasi seemed to have a clue about how to make a living. "Last Saturday, the Holy Ghost got all over me," Daniel said of one of his handling experiences. "All of a sudden, it went limp." He had not been bitten yet—although once he was rash "and the anointing wasn't yet on me," and a snake nearly got him.

I asked them how the anointing feels. "I go numb from head to toe," Daniel said. With Kasi, "the fear leaves and I feel a calmness that everything's going to be all right," she told me. He had friends still on drugs, and "I try to talk to them about the Lord but they ignore me," he lamented.

I gave them a lift to the Friday night service at Andrew's church. The *Journal* piece was framed on the wall. Andrew played electric guitar as an older woman with blond hair belted out a song with unintelligible lyrics. Micah was nowhere to be seen, but Daniel and his dad were standing with Andrew up on the altar. Two crutches were pinned up on the left side of the church in the altar area. As the worship went on, Daniel grabbed a bottle and lit the wick and danced about with it. Then his sister, a fifteen-year-old with long, dark, wavy hair framing a luminous face out of a Renaissance painting took it from him and danced. Charity Powers was barefoot and wearing a long blue dress, and there was an unearthly beauty about her. Andrew began to preach and stride about, working up a sweat. He was now "hacking," a way of preaching common in Appalachia where the speaker punctuates his sentences with an "uh" at the end. There were about thirty people there, including a photographer, but the evening was young. Veeka happily played outside with Payton, whom she clearly adored. I remembered that Ralph Hood had told me that word on the street was that Andrew was too reckless. "There is an art to handling," he said. "One thing about Andrew is he's likely to get bit and die young if he's not careful. There's an anointing as to when to handle the snake and when to put it down."

The next day, Veeka and I explored the lovely old homesteads at the Hensley settlement, a historic village atop a ridge at the Cumberland Gap National Historical Park. We retraced the steps the pioneers took on the gap trail through the park, but by 6:30 we were headed towards Jamie's church on the outskirts of Middlesboro. After a few false turns, I called Jamie on his cell phone, and he kindly directed me to the place. Resplendent in a sparkly striped shirt and satiny vest, he was greeting folks in the driveway of the plain, white, vinyl-sided building. I walked in to find Trina sitting in the back row, so we started to talk. She had long brown hair that fell below her waist. She was wearing a skirt but her toenails were painted, a sign of her having "backslidden," she told me. She said she was still in shock at having split up with her husband.

"He didn't want to work," she said. "I told him he had to be a husband." They were living with her parents, subsisting on almost nothing until "he just told me he never loved me." Fortunately she had not gotten pregnant, but they were separated. She could not afford the several hundred dollars it cost to get a divorce.

"Everyone knows about it, and they have their comments," she said tartly about what her church friends were saying. "Some of them say I should take him back." I told her she was nuts to think of that, and she agreed that reuniting would only continue the abuse. She said she'd love to go away somewhere and go to school or get a job, but there was no money and precious few local jobs. She told me the typical church offering was usually only a few dollars so there was no money from that quarter. As for getting to a job, her family only had one car, and her father needed it. All this was a far cry from the days when she took up her first serpent on an Easter Sunday when she was eighteen.

"The anointing moved on me," she said. "I began to cry. I felt no fear." A woman approached us to greet Trina. This was Michelle Gray, who lived in London, a small Kentucky town about an hour north of Middlesboro. She told me that her two boys Jonathan, thirteen, and Dillion, seventeen, both handled serpents. When I expressed surprise, she responded, "The Lord doesn't have an age limit, honey!" Micah and Tonya Golden arrived, both carrying snake boxes. I'd never seen his and hers snake boxes, but sure enough, she was carrying a smaller, white, decidedly feminine one. There were more than a dozen snake boxes up front but they only came out at the beginning of the service when folks were also handling fire. The pyrotechnics stopped soon after, and there was no more that evening. I spotted Ralph Hood, who told me that Andrew had gotten involved in some kind of immorality, for which Jamie rebuked him, and that he and Andrew had parted ways. This explained why Micah was at Jamie's church and not with Andrew.

Jamie's congregation belonged to "Jesus name" churches, which believe that one should be baptized only in the name of Jesus. The other sort were called "Trinitarian" churches, where converts are baptized in the name of the Father, Son, and Holy Spirit. For me, this was a minor debate, but Pentecostal churches in this region had split over this doctrine. Veeka was acting up, so we went outside, and I engaged a trio of people—one of them Jamie's uncle—who were smoking up a storm on an informal smoker's bench. The Holiness lifestyle doesn't preclude tobacco, so these folks were packing them away. With black lung so prevalent in one of the country's main tobacco-growing states, what are a few cigarettes? One of the men said the locals were worried that all the coal-mining jobs would be shut down. We briefly talked about mountaintop removal, but Veeka was acting worse, so I tried to leave. Unfortunately, four cars were boxing me in. So we stayed, which turned out to be providential as one of the young men I met at the end of the service was Nathan Evans. The twenty-one-year-old was a coal miner and the same young man who was bitten the day Mack died. He confirmed that he was the great-great-grandson of Bob Elkins and that he first handled snakes in March 2009, when he was eighteen.

"It's the word of God whether or not my family is in it," he said, as we went out on the porch to talk. But that resolve was tested when he was bitten by a rattlesnake that fateful day. He began throwing up blood, so he went to the hospital.

"I let myself down," he said unhappily of his decision to get the antivenin treatment. "Like Peter, I fell on the water." I suggested the hospital might have saved his life. "Without the Lord, I wouldn't be here today," he retorted. I noticed his twenty-three-year-old wife, Tiffany, standing there. She stood out from the crowd in her long denim skirt and high-heeled red shoes, her black hair up in a chignon.

She told me she worked with Nathan at a Walmart, and he invited her to church. They married in April 2010. She'd grown up in a five-hundred-member Assemblies of God church, so switching to a Holiness church of a few dozen members was a huge change for her. "I told the pastor they were all crazy, and I wasn't handling no fire," she said. But during a visit, "I could see the Spirit on all these people and I wanted that." After a few services, "the Lord moved on me to handle fire. It's kind of like cold water—it feels windy. It doesn't burn and it's not even warm." Nevertheless, "I still wasn't sold on serpent handling at that point. The last time my husband got bit, he should have died."

She told me about the terrifying drive to Bristol, where her husband had been helicoptered to Richland Hospital. "It was the longest hour ever," she said. "They didn't know what to do. They had to look up snake bites on the internet. They treated him for a cottonmouth, but he'd been bitten by a black rattler. It was really bad. He was in ICU for six days. They needed eighteen vials of antivenin and two packs of platelet transfusions."

Then she turned philosophical. "Whether you live or die, it's up to Him," she said, adding that only just last weekend she had handled a snake—a copperhead—for the first time. "The Lord said it was time. There is no way to explain the high you feel."

On Sunday morning, I got to the service early and snapped a photo of a "My rattlesnake is smarter than your honor student" bumper sticker on one of the cars. There were seventeen serpent boxes up at the front of the church. The men were clustered around the boxes, gazing at each others' reptiles. Two of the men showed me where they had been bitten. Jamie, who was wearing a screaming orange suit over a black shirt, was holding a box with a very unhappy-looking rattler inside. Its mouth was open in a menacing snarl. Jamie told me he fed them hamsters and small birds and that rattlers typically last only a year in captivity. (I later learned that snakes can live up to thirty-five years in captivity if treated properly.) Next, Jamie said they seem to die out of sadness and that when handled, the spiritual power overloads their circuits and they flame out. I noticed Trina sitting in the second row at this point, no longer skulking in the back. The service started, and twenty-five minutes into it, the snakes came out. Trina went and got a tambourine.

The preacher that day was twenty-six-year-old "Big" Cody Wynn, from Harlan, about forty-one miles north of Middlesboro. "We younger people need to stand against sin," he began. He weighed 312 pounds, had short black hair, yellow suspenders, and an open, friendly face. "If I would've been in this for money, I'd have stayed a drug dealer," he added. "Just a little bit of sin will take us all out. . . . If we don't stand against sin, there will not be a serpent-handling church in the land." It was an earnest ten-minute speech imploring people to live a holy life. I sensed this speech hadn't come out of thin air and that something was going on behind the scenes.

Nathan stood up. "The church has lost the power and I want to get back to it," he said. "The church needs to have the faith to raise the dead." Sitting in the congregation, I did a bit of reflecting. There was something about these people I didn't see in other churches I had visited. There was a freshness there, a desire to follow God that I didn't often run into in any religious setting. No one was jaded here. Bob Smietana had written that serpent handling was Christianity's wild, untamed side, and he was right. These folks were on the edge.

Eventually everyone headed for a potluck lunch at a local community center, and it was there that I snagged some of the men for better quotes. Big Cody told me that he had done drugs, been in prison fourteen months, and was in rehab when his grandmother invited him to church. He was twenty-three at that point. He went to a church led by Bruce Helton, a well-known serpent handler in Evarts, a tiny city in Harlan County to the northeast. "I prayed," he said, "and I didn't even make it to my knees. I grabbed the pastor and wouldn't let go." He also took up handling snakes and told me he lost his job after a cottonmouth bit him on the cheek the previous fall. He showed me a significant scar on his right cheek and pointed out he had no nerves there. For that, he spent fourteen days in a hospital. "They fired me," he said, "because they said I couldn't lift what I was supposed to lift." Out of work, he became a full-time evangelist, an occupation in those parts that pays nearly nothing. Like Andrew, he'd been a guitarist in a rock band. He got into snake handling when, "I said one night, 'God, if this is where you want me at, send me a sign.' I opened my eyes and a Jesus name pastor handed me a big black rattler. From that day on, I dug in and went. I just keep on going."

Lastly, I talked with "Little" Cody Coots, so named because of his five-foot, five-inch stature. He was turning twenty that weekend. His real name was Dakota, and he had an earnest face, short brown hair, and brown eyes. He was pushing the envelope far more than his dad when it came to "signs following." None of that wick-in-a-Coke-bottle stuff for him. He used a propane torch for fire handling. Strychnine was too tame, so he wanted to quaff Red Devil, a drain cleaner he bought off the internet. "The Bible says any deadly thing you drink won't hurt you," he informed me. "I've drunk strychnine. I just believe the Bible." The one person he knew who had drunk Red Devil destroyed his vocal chords. "He didn't have the anointing of God," Cody said smoothly. "He missed it."

I asked him when he started snake handling. He had had a falling-away from God between the ages of thirteen and seventeen, but he got back on track and started handling when he was eighteen. Most people start out with copperheads, which are poisonous but rarely lethal. Cody started out with a rattlesnake. "It's better than any drug," he told me.

He continued, "I don't go to doctors, I don't take medicine, and I got brake fluid in my eye the other day and the side of my face was burning from the inside out. I prayed and went to sleep and when I woke up, it didn't hurt. The Lord healed my leg. I was stacking some long strips of tin weighing five hundred to six hundred pounds, and they slipped off and hit my leg. I wouldn't go to the doctor. There is still a knot there, but it doesn't hurt and I know the Lord can heal.

"I want to cast out devils and raise the dead. My great-grandfather used to cast out devils. No one in the Coots family has done it since. I want to do that. I want it all. Anything in the Bible that's been done, I want to do it." He'd been bitten twice in the past year by cottonmouths, and he showed me his left knuckles. The effects of the venom were such that he could hardly bend any south of his forefinger. "I know God can protect," he said.

There had been a bell ringing in my mind as he spoke. I remembered all the years I spent researching charismatic churches for another book and how breathless and new and exciting were the early days—mainly in the 1960s— when people were being converted left and right. I remembered Christian coffee shops sprouting up around the Seattle area, where I attended high school, and public baptisms in Puget Sound. Years later when I was in Houston, I witnessed the awesome commitment among Christians who shared their possessions and homes in a twentieth-century reenactment of Acts 2. There was a sweep and a drama and a thrill during those days that I had not felt or seen replicated in twenty years. And now here were folks whose serpent-handling practices were way off the Christian mainstream. Yet, when was the last time I had heard anyone speak longingly about casting out demons, much less raising the dead? At least these folks cared about the supernatural.

My last conversation that day was with Jamie about the reality show offers he was getting and what he should charge. He said he was not paying his bills as it was, and filming anything for TV ate up his time. I recommended an agent friend of mine in Los Angeles. Jamie called this friend and ended up negotiating $5,000 per episode, which he had to split up among various family members. I also asked him about this split with Andrew. The problem, Jamie said, was not Andrew. It was Liz. My mind did not compute. Liz was pregnant with her fifth child. She could not be the problem.

One person I didn't get to talk with was Linda, Jamie's soft-spoken wife who was all of four feet, eleven inches tall. She had met Jamie when she was twenty-eight, fresh out of a twelve-year marriage that had begun when she was fifteen. At the time, she had bleached blond hair and a dark suntan and loved wearing short shorts, makeup, piles of jewelry, and high heels. Usually Holiness people are not allowed to marry someone who's divorced, or what these folks called "double-married." But Linda was considered an unbeliever at the time. Once she was baptized a month before she and Jamie were married, it was as if her spiritual life was put on reset. But all the jewelry and makeup had to go, especially when Jamie's father, Gregory, turned the church over to Jamie when he was twenty-two. What none of us knew was the trial Linda was shortly to undergo. A day after we all said good-bye at the community center and I drove back to West Tennessee, Linda's brother, Michael Smith, and her nephew Dustin were shot and killed by a deranged man who was a local judge. The story was something out of a twisted soap opera. The judge, one Raymond Smith (no relation), had come to the Smiths' home in nearby Pineville searching for Dustin's sister, also named Linda, with whom he'd had some sort of relationship. Linda woke up to hear the judge shoot his way into the house, killing her fifty-year-old dad and then approaching her bedroom to do her in. As Dustin tackled him, Linda ran out the door and hid outside. Dustin, who was twenty-one and set to head out for college that very week, was not so fortunate. After killing Dustin and not being able to find Linda, the former judge drove ten miles away to a cemetery—where his father was buried—and killed himself.

The scandal led the local news for days and rocked folks in Knox County, where the judge was from, and neighboring Bell County, where Linda Coots's relatives had lived. The funeral was a few days later at Creech Funeral Home in Middlesboro, and Jamie, as the brother-in-law and family spokesman, found himself in front of TV cameras trying to make sense of it all. Andrew Hamblin, who drove there to be of some support, also ended up on TV. Meanwhile, Linda Coots was telling reporters how close she'd been to her brother, who was only a year younger than she was.

"It's just heartbreaking," she said, dressed in black, her hair up in her usual bun. "It's been one of the worst weeks of my life."

"After today," said Jamie, standing outside the funeral home and wearing a grey suit with a rose in his lapel, "it's just picking up the pieces and trying to put our lives together and always in our hearts wondering why."

CHAPTER SIX

JIMMY MORROW'S CHURCH

It is just as well that my new job kept me busy the rest of that year, as the Hamblin and Coots families signed contracts with the National Geographic Channel and were shadowed by their cameras for much of that fall and well into the spring of 2013. I knew the TV folks weren't wild about having other media interfering with their work. I would monitor all the main players' Facebook feeds, seeing posts like this one from Liz on November 11: *Really wishes that people would stop saying that we need to leave serpent handling alone. i stand firm on the whole word of god!! asking us to do that is like asking me to not pray for the sick anymore. if u dont believe like me please keep ur opions 2 urself. i dont push the way i believe down peoples throats. so be kind and drop it.*

Her daughter Madlyin was born the following January. On April 11, she'd posted a note—*Really needin prayer!!*—followed by another note saying she was heading to her mother's with the kids. Later that day, Andrew had posted a note: *If anyone hears from my wife, please let me know. she was headed to ky 2 hours ago to pick up our daughter but the women that has her has still not heard from her. im worried sick. please someone let me know something.*

On April 12, I saw that Elizabeth had posted a note saying that she and Andrew had separated and that she didn't want people judging her. A bunch of her friends had responded with horrified comments. I was in a hurry to teach a class and forget to cut and paste her comments into a Word document. By the time I got to them twelve hours later, she'd removed them.

But a friend had written: *God has grate thangs. would like to help you tho this time. one thing is important is that you find resins to love each other. you need to fight to stay together. this can be hard but you love him as a man not what he doses so tray to give out more i love yous or your the best ever.*

Andrew wasn't letting on that anything was amiss. On his page, he had posted a song demo called "Punkin Brown" that showed footage of people handling snakes at a Pentecostal service. It wasn't clear which person was Punkin, a legendary serpent handler who died in 1998 of snakebite.

A few weeks later, the Facebook chatter was about a snake-hunting trip that had gone horribly wrong. The TV crew had taken Andrew, Jamie, "Little" Cody, and "Big" Cody snake hunting in a swamp near the Texas-Arkansas border. When Andrew plucked a cottonmouth out of the water with a snake hook, he turned too suddenly toward Little Cody. The reptile bit Cody, and as the series would show months later, he had an agonizing twenty-four hours weathering the aftereffects. He refused to get medication. Meanwhile, the wives of some of the men were discussing the incident on Facebook.

Just to let everyone know my husband did not throw a snake on someone and caused them to get bit, Liz wrote on April 24. *Andrew had it with tongs and turned around and it bit the boy. It is on film to prove. lord have mercy cant people tell the truth at all.*

OMG where did they get that from, wrote Brittany Coots, Little Cody's wife. *I've told everyone that's asked that it was an accident. He didn't mean to get my husband.*

LOL. How is he doing, Elizabeth messaged.

He said he is fine but is swollen, Brittany responded. *I've worried myself sick over him. Its killing me. I cant wait for him to get home!*

Andrew's church had its second homecoming the first weekend in May, and I made it to the Saturday night service. It was pouring rain in LaFollette, and the service was so quiet, I took no notes. I barely got to talk with Liz or Andrew. Life didn't calm down for Elizabeth, who on May 15 messaged: *Needin prayer and a move from GOD. if not im fixin to have a nervous break down :'(. cant take no more feelin like ive got the whole world on my shoulders.*

I was going through a similar crisis because my job at Union University was ending. A longtime friend in the D.C. area suggested I leave Tennessee as soon as possible, but I hesitated. I felt that part of God's reason for my being there was to write about the serpent handlers and to show the world who they were, why they believed as they did, and how similar they were to the rest of us. I had amassed piles of notes, but that task was undone.

And there were cautionary tales. In the *Southern Literary Journal,* I encountered an essay by Michael Odom on the book *Salvation on Sand Mountain* and how its author, Dennis Covington, had ended up writing a "southern memoir" about his experiences while on assignment for the *New York Times* covering a murder trial that involved a snake-handling pastor in Alabama. The earnest faith of these members of a marginalized religious culture profoundly influenced the sophisticated visitor, who embarked on a spiritual journey through immersion in rural America and hanging out with snake handlers. Whereas most visitors would find the serpent handlers grotesque, Covington was charmed by them. And they converted him, after a fashion, to the point that he picked up a poisonous snake in church. End of story.

Well, no way I was going to do that. But I had to at least explore what else was out there other than just the churches in Jolo, Middlesboro, and LaFollette. Ralph Hood had told me of several similar churches in Alabama, Tennessee, and North Carolina and suggested that I visit them to get a better grasp of this culture. Two of these churches had homecomings in June. I had taken some vacation time, so when I arrived home on June 6, I realized that one of those homecomings in Del Rio, just east of Knoxville, was two days away. I had not even started looking into possible hotels. On the same day, I got an e-mail from a man who lived northeast of Knoxville who admired one of my previous books. He and his wife would love to host Veeka and me, he said, should we ever be in the area.

I e-mailed him back: "How about this weekend?"

Two days later, the first thing I noticed in the Edwina Church of God in Jesus Christ's Name were the paintings. They were in brilliant colors, each about four feet across and maybe two feet high. The one closest to me showed a crowd gathered by a sky-blue river with several of their number being baptized. Various sayings and verses were scrawled on the hills, water, and sky, and one showed a black-and-white-striped log cabin with "Jesus Church, Naillon, Tennessee 1740" painted on it. The date referred to the painter's ancestors, who emigrated from Ireland and were already living in Tennessee's eastern mountains when it became a state in 1796. It was very much in the style of Howard Finster, the late American primitive artist. The painter was none other than the pastor, Jimmy Morrow.

I had brought along the host who had offered us a place to stay. He worked in the local school system, and as we drove south on I-40 that Sunday morning, he described the trailer homes, the welfare culture, the family trees that went straight up, and the people who sold off their kids' meds to make a buck.

We took one of the Newport exits, turned left onto the underpass, took the second street—Picnic Road—to the right, went about three hundred feet, turned left on Bloom Drive, splashed through a creek that ran across the road, and drove another quarter mile to the church. It was the same countryside written about in Catherine Marshall's best-selling novel *Christy,* and Jimmy Morrow later told me that his father, Albert, appeared in the book. The area was beautiful.

Jimmy was fifty-eight, a year older than I was. He was standing in front of the small church greeting people who were there for his homecoming. Besides me and the host, Ralph Hood was there along with another college professor, Jenna Gray-Hildenbrand from Middle Tennessee State University in Murfreesboro. I had called Jimmy a few nights before to ask about allowing photos. He politely refused to allow my camera and then told me he knew of at least eighty serpent-handling churches, eight to ten of which were in Tennessee. He was a tall, grey-haired man with black pants and a long-sleeved black shirt with white stripes, over which he wore a black sleeveless T-shirt with these white letters emblazoned on it: "Jesus Name / Acts 2:38."

That verse is a rallying cry for Jesus-name-only Christians because in Acts 2:38, the Apostle Peter instructs that baptism be done "in the name of Jesus Christ." A brown wooden pew was up front by the pulpit. Painted on that was "Jesus the name of God," "Jesus is above every name," and "The angel said, 'Call his name Jesus.'" In back of that, a grey wooden wall, about four feet high and with two small openings, blocked access to a large seating area where the elders, musicians, and pastors sat and the snakes were kept. It was the first church I'd seen that made it impossible for small children to get anywhere near the reptiles. The wood floor looked fairly new, and the whole interior was plain but kept up. The paintings added something I never saw in similar churches: beauty. The person overseeing this church obviously cared about matching colors, balance, and harmony.

Opening the service were a succession of women who came up to the microphone to sing "Ain't Gonna Let Nobody Turn Me Around" to guitars, drums, and tambourines. I later learned it was a well-known civil rights melody. Also up front was a small chalkboard bearing these words: "Church Homecomin / June 9th / Sunday at 11: AM."

"It's good to be in the Lord's house today. There's a good spirit, thank you God," said Jimmy. His wife, Pam, a sweet-faced woman with her red hair pulled back with a black bow, sat next to me. Unlike most Pentecostal women, her hair was short—just below her shoulders. Almost all the other women there had long hair, mostly pinned up on their heads. More typical was the fact she wore no wedding ring on her left hand. With Veeka bouncing around, I asked Pam if she had kids. She said no. Later I learned she had miscarried. Despite the heat, she was wearing long sleeves.

I looked around. One young man wearing a purple shirt hobbled in on a crutch. His left foot was quite swollen; he'd been bitten the previous day by a copperhead while out in his yard. People gathered to pray for him, and I learned his name was Jeremiah Brown. The music started up again, and I could see the men up front hovering over the snake boxes. I'd been around long enough to know what was next. Jimmy pulled out a rattler and handed it to John Brown, Jeremiah's grandfather. The snake's tongue was flicking about. Pam briefly grabbed it, as did Jeremiah. Suddenly something clicked in my brain: the young man was one of Punkin Brown's five children, who were left orphaned when he died of snakebite fifteen years before. The story of how Punkin and his wife, Melinda, both died of snakebite in church services three years apart made national news, as did the custody battle over where the children would live. So did the story of the judge's decision that none of the five kids could be at a service where snakes were being handled. I quietly asked around, and I learned that, sure enough, Jeremiah was one of a set of twins the doomed couple had.

I had heard that Punkin and Melinda's children were handling snakes and here was living proof. Jeremiah was not only hobbling about with a snake in one hand, he was also joining others in singing "I've Got the Devil Under My Feet." Then a woman wailed in tongues near the front for several minutes, her body trembling to the point that Veeka asked me what was wrong with her. The woman said something in English I could not make out.

"I see all things. Nothing is hidden," my friend told me she was saying.

Then Jimmy Morrow gave a short speech about our constitutional right to freedom of religion and threw in a sentence about a 1975 Tennessee Supreme Court ruling on serpent handling. Known as *Swann v. Pack,* it prohibited not only the handling or display of poisonous snakes but also the drinking of poisons such as strychnine. And it was a ruling that Jimmy Morrow chose to ignore.

"Stand for your beliefs," he told us.

Everyone headed outside for lunch, and I found Jeremiah. Yes, he and his brother Jacob were the two Brown twins. He started handling when he was eighteen because "I believe it's right," he said. "I believe it's the Word." But he was uncomfortable being interviewed, so I let him be. I found another young man who handled that day. Andrew Harley, twenty-one, was clean-cut, had brown eyes, and looked a lot like Andrew Hamblin. He lived in Morristown, about a half hour north of Del Rio. He had a nineteen-year-old wife and a two-month-old baby. He had handled two copperheads "because the Bible says so." It was tough to get the younger guys to talk much. I also located John Brown, who was much more talkative and was one of the patriarchs of the serpent-handling movement. He didn't want to discuss snakes but did insist I should be rebaptized in Jesus's name only, as my previous baptism didn't "take." This annoyed me, in that I had been baptized as an infant and rebaptized in a local pond at the age of seventeen. I wasn't about to entertain the notion of doing it again. He then invited me to attend the homecoming at his church in September and gave me directions (very exact ones as it turned out) on how to get there.

Later, Ralph, Jenna, my friend, and I got a tour of Jimmy Morrow's gallery, which was filled with more primitive-style paintings. There were also dolls he'd made of people holding snakes. If these were in a secular gallery, he'd have made a fortune. Ralph told me that Jimmy took no money for himself but funneled any profits back to the church. The bright-colored canvases showed people handling snakes and being beaten and put in jail for this belief. I got an idea.

"Jimmy," I said, "can you paint me one like that baptism painting in the church?" We agreed on a price. He said he'd even work Veeka and me into it somehow.

CHAPTER SEVEN

SAND MOUNTAIN

• •

It was a beautiful evening with temperatures in the seventies and a sinking sun casting slanting evening shadows over a lovely gorge through which ran the smoky blue Tennessee River. I was driving south on Route 35 up Sand Mountain in northeastern Alabama. I'd been in the area once before in 1997—in Gadsden, a small burg where I'd met Judge Roy Moore when he was a circuit judge. That was just before he began his meteoric climb to fame for his refusal to remove the Ten Commandments from his courtroom. He became the chief justice of the Alabama Supreme Court a few years later, then got into hot water for installing a monument to the Ten Commandments in the Alabama Judicial Building in 2003. For that, he was removed from office. But in 2012 he ran for chief justice again and was elected, only to be suspended four years later for ordering probate judges in Alabama to refuse marriage licenses for same-sex couples. After meeting him in 1997, I'd traveled west a few miles to interview a principal who was insisting on keeping prayer in his public school. Alabama was chock-full of great religion stories; I realized then and there that a colorful character stood behind every kudzu-covered bush. Sand Mountain—isolated, independent and largely poor—was a state of mind.

I'd forgotten how pretty the area was. There were pink mimosa blossoms—those shocking-pink flowers with ultra-delicate tendrils that look like a firework in process—on trees everywhere. The surrounding forests and lakes were lovely, which is why John Morgan—a friend—and I pulled over at the Washington Park scenic overlook halfway up the mountain. Meandering down a path with a view of the river and nearby Guntersville Lake, we saw some dressed-up people approaching us. One blond-haired woman in a shocking pink dress greeted us, saying her sister was getting remarried and would we like to listen in on the ceremony?

"We can't," I informed her, adding that we were heading up Sand Mountain to attend a serpent-handler church.

"Everyone's heard of that church," she told me, noting that its pastor, Billy Summerford, helped clear away some brush behind the school where she was the principal. Apparently that was a side business of his, as most Pentecostal churches in the area didn't take in enough money for a pastor to live on. Summerford had also instructed her to call him if she ran across any poisonous snakes, as he'd come by to pick them up. Saying good-bye, John and I headed up Route 35 to a small intersection and a light. That was the town of Section. We turned right on County Road 43 and drove another five miles south past hayfields and homes, churches, and a tiny settlement called Macedonia, which had a stop sign to mark it. Driving slower, we approached County Road 415, then took a right. We drove another block through the cornfields and through another stop sign. From there I headed straight down the road to Rock House Holiness Church, the place immortalized in Dennis Covington's *Salvation on Sand Mountain*.

Back then, the area had lots of unmarked dirt roads, making the church hard to find. Twenty years later, all the roads were paved, and there was a bunch of new hotels in Scottsboro, a city about ten miles away. Years before, a lot of media were staying in those hotels. That's when the church got even more notoriety, as this was the place where Punkin Brown had died the evening of October 3, 1998. Punkin had been striding around the stage carrying a three-foot, yellow timber rattlesnake in his right hand and at one point hopping across the room on one leg. Then the snake bit his middle left finger. A videotape was running at the time, helpfully chronicling the stricken man's last moments as he walked behind the pulpit. By this time, the congregation knew something was definitely up.

"God's still God, no matter what comes," Brown had said. "No matter what else, God's still God." He didn't—or couldn't—speak again. Billy

Summerford was at his side, supporting him as Brown lifted both hands. He was then lowered to the floor by several people, then asked if he wanted a doctor. He shook his head and pointed upwards. Jamie Coots, his best friend, gathered Punkin in his arms, but Punkin was fading fast. Five minutes after the bite, he was dead at the age of thirty-four.

What made things particularly heartbreaking was that his wife, Melinda, had died three years before after being bitten during a homecoming at Jamie's church. She had been twenty-eight, and Punkin had handed her the snake that killed her. Jamie and Linda took her to their home to recover, but instead she refused any medical help and died after two agonizing days. What hit the fan in 1998 was not so much Punkin's untimely death but the fate of his five children. The oldest was twelve, the youngest was four, and the twins were seven. The courts had taken away custody of his children from Punkin after Melinda died, but he'd managed to get them back. And now two sets of grandparents were warring for the kids. Punkin's parents ultimately got the children, but a judge ruled they could not take the children to a church service where there were snakes. (It was Punkin's dad I'd had the argument with about rebaptism.)

I hadn't wanted to go as far south as Sand Mountain as I felt that Covington had done a thorough job portraying southern Appalachian snake handlers, and there was no way I could outdo that. But I'd been told that if one was to cover this phenomenon, the Sand Mountain church was a must-see. I arranged to stay with friends in Huntsville some fifty miles to the west, who agreed to babysit Veeka. I located John, a native Alabamian from Chilton County south of Birmingham who was dying to have a good adventure. He'd driven up that morning and met me in Huntsville, and off we went.

We stopped the car. It was just past 7:00 p.m., and the service was clearly underway. Sand Mountain's annual homecoming was every Father's Day weekend, so we were there on Saturday night, June 15. The light-yellow church was bathed in the golden twilight that washed over the nearby fields. The air was gentle and welcoming, and John snapped a few photos, as none were allowed inside the church. We walked across the gravel parking lot and up a tiny porch. I took a breath, then turned the knob on the door.

About sixty people sat inside. It looked like most other churches of the type: some religious art slapped on the walls, news clippings of people handling serpents, two hanging plants, and a gold-brown lattice-type material strung along the ceiling in an attempt to give the place a homey air. A woman was singing "I Want to Know How It Feels" in back of the pulpit, which was surrounded by a semicircle of pews facing the congregation. Billy Summerford, I noticed, had his own cathedral chair near the pulpit. He had grey hair and was wearing wire rims and a plaid long-sleeved shirt. Then I saw Jeremiah Brown, the twenty-two-year-old handler I'd interviewed the week before, sitting in the semicircle. He was still having trouble with his leg. Jamie Coots, in a black shirt, was seated toward the back near a few other faces I recognized.

A half hour of worship followed, and then I noticed the men in the semicircle whispering to each other. The pastor interrupted the service to ask us to pray "for someone who's been bit bad," at which point everyone dropped to their knees and fervently prayed. This was a fate any of them could undergo. I started asking around. Some of the women told me that Bill Pelfrey, a long-time handler who was in his seventies, had been bitten about an hour before at Bruce Helton's church in eastern Kentucky. Pelfrey was featured in Covington's book. His dad, Oscar, had died of snakebite in 1968, so Pelfrey knew the dangers. He was vomiting horribly, they told me, and parts of his body were going numb.

How odd, I thought. The Rock House church was also the scene of a famous bite: the one that killed Punkin. And now here was his son seated not ten feet away from the very spot. A Tennessean named Allen Williams then got up to preach. He had a stocky build, a paunch, and short brown hair.

"Do you believe God did those tornadoes in Oklahoma?" he asked, referring to two horrendous twisters that had devastated the Oklahoma City area a month before. "God will do what it TAKES," he shouted, "to get peoples' attention. You gotta stand for what you know to be true and don't waver on it! Don't compromise with them. Do not accept the friendship of the world!"

"Amen," the people said.

"Don't wonder if people tell you you're crazy because you're living clean," he continued, segueing into how women should have long hair and men should not. "When I was growing up, boys had short hair and girls had long. Now little boys have pierced ears, and they grow up to be homosexuals. When children sass their mommy, they should get a spanking. By the time these kids are ten or twelve, they're in jail because their daddy wouldn't whoop their hiney."

Eventually he stopped, and we swung into "Four Days Late," a well-known gospel song about Jesus arriving four days late to raise Lazarus from the dead. At 8:45 p.m., the snakes came out, all of them rattlers. Only three or four people handled them, but I noticed that Jeremiah did, briefly. But my eyes were fixated on a little boy with short blond hair in jeans and a blue polo shirt. He was carrying a snake box, and he was heading for the pew in front of us. John and I prepared to leapfrog backwards over our pew. But first I peered over the kid's shoulder.

"That's empty, right?" I asked, pointing to the box. Inside was a bright chartreuse plastic snake.

"A training snake," John cracked.

The service was soon over and everyone was pulling out their cellphones to find out Bill Pelfrey's fate. He was bitten at 7:24 p.m. Eastern, people told me, but he was hanging on. Little Cody was driving north to be with him, and there was still vomiting and paralysis but other symptoms were fading. John and I headed out into the parking area with only a sliver of a moon for company but no street lights.

The next morning, we arrived a few minutes before 11:00 and learned that Bill Pelfrey would live but was still not eating. I wandered up to the snake boxes, where I saw a nasty-looking black timber rattler, some yellow timbers, and a canebrake. Big Cody, the jovial young man I'd first interviewed at the Middlesboro homecoming was there and told me he was still without a job; he'd used the last of his petty cash reserves to get to Sand Mountain, and he had drunk Red Devil four months ago for the first time. It went down like ultra-greasy baby oil.

"It's the worst stuff I've ever tasted," he reported. "Stayed with me two weeks."

Ralph was there, and John and I sat next to him in the front pew. He said he'd seen people quaff not only Red Devil but also car battery acid and lye. The latter can burn a hole in your throat. We were in the left front part of the church—about a yard away, Ralph told me, from where Punkin expired. Looking at the group of men taking their seats up front, I noticed a different face: a thin young man wearing grey pants and a purple plaid shirt. This was Jacob Brown, the other twin. *The Serpent Handlers* by Fred Brown and Jeanne McDonald, had an interesting note about him. During one of the custody trials for the children in 1995, Jacob, then five, was said by a court-appointed psychologist to have emotional problems and to be "an extremely anxious little boy," who was fearful of snakes and who talked about them being hidden in different parts of his father's trailer. Then four years later and further into the book, nine-year-old Jacob said he wanted to handle snakes like his dad.

Now he was twenty-two and the guest preacher. The crowd was thinner—maybe forty-five of us were there—but Jacob was already shouting into the microphone and striding about and sometimes scowling. Ralph told me Jacob had inherited his dad's mannerisms.

"C'mon now!" Jacob exhorted us. It was clear that the sound system, which emphasized the bass but not high frequencies, was geared for musical instruments but not voices. Even though we could not understand much of what he was saying, the men up front were shouting out encouragement as Jacob paced. He asked Jamie to read from Matthew 7:15–20.

"You're either in or you're out," he told those up front. "You can't straddle the fence. You can't go out here and sleep with whatever woman you find, whatever man you find, and preach the Gospel too."

He added, "People think I'm crazy for preaching what I preach. People think I'm crazy for taking up serpents. I've seen devils take up serpents. I've seen devils speak in tongues. The devil can do that and worse. The devil can take up a snake and speak just as pretty as someone filled with the Holy Ghost." His stream-of-consciousness ruminations on false religion continued for some time until I completely lost track of the point of his talk. I couldn't get over that it was Father's Day, and here was Jacob preaching inches away from where his dad died.

"I believe in living right!" he eventually screamed. "I believe in the Word of God. If you don't believe in this, get out!" He grabbed the black timber rattlesnake at this point, passed it to a few of the men up front, then took it back, and shoved it into a snake box. He continued on a jag through Matthew 7, hitting verses 24 and 25.

"I've been through it," he said. "And you know what you find out about Jesus? He won't leave you. I ain't here to scare you. I ain't here to cast you to hell. I'm here to preach the truth."

At just after noon, Big Cody started some riffs on the guitar as a way to gently urge Jacob to end it. Jacob didn't take the hint but continued to preach as more instruments joined in and the din got louder. Finally he put down the microphone to pray over someone who had come up for prayer. We swung into "I Call Him Jesus," and the place came alive with everyone dancing, praying, laying hands on each other for healing, or all three. One man lit a small torch and held the flames to his chest as he danced around. The men reached for the snake boxes and brought out several reptiles. Jamie, resplendent in a bright gold shirt, slung a yellow timber rattler around his neck. Several of the men danced with other snakes. Then Jamie held up two yellow timbers and spent the next few minutes balancing the slithery creatures. There was an unearthly calm about him as though he were in another dimension, far away from the present din.

"He'll heal your body!" people were screaming, and the place was electric. The pastor approached Ralph and held up a yellow timber rattler. Ralph quickly backed off. Everyone had congregated up front and was dancing and passing snakes around. One man in a blue shirt brought his little boy, who looked all of two years old, up to watch.

"The Lord willing, they won't bite," I heard Summerford remark as people were mopping their foreheads. It had been a good day—lots of snakes handled and no fatalities. We also learned he was turning sixty-five that day. Everyone headed into an adjoining room where the tables were laden with plates of ham, baked beans, chicken, green beans smothered in a sauce, cranberry, deviled eggs, and various southern dishes I could not place. The dessert table was packed with chocolate pies, banana puddings, piles of cookies, and cakes. I approached Jacob to get his phone number as I knew he was anxious to get home to Georgia.

"No, I only preach the Word of God," he told me.

"The media is a way to spread God's Word," I responded in an attempt to speak his language, but he shook his head. Other people told me that Jacob worked as a welder near Atlanta and already had two kids, but I was unable to spot them or April, his wife. I wandered outside and talked with a few twenty-something men, who told me the Summerfords never had kids of their own but informally fostered them as teenagers. But they didn't handle snakes "except to hunt them," one volunteered. My estimation of Billy Summerford went up as John and I lingered afterwards to talk with him. He was a guileless man of the earth, someone who walked the walk—especially if he was taking in homeless teenagers—and sticking with a church over the years that obviously was not a big income source. He'd been bitten ten to eleven times and had the scars on his fingers to prove it.

I asked Ralph if Jacob scowled and paced like his dad.

"Yes," he told me, "although Punkin would wave around a snake for far longer while preaching. Ten minutes at least."

I pestered Ralph with more questions. Serpent handlers don't delay gratification, he told me. When they get money, they spend it. This attitude extended to the undercurrent of sexual trespass that I was sensing. It seems that when people decided to "backslide," it was a time-out, when they could do what they wanted, then repent later. I'd already heard rumors about various people, but I had no idea how accepted it all was. The whole culture was strange to me. Many handlers homeschooled their kids, but in these parts the parents didn't do so great a job and the kids ended up being virtually illiterate. That explained the horrendous misspellings on Facebook (reproduced without correction throughout this book). A lot of them couldn't even read street signs, Ralph said. The best jobs had been in the coal mines, but that was a dead industry. Places like Middlesboro were dying towns. The friend who accompanied me to Jimmy Morrow's church had told me about some of the kids in the area. "I tell them to go into the military," he said. "It's their one ticket out of there, and they'll get a free education and training for a decent job."

Finally grabbing a plate of food, I sat down between Jamie, who seemed intent on ignoring me, and a quiet man sitting off to one side of the bench. This was Gregory Coots, Jamie's dad. Gregory had made his living in the mines and never felt all that cut out to head up a church. It had been his salary that helped support Jamie, Linda, and their children through the family's ups and downs. Gregory looked quite elderly, but he was only a few years older than I was. Across from us, Big Cody took a seat and informed me he was done with the media and didn't feel like answering questions. I guessed he'd been talking nonstop to the National Geographic folks for the last few months during the filming for the reality show and, I assumed, was getting paid for his appearances. Again, he mentioned that he'd spent his last dime to get to the Sand Mountain homecoming.

It's obvious these folks think God is always going to come through for them, I thought. I informed Big Cody that he would need gas money to get home and slipped him twenty dollars.

He took it.

CHAPTER EIGHT

THE
REALITY
SHOW

By August, National Geographic was sending out advance PR for its reality show, and Liz and Andrew were already feeling the effects. On August 14, she posted a letter from a man in Ilawa, Poland, on Facebook asking for prayer for his dad.

This is the 2nd letter this week, she wrote. *Many may not like or agree with what we do, but this is what its all abt.* The week before, she added, they'd had visitors from New Zealand who had seen online videos about the church. *Time* magazine had even showed up to do a piece.

The editor of Speakeasy, the *Wall Street Journal*'s entertainment blog, said he was interested in a story about the show, so I contacted the National Geographic folks for an interview. They'd been sending me numerous emails about doing a story, but when I finally got an assignment, they insisted on my going through them to talk with Andrew and Matthew Testa, the executive producer. Their PR people listened in on our conversations, a real turn-off.

Matthew revealed that the filming had begun the previous September and had ended in July with the bulk of it shot March through June. He waxed enthusiastic about Andrew and Jamie.

"They're both natural leaders, naturally charismatic," he said. "They are very intelligent, very well spoken and very deeply committed. You would automatically assume they are fundamentalist and not very broad-minded and strict and maybe wary of outsiders, but that is not the case. They are very personable. Where they draw the hard line on certain religious things, they were very open with us. They opened their lives to us in a very trusting way. You expect a lot of fire and brimstone but they are very easy to communicate with."

I asked him how they dealt with being so close to snakes, and he told me they put cameras on the ends of boom poles to get near the reptiles.

"I enjoyed being close to them," he said. "They are really beautiful. I like watching their behavior. They are spectacular animals."

He revealed there were two shows about Trina and her divorce. I figured she must have found the money somewhere to go through with it, and sure enough, she got no end of grief from her family because "signs following" churches only allow believers to marry one person for life. The fact that George Hensley, founder of the movement, was married four times wasn't in their collective memory. Even though Linda had been married before she and Jamie got hitched, being a pastor's daughter meant that Trina was held to higher standards.

"In an unusual feminist move, she broke up with this guy," Matthew was telling me. "Everyone said she'd never be able to remarry and stay in the church. Her dilemma is whether to remarry and leave the church or stay in the religion. The church is like a family business. They are all in it together. There is disagreement among the congregants as to whether she should be allowed to remarry. Little Cody doesn't think there is a loophole. He preaches against 'double marriage' from the pulpit, almost as though he is preaching against her. Those are two of my favorite episodes. People are vying for their own happiness and trying to adhere to these rules they believe very deeply, and it's hard to balance the whole thing."

Sure must be lovely having your own brother preach against you, I thought. Next, I was connected with Andrew. He was unhappy with *Snake Salvation* being the name of the show. "It put a lot of people off," he said. "I don't believe people go to hell because they don't handle snakes."

The hardest part of the filming, he said, was having constant cameras along with five children underfoot. "Problems were arising in the church that couldn't be filmed and just finding something to film was the hardest part of it."

Then he revealed something I'd picked up hints about on Facebook: he and Liz had moved out of that awful apartment to a house and then were moving again.

"We are fixing to move to a house that was given to us," he enthused. "Some people from Wisconsin heard about us through the *Wall Street Journal* and YouTube. They found a house and bought it. It's a beautiful home: Five bedrooms, two stories on two acres. It's in beautiful country, and there's a big deck around it."

The buyer, he said, was an elderly woman from Wisconsin who offered to front the purchase price on the condition that she could stay there whenever she visited the area. Meanwhile, other visitors kept arriving.

"We've had people from Houston come," he said. "A pastor from India came. Three people from New Zealand. They've come from New York, California." A visitor from England asked to take home a prayer cloth, he added. But there was a downside to it all.

"We get hate mail: people saying, 'You should be in jail, dead.' I've had people write that my children should be taken from me. I write back and say I am sorry you feel this way, but we have a right to do this. And by the time I am finished talking with them, they've changed their minds." Most of these conversations were through Facebook.

I remarked about how things had changed since I first met him.

"You have no idea," he said. "I am a fulltime pastor now. I helped lead revivals throughout July and August." Moreover, he still had no laptop for all his correspondence, and he and Liz shared a cell phone. They couldn't afford cable TV, so he was planning to watch the show at his grandmother's place. Odd, I thought. He must have gotten some decent money from the National Geographic folks. And he still couldn't afford a second cell phone?

"The only thing I want out of this is not money, not glory, but to see someone get saved," he was telling me. "Not to handle snakes or speak in tongues but that people might know there is the realness of God, and there is something to take the place of drugs, alcohol, and depression. The only reason I let National Geographic in was to show the light of Christ to the world."

He added, "I want us to be like Jolo was in the 1960s and '70s. At one time, West Virginia state police would have to direct police for the hundreds who came out."

He's still fixated on being a second Bob and Barbara Elkins, I thought. But the rest of the serpent-handling world didn't see him as representative of them at all. Andrew seemed to guess at my thoughts and ransacked his memory for legitimacy.

"Randy is the one who pushed me into the cameras," he said, referring to Mack Wolford's other name. "'You need to do it, Andrew,' Randy told me. The Lord then called him home and his work was done. I miss him every day."

I put together a story for the *Journal*, then started calling around to get photos for the piece. Oddly, the chief spokeswoman for the show had chosen the week just before the series launch to vacation in France. Her deputy then left on a business trip, which left me on the day of the launch scrambling to get photos sent to the Speakeasy editor. I got in touch with a photo researcher who sent me files on a zip drive I couldn't open. The issue was finally resolved, but it was the first indication I had that National Geographic didn't see a future in the piece.

As I was wrestling with zip drives, Andrew posted this: *At 9:00 tonight millions of people will see me, my family, and my church living our lives and worshipping and serving God. Yes we will no doubt get negative feedback, persecution, and just over all bad stuff said about and toward us. But with that being said, if just one person's life is changed it will be worth it all. I believe this is gonna open doors to the lost and maybe something will be said or done to help them. So I hope everyone enjoys it and for the ones that don't, I'll never apologize for spreading the Gospel of my Lord and Saviour Jesus Christ.*

What he didn't know was that his name was mud among other serpent handlers. The weekend before was homecoming at the House of Prayer in the Name of Jesus Christ, the church pastored by John Brown in far western North Carolina. I was apprehensive about visiting the place, as it had the reputation for being unfriendly toward media. The church had endured bad publicity surrounding Punkin's death, not to mention the never-ending coverage about the custody battle for his and Melinda's children. With Veeka in tow, I drove to Newport, the nearest large town across the state line in Tennessee, to stay Friday night at the Motel 6. The next morning, I met up with Jimmy Morrow, who had completed the painting I had commissioned. It showed a river, a church, and a crowd of believers watching a baptism. Jimmy had, per my request, painted in a serpent handler, then put in two stick figures that resembled Veeka and me standing at the edge of the crowd. That kind gesture gave me the courage to drive over the mountains toward Marshall, the small town in which the House of Prayer was located.

It was early evening when we arrived at the place, which was tucked into a hollow off Lower Brush Creek Road. John Brown's instructions were on the money, so we were among the first to arrive and join a handful of people seated on the church's covered porch with cushioned benches, graceful lantern light fixtures, and hand-carved railings. The first woman to greet me was Katie Allen. Her first husband, she said, died in 1973 of drinking strychnine, leaving her with several children. He was one of two people to die that night of poisoning.

"Must've been a bad batch" was all I could think to say. About thirty people, not including numerous children, filtered into the sanctuary. I noticed no one had snake boxes. I gaped at the gorgeous interior, which was a real departure from the typical serpent-handling church. The oak wood floors—no cheap carpet here—had a cross inlaid in lighter wood right before the pulpit. There were new ceiling fans, new bathrooms, cushions on the pews, and a porch outside the back door overlooking a stream. There were two cross-shaped windows set in the wall separating the narthex from the nave. Katie informed me that her family had donated the land for the church and that Charles, her second husband, had done much of the remodeling. There were tissue boxes placed strategically about. Some thought had gone into this place.

Veeka found a tambourine and began pounding happily away. Unable to find a blow dryer at the hotel in nearby Hot Springs, my hair was partly pulled back and scraggly. I had on no make-up except some tan lip gloss, and I wore a long skirt. We fit right in, I thought.

The service began and one speaker said he remembered the days when the parking lot was so full that there wasn't room for all the cars. There was plenty of room in the parking lot now, of course. "It's not just a snake-handling church," he concluded a bit defensively. "It's people coming together with faith and love."

The service ended at 9:30 p.m.—early for that crowd. I saw John Brown afterwards, and he was a bit down. "It wasn't coming together tonight," he told me. "People were divided."

The next morning, Veeka and I were breakfasting at the Smoky Mountain Diner in Hot Springs when we spotted Ralph (in the trademark jeans and light blue shirt he wears to all these services), Jenna, Jimmy and Pamela Morrow, and several other outsiders in town for the homecoming. I felt less alone. We gathered at 11:30 at the church, where there were about forty adults present. "There's a good spirit here," John shouted, as we began a medley of country praise songs, none of which I recognized. The front pews filled up with all men, who served as the amen corner. I noticed Pamela was sitting alone, so I beckoned her to come join us. The din of screaming babies and toddlers was insufferable. One little kid banged two cymbals continuously for the two-and-a-half-hour service. The worship followed the typical pattern: people going up to the front for healing and anointing with oil, various prophecies, several brief sermons, and dancing.

"These people up here are not jumping around for nothing," John Brown told us at one point. "They're jumping around because they've got something to jump around about." And everyone was into it except for a teenaged girl who sat next to us. She wore a jean skirt, T-shirt, sneakers with mismatching socks, and a dark brown ponytail pulled to one side. She just sat there stolidly. Was she bored? Sad? Forced to be there?

I heard the keyboardist walking around the church interceding loudly in his prayer language over people.

"How do you pray in tongues?" Veeka asked me.

I puzzled over how to give her a short answer now and a longer one later, then realized there had been no snakes. I was wondering if anyone there was aware that the reality show was premiering in two days when John stood up in the last few minutes of the service. The first thing he brought up was the show.

"This church has nothing to do with it," he said. "Salvation is not for sale. You don't get it through a snake. You get it through Jesus Christ."

So Andrew was right in fearing that other Holiness churches would take the title of the show in the wrong way. I talked with John afterwards, feeling strangely drawn to this frail-looking man whose son and daughter-in-law had died of snakebite and who had suffered so much. He explained that he'd put "a fleece out to the Lord about serpents at the service and God said no." ("Putting out a fleece" is a Christian expression signifying a request for a visible sign from God for direction.)

I then asked him about how Punkin's kids were doing.

"We've never gotten over it," he said tearfully. The bad publicity, the being talked-about all over western North Carolina and eastern Tennessee—fifteen years later, it still broke his heart. I asked him which of the kids handled snakes. All, he said, except for Daniel, now nineteen, the youngest. There was a picnic afterwards up the mountain in the small town of Walnut. Usually I was at these meals with my notepad out, interviewing people. I kept it stowed away this time.

Two days later on September 10, appreciative comments were pouring onto Andrew's Facebook page after the show ended. *Very cool show,* wrote a man from Washington D.C. *I was a bit worried that it would not be done tastefully but I am happy to see it is well done and not trying to exploit your faith.*

Others wrote in with prayer requests, requests for service times, or congratulations. Jamie's page got a handful of comments. Liz and Andrew's page had far more traffic, mainly because of its never-ending drama. On September 13: *This is elizabeth if anyone has wrote me and wonder why I have responded its cause I'm blocked from doing anything on facebook cause someone felt the need to report a picture of my son using the potty for the first time. I also won't to add it didn't show nudity in it at all. he was covered up.so I'm not ignoring u lol.*

On Saturday, September 14: *Elizabeth again ~ once again someone reported two more of my kids photos so now I'm blocked for two more days. please say a prayer for me and please pray for the person that's doing this.*

She then posted: *The person claimed it was pornographic! how childish can someone get. poor lil me lol.*

Said one sympathizer: *They have dirty minds, pure devil.*

Liz: *Amen. they need to get there minds out of the gutter.*

Another person posted: *Someone probably did it just for spite. people are terrible.*

Liz: *my boys have been known to b lil streekers at times lol.*

Indignant posts poured in. A neighbor in LaFollette posted: *Some people are so filled with turmoil and hatred, that they want to make everyone else suffer like they are. Whomever, just wanted to cause you trouble. There are people out there that just plain enjoy doing such. The Lord knows your heart.*

Liz: *thank u. i aint letting it get to me. people are just miserable and cant stand to see someone else happy.*

Said another poster: *Wow. All I can say is wow. With all the junk on Facebook and they block you for that.*

Liz: *i got on facebook last night and they reported 5 more photos they went as far as reporting one of my twin boys playing in the floor at church at 6 months and reported it to be violent and disturbing. so it will be a while befor its up and running. It will let me on it but cant message or write or like anything.*

I messaged her to ask if she'd contacted Facebook. I was also scrounging about in my files to find the name of Facebook's media contact, which I had somewhere.

Liz: *i tried when they reported the photo. but it didnt work. my sister saw on one of our pics of the nat geo show that someone had tagged in the post the link to my facebook. people are taking this to far.*

I messaged: *Did you get ahold of anyone or just leave a message? Meanwhile, contact the NG folks about this mess, as it will only get worse as more shows air. They can pull strings that you cannot.*

Liz: *i went in and set it to private . . . so hopefully this mess will stop. i looked for were they put the link but couldnt find it there was to many comments and it wouldnt show them its just the devil a trying to fight. for the mean while im taking over andrews lol. and i left a message on the feed back.*

A Nashville woman wrote: *It is the devil. I see this countless times in people in ministry getting reported. Hang in there, the enemy wants you to delete the Facebook pages then they have won, when Facebook was one of your tools of evangelism to begin with and works. Don't give up!*

Liz: *i downloaded the photos before they took them off. i ant letting them win lol.*

I end up emailing the National Geographic PR folks myself to ask them if they were aware of the hits that Liz was taking on behalf of the show, but I got no response. The day after the show, Andrew wrote: *I want to thank everyone for their kind and encouraging words. My Facebook had exploded lol. Hope everyone that has wrote me comes out this weekend. Were gonna see people saved, helped, delivered, and get a blessing from the Lord.*

On Saturday, September 14, he wrote: *Had a great service. People came from all around. The altar was full of people praying. That's what its all about. We must be doing something right. Hope more come out Sunday.*

On September 16, a man from Fairfax, Virginia, wrote on Andrew's Facebook feed: *Thanks for accepting my friend request! I just began watching your show on NatGeo and I am very impressed. Not sure what is tougher . . . snake handling or 5 kids—you are a rock star.*

I think the snake and children are equally amazing LOL, said an adjunct history instructor from Columbia State Community College in Columbia, Tennessee.

Andrew responded: *my kids are meaner than any snake that crawls lol.*

On September 17, a Thomas Crouch wrote: *Some of my own fellow snake handlers have block me on f.b. due to me saying that your show wasn't a reproach but the ones watching the filth on t.v. was really the reproach . . . shame on you, makin me loose my friends like that . . . you bad, bad feller . . . hahaha!*

I searched around Facebook to see if I could find posts that supported Crouch's assertion, but if other serpent handlers were trashing Andrew, they were doing so on inaccessible feeds.

After the Friday service on September 20, Liz wrote: *there was really no were to sit at the beginning it was packed. we had one to pray again. so things are going great. and the preaching was out of this world.*

By September 21, Andrew's Facebook friends list had skyrocketed to 2,223. He announced that lots of people had contacted him about church, that the people who were offering to donate could send money to his home address (which he listed), and that other networks had contacted him to do some filming.

He wrote: *Fabulous, amazing, wonderful. Thats all I can say about service last night. The church was packed and people came threw the doors shouting. Can't wait to see what God has in store tomorrow. Everyone that can and will come be with us.*

Meanwhile, Jamie had his own fish to fry in the name of religious freedom. On October 3, the *Wall Street Journal*'s Houses of Worship section published his essay about how state laws against handling snakes in church "has forced me to question America's commitment to religious liberty." If Christian Scientists are allowed to refuse life-saving medical treatments, why couldn't he handle poisonous snakes? he asked. Because snake handlers tend to inhabit backwoods Appalachian towns like Middlesboro, which is "racked by widespread drug abuse and economic hardship," he wrote, "this makes our church an easy target for mistreatment by authorities." Freedom of worship needed to extend from just protecting the well-known faiths to obscure ones like his, he concluded.

What really bothered Jamie was his arrest the previous January. He was heading through Tennessee on his way home from buying five snakes (rattlesnakes and copperheads) in Alabama. At first, a cop had pulled him over for having tinted windows, but then noticed the four snake boxes in his back seat. The Tennessee Wildlife Resources Agency was called in, and Jamie found his snakes and boxes confiscated and himself slapped with misdemeanor charges for transporting illegal reptiles and having those reptiles in improper containers. It was legal for Jamie to buy the five snakes for $800 in Alabama and legal for him to own the snakes in Kentucky, but the state of Tennessee judged it illegal for him to possess the snakes while driving through Tennessee on I-40. Jamie was okay with his snakes being confiscated—one can always find others—but not with the snake boxes being taken as well. One had belonged to Punkin, and Jamie wanted—and finally got—the boxes back.

The only upside to it all was that the National Geographic film crew were on hand to film his subsequent court appearances, which made the Tennessee law enforcement officials look ridiculous and Coots noble in comparison. Ralph Hood found Jamie a pro-bono lawyer who got him one year's probation after pleading guilty to possessing poisonous snakes in Tennessee. That explained why he wasn't handling when I saw him at the LaFollette and Del Rio churches that spring. Both churches were in Tennessee.

I was beyond fascinated with the sixteen segments, which caught parts of Jamie's and Andrew's lives that I'd not had the time learn about. The episodes switched between Middlesboro and LaFollette, two cities thirty-seven miles apart with dramas occurring in each family. Episodes with Andrew showed him continuously hunting snakes. I noticed Liz was in very few of the episodes, and neither were the kids, except for brief glimpses of them when they were at the pet store with their dad while he was buying mice for snake food. The film crew pounced on a bystander who met Andrew at the pet store and followed him when the man ended up visiting Andrew's church and was clearly appalled by what he saw. They were clearly scraping the barrel to get some action going in LaFollette.

Middlesboro was quite different. At the time the episodes were shot, most of the Coots family were unemployed, and one episode showed Little Cody wondering if he should sell drugs to make money or go work on an oil rig. The possibility of giving into various sins while on a rig scared him away. The family was fixated on Katrina's situation, as she had finally gotten a divorce, and now the question was whether she could ever remarry. Trina, as she was called in the show, got a whole episode to herself and her eight-month stint of "backsliding." It seemed to me that the poor girl just wanted a break, and for a while she wore pants and makeup and got new clothes that scandalized her family. Both Cody and Jamie were suggesting that Trina would go to hell unless she repented. It was an impossible choice: staying single for life and in her family's good graces, or remarrying with the chance for children and a life but with her family turned against her. Jamie came across as far more compassionate than Cody, and at the end of one segment, he extended the olive branch—actually a serpent—to his daughter during a service. She took it, breaking down in tears. That was the sign that she had repented. "I may never get married again but at least I'll be right with God," she told the camera.

The success of *Snake Salvation* brought more reporters to the area, including National Public Radio's John Burnett, who showed up in Middlesboro for two segments, the second of which trashed Jamie for how he treated his captive reptiles. NPR interviewed various snake experts, all of whom said the snakes used by serpent handlers were usually kept in such poor conditions that they ended up dying young and were too weak to bite. Such snakes were dehydrated, underweight, and sick, they said, and their venom was weaker and less apt to kill. That would have been news to Mack Wolford, I thought, but the piece did answer some of my questions about these snakes, which were cooped up in aquariums, Tupperware containers, or cages. A snake kept in a zoo could last for years but Jamie's and Andrew's snakes often died after a few months. NPR said that snake experts had contacted them after their first segment with information implicating the serpent handlers. They had some good points, but Pentecostal serpent handling had been around for more than one hundred years. Why all the fuss now?

Another visitor was Gemma de Choisy, an Iowa-based freelancer for Buzzfeed.com, an edgy website not known for religion reporting. But Andrew and Jamie were breaking out of the religion ghetto to be pop culture icons for at least a few brief weeks. Gemma had a beautiful writing style and came up with a fresh batch of observations about Andrew on things I hadn't known about. She found a host of visitors at Andrew's church who didn't fit the Holiness profile: recovered drug addicts and women in denim, rhinestones, and white leather boots. This was Andrew's dream—to reach the unsaved—and even though many were simply gawkers for a snake show, there were some serious seekers there. Gemma was in LaFollette near the end of October, when National Geographic inexplicably decided it was done with the snake handlers and crammed the show's last four episodes into one day. It was as if someone had turned off a switch, and the channel was trying to dump the series as fast as it could to make way for other shows. I called Jamie, who was clearly nettled by such treatment. He had been told their contract had not been renewed because of a dearth of viewers. Gemma managed to get a spokesman to reveal that the series had averaged 300,000 viewers per episode, which was not enough to guarantee a second season. (When I talked with National Geographic's spokeswoman about this later, she told me she didn't know where Buzzfeed had gotten such a figure. When I asked her to tell me what the true viewership was, she declined.)

The cancellation's effects were immediate. The Sunday after the last episodes had run, the crowds at Andrew's church had petered out, as Gemma recorded only twenty-two people there. Clearly a second act was called for. And this time, it would show up at Andrew's front door.

CHAPTER NINE

THE ARREST

* *

It was a cool fall morning with cloudy skies when two men from the Tennessee Wildlife Resources Agency showed up on Andrew and Liz's doorstep. It was about 9:30 a.m. on Thursday, November 7. They knocked. A cheery-sounding Andrew answered the door.

"How are you doing sir?" he asked. "It's good to see you."

"How are you doing, Andrew?" one responded. After some chitchat, he said, "We wanted to talk. You kind of expected us to show up at some point. Well, we've showed up. We need to talk with you about the snakes. I assume you're still practicing?"

"Yeah."

"You have snakes, I assume?"

"Not here at my home."

"You don't keep them here at your residence?"

"No sir," said Andrew, "I keep them at an undisclosed location. They are under lock and key, well taken care of and everything else."

"Where is that at?"

"Well . . ."

"Are you keeping them at the church?"

"Yes."

"You're keeping them in the church building?

"Yes, they're secured there."

"Can we go there and take a look at them and see what you have?"

"Well," Andrew hesitated, "Can I speak with my wife first?"

"Absolutely."

"It will be just a sec," Andrew promised, leaving them at the door. While he was gone the officers talked. One reminded the other to make note of the tags on Andrew's vehicle. He wondered out loud whether they had any bolt cutters.

"It may be necessary," the other responded, "but I don't think it will be." As minutes dragged on, they knocked again. Andrew, who was inside frantically contacting Jamie for advice, had kept them waiting sixteen minutes. Finally a child shrieked, "Daddy's downstairs!"

An officer tromped around to the side of the house, where he knocked several times on another door. No response. The other poked his head around the corner to say that Andrew had reappeared at the first door and was ready to head for the church.

"The wife is getting the young'uns ready and we're heading to church. The most I've got is copperheads and some rattlesnakes, too," Andrew said. "Will they get taken?"

"We'll decide when we get there," was the response.

Once at the church, Andrew led the officials inside, unlocking two doors before they arrived at the snake room. Once there, Andrew was informed that the snakes were being confiscated. As officials carted them out, Andrew began texting his friends and fan base: *Anyone and everyone that will please begin to pray now. 4 game wardens have me at my church now. I don't know what the out come will be but Liz will keep everyone posted. Mark 16:18 is still real.*

He got 165 comments and 269 likes. Meanwhile, Jamie was also spreading the word: *Everyone pray for Andrew Hamblin TWRA officers are at the church with him now they will most definitely take his snakes and possibly take him to jail. And before some of you decides to make you smat elic comments just remember you may not agree with our religion but they are taking all our rights away a little at a time. Prayers out of school ten commandments out of courthouse pledge of allegiance just on religion gun rights. So just consider you may not like what we do but some people don't like guns either.*

One woman responded: *Didn't u all realize if u went public with this program that the authorities would come in and take the reptiles? . . . and I'm shocked they haven't come in for child endangering.*

Jamie shot back: *I went on television because as the apostle Paul said "I am not ashamed of the gospel of Christ for it is the power of God unto salvation not to the Jew only but also to the greek."*

Some 158 responses rained in fast and furiously. Posters ranged from a rural mail carrier in Minnesota to a paramedic in Powell, Tennessee. Most said they disagreed with snake handling but defended the right to do it. *I've watched the show many times and they are not putting the children in danger,* one woman wrote.

It's your snakes today, our Guns tomorrow and it's not getting better, messaged a woman from Hazard, Kentucky. *This current government is out to seek and destroy.*

Don Burnett, a man in charge of information services at the nearby Lincoln Memorial University, wrote, *Jamie, sir, you know I am Lutheran and do not interpret Mark the same as you, but as a Law Enforcement officer I personally have tended to your animals myself many years ago. It is a violation of religious freedom. Prayers my friend!*

Jamie then posted a number of photos of wildlife officials and what looked like police carting out the snakes in glass aquaria. A female reporter stood on the church porch taking notes. Everyone was wearing a coat except Andrew.

One woman then posted: *Well I will call some good old boys of South Carolina to go out and pick up some more for you. We praying.*

A woman from Parsons, West Virginia, posted: *If you want some big timber rattlers, come up to the hills of Tucker County in West Virginia. We have lots.*

Then Andrew posted some updates: *They came in my church and took every serpent we had,* he wrote. *My court date is November 15 at 9:00. I encourage everyone no matter if we believe alike or not to come show your support of a fellow CHRISTIAN. But one thing is for sure. I've still got VICTORY!!!!!!* This got 167 comments, ranging from a reader in Piketon, Ohio, to a vocational tech in Philadelphia and a University of Cincinnati neuroscience student. People suggested petitions and asked if there would be a legal fund. The people commenting ran the gamut in terms of race, age, and occupation. A fan from an herbal retreat center in Barre, Vermont, offered to donate. A senior security analyst at the University of Texas–San Antonio, a man from Pueblo, Colorado, and a woman from Houston all expressed support.

Guess the state has nothing else better to do than harass these folks! wrote a paramedic in Lafayette, Louisiana.

I'M sorry I'M mad. Somebody turned this man in and I dont trust anybody but pastor andrew and pastor Jamie, another person wrote.

Later in the day, Andrew posted: *I want to take a few minutes and thank everyone whether you believe like me or not for all the messages, comments, and most of all prayers. God will move you watch and see. This day I declare victory. Hold on children our promised land is just in sight!!!! Amen Thank GOD!!!!*

On Friday he wrote: *Thank God for this day. Keep the prayers coming. Write letters, send emails, make petitions. Let's nip this in the bud once and for all. Everyone also remember there WILL be church tonight and were gonna have a time. Hope to see you there.*

At this point Andrew's Facebook list had zoomed up to 4,915 friends. He was charged with possession of Class 1 wildlife (species inherently dangerous to humans), a misdemeanor punishable by up to eleven months, twenty-nine days in jail, and a $2,500 fine per count—which could mean some serious jail time if they threw the book at him.

Ready for my blessing tonight, he posted a bit later. *Hope everybody plans on being there tonight. Were gonna shout the house down. Come and see what God has in store tonight.* Some 231 people "liked" that, including one Ashley Hall, who messaged: *On our way we wasn't gonna miss this.*

Judging from comments on his page several hours later, his Friday night service was packed. On one of the TV clips, Andrew was playing it as a major religious freedom issue.

"To me, it's unconstitutional," he told one network. "To me, telling someone what they can or cannot have in a worship service is no different than telling someone they can or cannot have a Bible."

A warden interviewed sounded lamer. "A venomous snake can bite and kill a human being and especially the elderly and the young folks," he said. "You see both of these kind of folks around those snakes at his church."

That, I thought, wasn't really true, and it was obvious the wildlife police hadn't visited Andrew's church during services. Yes, there were kids in the sanctuary, including my now eight-year-old. As for the elderly, I could count on one hand anyone over fifty I'd seen at Andrew's house of worship. It was clear the state was going to use the danger-to-the-public argument, which might have been feasible if Andrew's church had been on a main street somewhere. But the Tabernacle Church of God was off a side road that was off a side road. One had to work hard to get there.

By this time, articles were appearing everywhere as journalists were dusting off their *Snake Salvation* press releases from two months back. "Serpent handler–TV star has a new cause: religious liberty," is what Bob Smietana wrote for Religion News Service. Over the summer, he'd left the *Tennessean* for a better-paying and more stable job, but he was still following Andrew's story. He quoted one person from the Becket Fund for Religious Liberty suggesting that if the TWRA allowed zoos to have snakes, they should allow churches to own them as well. An official for the Baptist Joint Committee for Religious Liberty brought up the 2009 Tennessee Religious Freedom Restoration Act, which allows the state to restrict religious practice only if it has a compelling interest and that it must do so by the least restrictive means. Totally forbidding snakes from the property of a serpent-handling church would be overwhelmingly restrictive. The *New York Times* took the same angle, quoting a Stanford Law School scholar, who suggested the state could not treat zoos one way and churches another.

Religious liberty had become a huge part of the national debate by the fall of 2013. States had been changing their laws against same-sex marriage since 2004, so in June 2013, the Supreme Court struck down a key provision of the 1996 Defense of Marriage Act, basically forcing federal recognition of gay marriage, along with marriage-related benefits. As more homosexual couples began having marriage ceremonies, they began approaching bakeries, wedding photographers, and wedding chapels to assist in their weddings. Or, in the case of a Lexington, Kentucky, T-short company, its owner was asked to make T-shirts for a local "pride festival." Caught in the crosshairs were some of the Christian owners of these businesses, who didn't want to participate in a ritual they felt was morally wrong. Starting with a lesbian couple who sued an Albuquerque photographer for refusing to shoot their "commitment ceremony," homosexuals were fighting back. One side claimed it was their civil right to be served in the way they requested, and the other said the First Amendment guaranteed them freedom to practice their religion, which meant not supporting anything to do with gay weddings.

Thus, Andrew's arrest was rich with great story possibilities. A bunch of local TV stations had also weighed in, using the angle that the snakes were a public safety hazard. The TWRA folks were quick to talk about how some of the serpents were already dead when they were taken to the Knoxville Zoo; others were sick. Eventually they would all be euthanized. Oddly, I saw nothing in the Knoxville paper. However, the *Chattanooga Times Free Press* was waking up to the fact that serpent handling had started a century ago in their neck of the woods and that Ralph Hood worked in their city, and yet they were doing precious little coverage on the topic. They assigned a team of reporters to start working on a project about serpent handlers. Things had progressed a long way since Lauren and I were the only people on the snake beat. Starting with the *Post* piece in November 2011, it was mainly us those first two years—along with Bob Smietana—but when the reality show hit, other reporters elbowed their way in. The Knoxville TV stations were finally doing regular stories on Andrew and Jamie, as was the LaFollette paper.

On Saturday, flush from the huge crowd on Friday, Andrew posted: *I'd like to encourage my fellow pastors and their churches of every denomination to come and support me on the 15th at Campbell county courthouse. I encourage* EVERYONE *that stands up for religious freedom to be there to. Today its us tomorrow it might the Baptist, Catholics, or Methodists. Thank you all and God bless.* A separate Facebook page, "Support for Pastor Andrew Hamblin and family—snake salvation," had eight hundred likes by early Saturday evening.

That same evening I called Jamie to see what he thought. He was still smarting from the NPR exposé about the condition of his snakes.

"Andrew has been there two years," he was telling me. "They knew where the snakes were. He don't let the elderly handle them nor kids." Jamie had gotten some fallout from the show as well. Kentucky law demands that one have a permit to keep poisonous snakes, and Jamie had obtained permits back in 2008 after he was fined $5,000 for keeping several dozen poisonous snakes and had spent several hours in jail.

"PETA [People for the Ethical Treatment of Animals] had sent a letter to the Middlesboro police, state police, the district attorney, and game wardens saying they needed to come out and check my building," he said. "But the Middlesboro police said Jamie has all these permits for these snakes and they've already been checked."

I asked about his family. Both Little Cody and Trina had found full-time jobs, and Jamie was driving a school bus part-time. *Snake Salvation* had not brought crowds his way as it had to Andrew's church, but he had two thousand Facebook friends, a lot of people had requested prayer, and his church had sent out prayer cloths to those who asked. (Pentecostals believe such cloths can been prayed over as a way of imparting blessings to those unable to be physically present at services.)

"And it has enlightened them to what our church is about," he added. I asked him about the show. "They thought it would go big and be popular," he said.

"The ratings were just too low. I talked to one of the executive producers who said, 'I know people are watching but not the people with the Neilson boxes on the back of their TVs.' I knew there was lots and lots of people watching." Then there were those last four episodes all in a row on October 22, aired as though the channel was trying to clear the series off its plate. Then again, National Geographic was showing reruns of the show through November.

"It didn't seem to me they gave it as much advertising as they should have," Jamie remarked. "They thought it was something really huge. Non-Christians don't want to watch something like that. Mainstream religions don't want to watch it. It seemed like it fizzled out pretty quick."

The weeks dragged by until Andrew's first court appearance. I'd gotten the nod from the *Journal* to write about it for them, so I left Veeka with some friends and drove across the state to cover the arraignment. There was also chatter on Facebook about Liz being in the hospital briefly after having a panic attack.

It was a clear, starry, late fall night, just hours before the arraignment, when I arrived at the hotel to pick up Jenna Gray-Hildenbrand, the MTSU professor I'd met at Jimmy Morrow's. Because Jenna was a specialist on serpent-handling laws, she felt she had to be at this hearing. I took her to Andrew's church about six miles away, as she'd never seen it. We had decided to share a room at a Hampton Inn just off the I-75 exit and down the road from the courthouse. It was a wonderful place with llamas in the back yard, a pretty view out front, and all sorts of local historic material in the front lobby. I remarked to her how the lovely, cool evening was so similar to that New Year's Eve almost two years ago when I first arrived at Andrew's church. And here we were: that same dirt parking lot overlooking the surrounding countryside with the cars parked helter-skelter.

A table for petitions was set up near the front of the church. My *Journal* article had been relocated to the narthex, and a large photo of Andrew handling a snake (from the *Tennessean*) was on the left wall of the nave with Mark 16:17–18 emblazoned on it. Someone told Andrew we were there, and he came in from a side room, wearing a red T-shirt that bore the same biblical reference.

All of his fifty-three snakes were local, he told us, with two exceptions: one Malaysian mangrove and one South American rattlesnake.

"I'm hoping for a miracle tomorrow," he confided. What really hurt him wasn't so much the TWRA but Dennis Powers, the state representative who had encouraged Andrew to approach the county commission in the summer of 2012 about supporting his bid to change state law forbidding possession of poisonous snakes. The commission had turned him down, but Powers, no doubt buoyed by the presence of the National Geographic film crew, still acted cordially toward Andrew. Then came November 7. After the TWRA and all the media had left his church, Andrew had gotten wind that Tennessee governor Bill Haslam was in the area that very day at a fundraiser. Andrew made the gutsy decision to appeal to the governor himself. He only got as far as Haslam's security detail, which referred him to Powers, who was also at the reception. Powers's conversation with Andrew was civil enough, but afterwards Powers told the *LaFollette Press* he was surprised "someone on food stamps" could afford the $100-a-plate reception. "I'm not really sure how he got in," Powers told the paper. Andrew saw the article and was still seething when we talked with him.

"It's a shame when a preacher can't talk with his own governor without being thought an extremist," he told us. "What'd he think I was going to do: pull a snake out of my pocket?"

He showed us some of the improvements he'd made at the church. The bathroom had new flooring, and there were the beginnings of a porch patio on the west side of the church. There were also instruments for a full band. Two years before, there'd been one keyboard, three guitars, and some tambourines. Things had gone uptown since then. Now there was a complete set of drums, four electric guitars, one bass, a keyboard, and of course the tambourines.

The next morning at 8:30, Andrew was holding a press conference on the steps of the Campbell County courthouse. Fortunately, the weather was mild and the morning was crisp and clear, so he stood there with his large Bible and in a red dress shirt and dark suit. Except for a few business suits and several media folks bearing notepads, the crowd seemed to be all locals. I spotted Liz in a long black skirt, red blouse, and a red bow in her hair. She told me they hadn't gotten to bed until 3:00 a.m. Jamie Coots had shown up wearing a maroon blazer, red tie, and red shirt. I spotted Michelle Gray in the crowd wearing a red satin blouse.

"How's the little one?" she asked me.

Jenna loaned me a red scarf, so I fit in. About forty people—many of them sporting some shade of red—had gathered on the steps to listen. The most eye-catching of the lot was a woman in dark pants and jacket, red blouse, and long blonde hair carrying a red and black "SNAKES TODAY, BIBLES TOMORrow?" sign. Standing behind her was another woman whose sign read, "Mark 16:17–18 is as real as John 3:16"; the latter was as pivotal a verse symbolizing evangelical Christianity if ever there was one. Seeing the TV cameras rolling, Andrew proved himself more than able to deliver a few dramatic flourishes, starting with a retelling of the story of Abraham not withholding his son, Isaac, from sacrifice.

"Today, I don't want to withhold the sixteenth chapter of the book of Mark from God," Andrew told us. "This is my God-given right in the United States. If God moves on me to take up a serpent, I take up a serpent."

We entered the courtroom where Ralph, Jenna, and I crammed into the front row. Andrew was paraded in along with a bunch of scruffy-looking men, and all were told the charges against them. Andrew pled not guilty, the lawyers conferred, and it was announced that his preliminary hearing would be at 3:00 p.m. on December 17. I inwardly groaned. Veeka's school Christmas pageant was that day. Andrew headed outside for another speech on the courthouse steps while Jenna and I, along with Gemma from Buzzfeed, entrapped Chris Jones, the pro-bono lawyer who helped defend Jamie in Knox County General Sessions Court the previous February. He was no friend of the TWRA, he told us, adding that in 1991, Tennessee had amended its wildlife code to require permits for the keeping of any wildlife, including turtles. He told us of people who had had to surrender their raccoons or tame deer. Someone's pet deer, he told us, was apprehended in the morning and shot that afternoon.

"They send storm troopers to peoples' homes," he added. "No state treats people like they do in Tennessee."

My Speakeasy blog on the hearing made it onto the "editor's picks" section that weekend. The *New York Times* had also sent a reporter there, raising the stakes. A few weeks later, NBC's *Nightline* had Andrew and Jamie on. The *Nightline* reporter was respectful but totally clueless about anything Pentecostal.

On November 25, Liz posted: *Wonts to thank the good Lord for a few things. first 4 months ago we lived in a two bedroom house with 5 kids. it was so hard we didn't have room for anything so we started looking for a bigger place seemed like every were we would call when u mention ur married to andrew hamblin or having 5 kids people would just hang up. 6 different places to be correct. Anyhow we drove around one day just looking and trying to find a place and we came across beautiful house but to much for us to afford. andrew stopped at one place and set there crying a said I would give anything to give u and the kids a nice house something like out of a magazine. I told him just hold on and in Gods time well get one. two months later the Lord blessed us with a 4 bedroom two bathrooms up stairs and down stairs red and white house ain't God good??? But then something came up that are vehicle had to go cause we couldn't affort the payments but God blessed again and the Lord moved on some good people and they baught us a van. not done yet!!! we had been looking for a couch and [love] seat and out of the blue God sent some more God fearing people along are way and tonight we got blessed with a couch love seat coffee table and end tables. I can't thank him enough!!!!!!!*

Then, on November 30: *Really wishes people would walk a mile in mine and andrews shoes then maybe they would give us a break I mean really we have a family of 7, church, church family, natural family, all that's going on with this court date. not to mention some unspoken matters. we don't have time to breath so please back off.*

She got a load of sympathetic replies from dozens of people out of the thousands now following her Facebook feed. The chatter continued into the next month. On December 11, Andrew posted: *Another sleepless night has come and gone but yet I'm blessed with one more day. Everyone keep those prayers going up. And remember I need everyone, no matter your denomination or beliefs, to come out and be with me on the 17th at 3:00 at the Campbell county courthouse to show your support for freedom of ALL Christians in America. Hope everyone has a blessed day. #freedom #prayers #faith #hope.* He got 174 likes and twenty-nine comments. One of his grandfathers died during this time—another major blow.

Someone asked Liz about how the police got wind of where they lived. *They came to our home that we just moved into and no one really new were we lived so were think we were set up by someone we know or they have been watching,* she responded. *they came to the house and then two more were at the church are landlord said the had been waiting for 30 mins before we got there. but they didnt read him his rights till after he showed them the snakes.*

A month later, we were back. Andrew seemed to be blessed with good weather on his court dates, as the skies were clear that Tuesday afternoon. The thirty-mile drive up I-75 from Knoxville was feeling downright familiar as I swept up toward the gorgeous green ridges and mountain lakes. Jenna was waiting by the courthouse. She came a few days early to attend the Sunday service. There, Andrew had joked to the congregation that if his snakes were brought in as evidence, God just might anoint him to handle them. I chatted up a few deputies, who told me which BBQ restaurant in town to patronize and which Boy Scout trail led along the ridge atop Powell Valley. I then ran into Matthew Cameron, the omnipresent TWRA spokesman, outside the courtroom. I pointed out to him that snake handling in churches had been around for 103 years, so why the fuss now?

"It doesn't conform to the law," he said of the way the snakes were kept. "It has to be a cage within a cage with a parameter fence around it guarded twenty-four hours a day by an expert." Only zoos and educational institutions qualified, he added. I wondered whether even the Knoxville Zoo had an "expert" guarding its snakes 24/7. I pointed out that no church could even hope to qualify under those standards. If Andrew went down, I asked, would his agency go after other churches, such as Jimmy Morrow's? He refused to say.

Some seventy-two spectators, many of them wearing red, filled the courtroom along with another thirty lawyers, sheriff's deputies, and other officials. Andrew, resplendent in what looked like a new suit with a red tie, cream-colored shirt, and red and black vest, entered the courtroom, hugging people as he made his way to the front. This case may have been a pain in terms of time and the $2,500 Andrew was having to pay for a lawyer, but in terms of free PR, it was a gift that kept on giving. I looked up the new address of their house, which real estate records showed was bought for them in September for $55,000. They'd definitely moved uptown.

To persuade the judge that there was enough evidence to send the case forward, the district attorney called on TWRA's Sergeant Joe Durnin, who was one of the two officers who visited to the Hamblin household. He was asked to tell of his subsequent discovery of the fifty-three venomous snakes in six containers at the church.

"We read him his rights, then took possession of the snakes," he said. "We tried to identify what we had in the containers." There were twenty-eight copperheads, he added, along with a collection of rattlers, cottonmouths, and some exotic species.

Next up was Andrew's lawyer, Mark Hatmaker, who made Durnin retrace his steps on the morning of November 7. Hatmaker was bald and wore a light grey suit and dark round glasses. We learned that the TWRA had collected six agents from adjoining counties for the raid with two of them at Andrew's house, two stationed at the church, and the other two on stand-by. Hatmaker asked Durnin to repeat the conversation at Andrew's house and Durnin blurted out that it was all on tape. A surprised murmur arose.

"You took a recording device to the Hamblins' home?" asked Hatmaker, acting aghast. "Did he know you were recording him?"

"I don't know," Durnin responded, adding that all agents like him wear portable cameras. Hatmaker acted as though he'd never heard of such a thing, at which point Durnin grinned.

"You find that funny?" snapped Hatmaker.

"Well, sir, if you're not aware of that, I find that amusing," Durnin said.

"Did you tell him at any time you were taping him?" Hatmaker asked.

"No sir." He added that the camera on his shirt was "pretty obvious."

"Pretty obvious to him?" Hatmaker groused. I sidled over to Andrew and asked whether he knew he was being taped. He shook his head. "Entrapment," someone in the audience murmured. The agent said the whole dialogue was on a file on a laptop in the courtroom, and several minutes passed while various lawyers tried to make the tape play. The screen was set facing the judge and away from the spectators. "America's funniest videos," someone in the room cracked. A woman in red raised her hands. "God is in the house," she proclaimed.

The tape finally started. Amid the twittering of birds and the continued barking of a dog, we listened to the two agents' confrontation with Andrew for nearly twenty-five minutes.

"When you went to Andrew's house, you were going there for the purpose of getting snakes from him, right?" Hatmaker asked afterward.

"Possibly," admitted the agent.

"Why didn't you get a warrant?" the lawyer asked.

"I was just going to inquire," Durnin replied. The lawyer clearly found it difficult to understand why Durnin assembled agents from several counties just to "inquire" about Andrew.

"Didn't you tell him he had a right to remain silent?" the lawyer asked.

"I didn't know he was in violation at that point," Durnin replied.

"Did you have any proof he was guilty of anything before October 7?" the lawyer asked, plainly confusing October with the November 7 arrest date.

"Not necessarily," said the agent.

Realizing he'd messed up the dates, the lawyer asked, "Did you have any proof before November 7 that he possessed Class 1 wildlife?"

"No," the agent said. Then he added, "There was all sorts of images on TV. There was all sorts of pictorial evidence."

"What if it was more than a year ago?" the lawyer asked, referring to a statute of limitations whereby the state cannot prosecute for an offense more than a year old. "You can't charge him with possession if was more than a year ago. . . . You went to his house to investigate him? You wanted him to admit he had snakes?"

"I had no personal interest one way or another," the agent said, adding that the TV shows were enough evidence for him. The judge seemed to think so, too, ruling that there was probable cause for the charge against Andrew. He announced a January 6 date for a grand jury hearing.

Afterward on the courthouse steps, it was dark, quite windy, and about forty-eight degrees. Andrew, who was floodlit by TV lights, remained upbeat. "I believe God has his hand on this," he said. "Everything went well. I feel the Lord will intervene."

Just before his arraignment on Nov. 15, 2013, Andrew Hamblin speaks to supporters and media on the steps of the Campbell County courthouse in Jacksboro, Tennessee.

After a preliminary hearing, Andrew Hamblin gives a press conference on Tuesday, December 17, 2013, on the steps of the Campbell County courthouse in Jacksboro, Tennessee.

In support of Andrew Hamblin, Jamie (center) and Linda Coots (immediate right of Jamie) stand on the steps of the Campbell County courthouse on November 15, 2013. The three women with them are (left to right) Rosie Nash, Flossie Brumitte, and Nana Lou Meadors and they attended Andrew's church.

A detail from a painting of Tennessee serpent handlers at a baptism by pastor and serpent handler Jimmy Morrow. Notice the "Jesus only" shirts as well as the snake and snake box.

Seen on a car parked outside of Jamie Coots's church in Middlesboro, Kentucky, in August 2012.

Jimmy Morrow, the pastor of a serpent-handling church in Newport, Tennessee, shows off a serpent-handling doll he made.

The path to the Pinnacle Overlook at Cumberland Gap National Historical Park, which sits on a ridge overlooking Kentucky, Tennessee, and Virginia. Taken on December 31, 2011. Olivia "Veeka" Duin is seated to one side.

Veeka at the Pinnacle Overlook at Cumberland Gap National Historical Park on December 31, 2013, two years after our original visit. The lake shimmering in the background is right in back of the Middlesboro church.

The couple in the center is Andrew and Liz Hamblin. She is weeping after he's handed her a snake during the New Year's Eve service on December 31, 2013.

Andrew and Liz Hamblin with their snake boxes. Photo by Joshua Lowery.

Andrew Hamblin holds aloft two handfuls totaling five snakes at a New Year's Eve service at his LaFollette, Tennessee, church marking the end of 2013. The woman on the right in the skirt with her back to the camera is Linda Spoon.

As Andrew Hamblin grasps two copperheads, he's flanked by Dillion Gray (to the left) and Derek Abrams. Photo by John Morgan.

Andrew Hamblin leads worship at his LaFollette, Tennessee, church. In the near background is Paul Gray. Photo by John Morgan.

Andrew Hamblin offers members of his Tabernacle Church of God a chance to do some snake handling during a service on December 31, 2013.

A disconsolate Andrew Hamblin holds a press conference inside his Tabernacle Church of God on February 22, 2014, to explain his reactions to the death of his mentor Jamie Coots a week earlier.

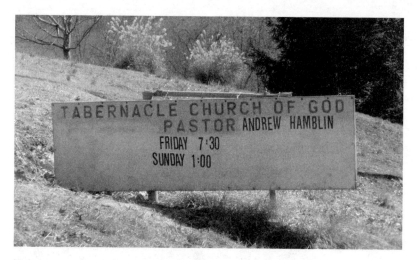

Tabernacle Church of God's sign stating service times and Andrew's name.

Veeka Duin and Payton Hamblin play outside of the Hamblin residence on Frontier Road in LaFollette, Tennessee, February 22, 2014.

Liz Hamblin and her three boys announce baby Hamblin number six.
Courtesy of Elizabeth Hamblin.

The Hamblin children, (left to right) Clayton, Caydon, Payton (picking up Dayton),
Haylin, and Madlyin, playing in Tackett Creek in Clairfield, Tennessee, in the spring
of 2016. Courtesy of Elizabeth Hamblin.

(Left to right) Jacob Gray, Michelle Gray, and Andrew Abrams at a closing party in May 2014 after a homecoming weekend at the Tabernacle Church of God.

(Left to right) Jonathan Gray, Andrew Hamblin, and Paul Gray at a homecoming at the LaFollette, Tennessee, church on May 24, 2014. Hamblin is handling two copperheads. Photo by John Morgan.

Tyler Evans (brother to Nathan) handles two copperheads. Andrew Hamblin
is to the left, Jeremey Henegar is to the right (background), and Paul Gray is
to the far right. Photo by John Morgan.

(Left to right) Michelle Gray,
Jullian Evans, and Elizabeth
Hamblin at the Saturday night
service of a May 2014 homecom-
ing at the Tabernacle Church of
God. Photo by John Morgan.

Nathan Evans, great-great grandson of serpent-handling pioneers Barbara and Joe Elkins of Jolo, West Virginia, handles a rattlesnake at a homecoming in LaFollette, Tennessee, in May 2014. Photo by John Morgan.

Veeka Duin, then 6, worships during a service at the Church of the Lord Jesus in Jolo, West Virginia, in September 2011.

Taylor Noe (left) looks on as Andrew Hamblin handles two copperheads.
To the right are Elizabeth Hamblin and Jullian Evans. Photo by John Morgan.

Adam Hensley married Elizabeth Hamblin
on March 18, 2017. Family Photo.

As Taylor Noe handles fire, her husband Derrick Noe places his hand on her back.
Tyler Evans is to the left. Photo by John Morgan.

CHAPTER TEN

NEW YEAR'S EVE

• •

We approached Cumberland Gap in the late afternoon with just a few more hours left of 2013. The early winter sky was a bright blue, and the day was clear.

My daughter and I retraced our steps of two years before, racing up Pinnacle Road to the overlook over Powell Mountain, the Poor Valley Ridge, and thousands of blinking lights as dusk raced toward us. So much had happened since I'd driven 530 miles from Washington on a whim. I looked west toward Middlesboro. On one of those twisty roads was Jamie's church. South down the Powell Valley was Andrew's new home. And way to the southeast was Jimmy Morrow's church. The Browns' church was across the state line in North Carolina, and beyond the horizon was the church on Sand Mountain. Way to the east was the Jolo church.

Everything was dusky blues and yellows. The landscape was more somber than on our first visit, and the sun was sinking fast in a blaze of puffed clouds. The reservoir—Fern Lake—behind Jamie's church glittered. The trees were completely bare. Icicles hung from the rocks. It was thirty-nine degrees when we climbed out of the car. Twenty minutes after we rushed back from the overlook, it was thirty-three.

Our thirty-mile drive back to LaFollette on Route 68 was interrupted by one thing: my curiosity about Andrew and Liz's new home. It was several miles north of town, so the skies were dark by the time we drove by. Sure enough, it appeared quite spacious and definitely out in the country. We were hungry, so we stopped by the Sonic Drive-In for a kid's meal and a banana split for old time's sake. Lafollette was still a maze of Food Lions, Dollar General stores, banks, insurance companies, and cheesy Christmas lights. Then we headed east on Tennessee Avenue, past a huge chicken at the gas station across from the police department parking lot where I first met Andrew and followed him to his church.

It darkened into a clear, cold night with a sky full of stars. Right away I noticed huge differences from two years ago. First, Andrew was standing outside with the smokers. I did not see him with a cigarette, but he'd been more open lately about the fact that he smoked even though people were criticizing him for it. The church was half full forty-five minutes before the service. Andrew had set out extra red folding chairs.

"No one under eighteen is to be messing with these serpents," he announced. "If you've come to fight and argue, go back to the house. We come to worship in spirit and in truth. We only want believers to handle snakes on this hardwood. I'm here to edify the body of Christ. I don't know what you're here for."

There was clearly a defensiveness and wariness that the twenty-year-old pastor of two years ago did not have. Now twenty-two, he had been through the wringer of having his name and beliefs broadcast around the country and having to deal with reactions from thousands of people. He went on to talk about the rules for pictures, and he asked those people who don't want to be in media photos to raise their hands. About five did so. About eighty people were there by 8:00 p.m., and the number drifted up to close to one hundred as the evening progressed. Andrew was dressed in a suit, a white shirt with cufflinks, and a black tie. A bevy of young men up front looked natty in dress shirts and suspenders. It was a better-dressed crowd by far, and Andrew told me later he wanted a classier look among his acolytes.

The band swung into "I've Got the Devil under my Feet," and Andrew did some wonderful riffs on a white electric guitar. A woman in her late 60s in a floor-length marron skirt with long, grey hair danced about, then prayed over a young woman in a long skirt and black sweater whose downcast face was covered by her hair. I didn't recognize any of these people but later learned the older woman was Linda Spoon, one of the stalwarts of the church. Before the service, I approached a few people to ask how long they had been coming, and no one had been there longer than a year. Eventually, I spotted Charity Powers, the teenager whom I'd seen handle fire at Andrew's church. A blue cloth flower pinned in her hair matched her blouse. Now sixteen, she was ultra-slim with long, wavy brown hair that fell well below her waist, and enough of a beauty to attract local suitors. In fact, I'd seen her August 16 wedding proposal on Facebook. But she told me the engagement was off and that she was not going to Andrew's church any more. Things, she said, had changed, and she liked it better the old way. Her brother Daniel and sister-in-law, Kasi, had left the church, and Kasi had just had her second child, a girl, ten days before. Her other brother, Charlie, and his girlfriend sat behind me. Charity may have been discontented, but toward the end of the evening, she was up in front worshipping.

Andrew asked how many people had come because of *Snake Salvation*. About five or six raised their hands. An informal poll I'd taken of some of the congregants before the service found that people came more by word of mouth and what they read in the *LaFollette Press*. Andrew then announced he needed prayer.

"Well, don't just stand there staring at me," he said before a number of people rushed to the front and placed their hands on him. Meanwhile, Veeka was bellyaching forty-five minutes into the service about the earsplitting noise. I refused to budge. She was the reason I left early two years ago and missed Andrew's being snake-bitten at midnight. She was eight and a half now and would just have to endure it. Though that may sound coldhearted, Andrew was now a celebrity, a lot of journalists were tracking him besides me, and I felt like I needed to stay on top of everything he was doing. Ever since I'd missed Mack's death and had the difficult job of assembling a story from hundreds of miles away, I wanted to be present if anything happened with Andrew. Of course, I was hoping for a quiet night, but as far as I could tell, I was the only journalist there.

The snakes first came out not even an hour into the service, and the way Andrew stood there holding them all in both hands reminded me of a priest holding up the bread and wine. I snatched Veeka's new iPad from her and found it took much better pictures than my digital camera. An old-time Chattanooga handler—who noticed me snapping away—sidled up and asked me to use neither his name nor that of a visiting handler from Georgia.

"I don't want people connecting me with being here," he said. Like everyone else there, he did not have copious amounts of money and was terrified of some TWRA officer showing up at his door with a newspaper clipping in hand and a lawsuit at the ready. "They'll try to close the door on our churches in Tennessee," he added. I asked him why Tennessee handlers like Jimmy Morrow and the Browns weren't lifting a finger to help Andrew, at least that I could see. If he fell, they were next in line.

"The Jesus name people are the most organized unorganized people you'll find," he said. "They are split among themselves about this. I've tried to get that bunch unified for a long time, but the slightest thing separates them."

Meanwhile it was chaos up front with several dozen people milling about. There were people weeping; at least two men were in a dead faint on the floor (this was known as being "slain in the Spirit"); others were getting prayed over; others were dancing. Numerous people were racing in circles around the podium, while other people were twirling and playing various instruments. All sorts of kids were wandering in and out. At 11:30, Andrew started to preach. He told congregants to act more Christian towards each other—"to suck it up and grow up," as he put it. About one minute before midnight, to my horror, he grabbed a handful of snakes and hoisted them up. No, you fool, I thought. Remember what happened at the stroke of midnight two years ago?

But Andrew handed three rattlers and two copperheads to anyone who'd take them. As the drums, organ, and guitars ground away, he danced from one person to another—at one point he was holding five snakes in his hands—offering them a chance to try serpent handling. Several people did so. Liz took a snake in hand and dissolved into tears. In fact, she had several snakes in her hands. She eventually stopped crying, and it jolted me when she wiped her face with one of the snakes. I headed up front with the iPad. Lauren was not there tonight to record this on film. Veeka, who'd been complaining all evening, found a small tambourine and got a second wind, dancing about at the front while I restrained her from going anywhere near that pulpit where God-knows-what snake might be in a box nearby. I remembered Andrew saying a month before that he'd be willing to construct a glass barrier, and I realized that, with this welter of humanity of all ages on that platform, a barrier was not going to fly. Ralph had told me that in 103 years, no bystander at these services had ever been bitten by a snake. I wondered where the TWRA folks were now and why they couldn't come to one of these services to see how the whole thing actually worked.

Eventually we were outside under the early morning stars, where we miraculously found Veeka's new Barbie doll on the sidewalk—where she'd dropped it—and it was back to the Hampton Inn. I was too tired to notice a speed trap, which meant that sometime after 1:30 a.m., one of Jacksboro's finest stopped me for going twelve miles over the speed limit and having an expired license plate. The evening cost me $175.

The next morning, Andrew texted me to meet at McDonald's, as I'd asked to talk with him. He had arrived early, which was pretty amazing considering he was up until about 5:00 a.m. After the service, he and Liz and a few church members had gone to a Waffle House to relax. He said he had a "thirty-six-hour day" in front of him, which I read to mean I had an hour with him at best. When I asked about his court defense, he replied that the snakes "belong to the church. So anyone who handles the snakes would have to be charged with possession." That was obviously something his lawyer had thought up—not a bad stratagem considering that the last thing the local court wanted was to take on more than one serpent handler or to be accused of raiding a church. I asked him about how things had been going in court, and he told me that Sergeant Durnin's remark about the bolt cutters had offended a lot of people. Again, that individualistic mountain spirit. No one wanted police at their door with bolt cutters. But Andrew's church was now two years old. Why now and why here?

"Word got to me that the DA felt I was rubbing their faces in it," he said of Lori Phillips-Jones, the district attorney for Campbell County. "They watched the show and asked for the cottonmouths I'd brought back from Texas." To create momentum for the show, the National Geographic Channel had created a field trip for Andrew, Jamie, and both Codys to go snake hunting in Texas. It was in one of the earlier episodes. Of course, he had liked the show but said, "I hunt maybe five times a year. The show made me look like that's all I did."

I tried to find out exactly what National Geographic paid him, but he dodged the question. I asked him about the nearly 100 percent turnover his church had seen in the past year. As for those who'd left, it was their fault, not his, he said. A revival he had in October—to take advantage of his new local fans from *Snake Salvation*—netted him a bunch of new members. People were standing outside back then, he told me, trying to get into the church, which squared with some of the Facebook posts I remembered from folks mentioning the crowds. His was now the largest serpent-handling church in

Tennessee, and he estimated that "hundreds" had become Christians through his ministry over the past two years. He could think of two churches (one in Texas, the other in Arkansas) that had taken up snake handling after hearing about him and that Pentecostal pastors were asking him for advice about when to take up a snake.

"They say, 'I was praying about it and I went numb in my hands and I handled a snake and nothing happened to me,'" Andrew said of those conversations. He wondered if he should start a new denomination. "That was our third New Year's Eve service," he said, "and look where we are now."

Now that he was on trial, I asked where the snakes had come from for his services.

"They come from here, there, and elsewhere," he said. This was not the innocent with whom Lauren and I had met two years ago at the Pizza Hut. He was now a media veteran, a man with a lawyer, a man who was in court and guarded his privacy more than he used to. He was under immense pressure.

We got into a discussion about Jolo. He wondered what was happening there, as it had held no homecoming in September. I'd called Harvey's home to ask the same thing, and the person on the other end—Harvey's wife, I thought—told me they'd stopped meeting during the winter. During warmer months, they held meetings on occasional Wednesdays. For Andrew, that proved the pillar of fire had left Jolo and come to LaFollette.

"Liz," he informed me, "is the new Barb Elkins." And he, of course, was the new Bob Elkins, and they would be the couple setting the pace for serpent handling in the twenty-first century.

A week later, I heard Andrew's grand jury appearance had been switched to January 8, the same day I was flying to Colorado for a conference. As soon as I reached my room in Boulder and logged onto Facebook, I saw Andrew's first post at 6:00 a.m.: *Today is the day of Salvation. I speak victory this morning, not only for serpent handling Pentecostals, but for religious freedom threw out this country. I don't know what this day holds but I know who holds it in his hands. Everyone remember me, my wife, my children and my congregation as I face the grand jury today. Always remember in some way or other the Lord will provide.*

And then, in the early afternoon, appeared this on his Facebook page: *BLESSED BE THE NAME OF THE LORD!!!!! The verdict is NOT GUILTY!!!!! God prevailed in Campbell County today. From the bottom of my heart I thank everyone for your prayers and support. Thank God for evermore.*

That post got 723 Facebook likes. Sure enough, when I clicked on WATE .com, the site of the Knoxville ABC affiliate, I saw the report that the grand jury had returned a "no true bill," meaning that there was neither probable cause nor evidence that a crime had been committed. The locals had lined up behind Andrew. I looked at some other news accounts and learned that Andrew testified on his own behalf during the thirty-two-minute hearing and that TWRA officials were saying thirty of the fifty-three snakes had died since their November 7 capture.

Mine was the 595th "like." I started scanning some of the 157 comments, which came from Poplar Bluff, Missouri, Douglas, Georgia, New York City, and lots of places around Ohio, to name a few.

Thank God that you prevailed today, wrote Terry Broberg-Swangin, a fifty-four-year-old woman from Fort Wayne, Indiana, whose profile said she got her MA in liturgical studies from the University of Notre Dame in 2008 and was a Democrat. *Although you'll never see this Roman Catholic handle a serpent, you have brought so many people together from different faiths to be united for religious freedom,* she wrote.

Much Respect for You Andrew, wrote Bruce Armstrong, thirty-three, from Hollywood, California. *Everyone Was Cheering For you in our Cubicles at Work Today! Southern Cali Loves Your Spirit, You are an Inspiration to All of Us.*

For the time being, Andrew was on top of the world.

CHAPTER ELEVEN

ANOTHER
DEATH

● ◉

It had been a tough winter, one of the worst in recent years, with snowstorms all over the Midwest and East Coast. Everyone was feeling the pain, including the Hamblins, whose court battle had proved quite costly.

Elizabeth posted on January 16: *are bills are a draining us. caught up on rent but backed up on elecrtric. but God can move in anything. were still holding on.* Then later that day: *Andrew got a J O B !!!!! Whoot whoot !!! Thank u Jesus my prayers has finally been answered . . . . . :') AINT GOD GOOD.* One of the church deacons, she explained, had opened up a grocery store where Andrew was now working.

The forecast over President's Day weekend said it might be in the sixties, so I made a reservation with a bus tour at Reelfoot Lake, a large body of water in the far northwestern corner of Tennessee not far from the Mississippi River.

It was February 16, a Sunday, the one day of the week that I don't check the internet first thing in the morning. My plan was to take Veeka seventy-four miles to the lake right after church, snag the early afternoon tour, and maybe see some eagles' nests. The place was known as a huge sanctuary for many bird populations, including bald eagles that made their home there.

We were bouncing along on an old school bus through snowy fields when I glanced at my iPhone and just on a whim clicked on my e-mail. I saw a message from John Morgan with a newspaper headline from the Knoxville TV station WATE: "Kentucky snake handling preacher, reality TV star dead from snake bite."

It was Jamie Coots.

Now I knew what they mean about your world going temporarily black when there is bad news. As the other people on the trip chattered about snow ducks and the occasional eagle, I was in shock. We were thirty miles north of Dyersburg, the nearest city of any size and a good seventy miles north of Memphis, so the internet was agonizingly slow.

I found a Facebook message from Cody Coots, the twenty-one-year-old son, posted at about 3:00 a.m. his time: *This Cody coots dad past away yesterday I'm miss him so much and love him please pray for use we have no live insurance on him if any one has anything to give to help would be greatly appreciate RIP dad i love hope to see you on the other side on day.*

The WATE story said that an ambulance had shown up at the church some time after 8:00 but that Jamie was dead by 10 p.m. My goodness, I thought, that was quick. Nothing like the agonizing eight to ten hours it took Mack to die. And what was it about these folks that they always die over a three-day holiday weekend?

I e-mailed the *Wall Street Journal*. Sure enough, the Speakeasy blog wanted an article. By the time the bus tour ended and I got home, it was 6:00 p.m. and the story was nearly twenty-four hours old. TV crews had shown up at Jamie's church that afternoon to get tearful quotes from Cody Coots and Big Cody Wynn.

I quickly learned that Jamie had been bitten by a rattlesnake on his right hand—the same hand that had lost a finger several years ago. And that Andrew had been there at the service. Odd, I thought. Andrew didn't usually attend Jamie's Saturday night services, so what brought him there?

I called the Middlesboro police and got someone to read the press release to me. They'd gotten the first call around 8:24 p.m., but whoever made the call was not a member of the family. Jamie's services usually started at 7:00 p.m., so it had been well underway by then. According to WBIR, the Knoxville station that seemed to have the most details, Jamie had been bitten on the back of his hand. He dropped the snakes (he was holding three at that point), then picked them back up. He then headed toward the men's room with Andrew and Little Cody because he felt sick. And after saying "sweet Jesus" to Andrew, he passed out.

The service came to a quick halt. It took five men to carry Jamie out. Cody told the TV station they thought it would be like before with the eight other times Jamie had been bitten. He would go home, feel sick for a while, and then get better. But this time, Cody must have known it was different. Jamie was out cold. When the ambulance crew showed up, Jamie wasn't there, so they hastened over to his house. Later, Elizabeth posted an explanation: *There was no saving him. He died 3 mins after he was bit. It hit a main artery and he refused to go. He told his family if he was ever snake bit, he wouldn't go. He made a vow before God he wouldn't. You have to respect his wishes.*

It took me nearly three hours to get through to Jeff Sharpe, the local police chief, at about 9:40 p.m. his time. He was plainly exhausted. One of his lieutenants had told me he had been answering press calls all day, so I was probably number seventy at this point. He had some interesting details I'd not gleaned from the TV. When Sharpe arrived at the Coots home, it was full of church members and family holding vigil. Jamie was seated somehow—even though he was unconscious and dying—in his favorite chair. Meanwhile, Linda Coots and Cody were signing a form waiving medical treatment.

"He'd already said before they took him home that he didn't want to be treated," Sharpe said. "He'd made his feelings very, very clear about what should happen if he was bit." Officers left the house at 9:10 p.m., he said, and less than an hour later, they were summoned a second time, as Jamie had died. And so the chief returned with Jason Steele, the local coroner, in tow. I had a feeling that the chief knew that Coots's death would be a huge deal, which is why he showed up twice at the house, but he told me that he made it his practice to show up at the scene of every unusual death.

"Whoa," I said, "it only took him two hours to die?" I told the officer about Mack's agonizing death.

"Something made this happen faster than normal," Sharpe said.

I asked him how many from the press had called. "Lord," he said, "I have no idea."

Had Andrew been there? Yes, he responded, Andrew had been at the Coots house.

God, I thought, what must have been going through Andrew's mind at that point? That he's next? Arnold Saylor, a longtime snake handler living in Fort

Wayne, Indiana, was in the area that night when he received a phone call from Andrew. Saylor began speeding toward Middlesboro as Andrew peppered him with more calls, asking what to do because Jamie wasn't responding.

"Walk him. Don't let him freeze up," Saylor commanded Andrew over the phone while trying to steer his car. When he arrived at the house, he tried to hoist Jamie out of the chair. The second he did so, he sensed Jamie's spirit leave his body.

"He's gone, he's gone," Saylor cried as he lowered Jamie back into the chair.

I looked up various Facebook feeds. *in need of prayer,* Elizabeth had posted some time around 11:30 p.m. Saturday. *I looked at jamie like a daddy figure he has always been good to me and my family. I love u and miss u so much already.*

She got several dozen replies and grief-stricken expressions and 227 likes. *I honestly feel like I'm in a bad dream and can't wake up,* she wrote.

What a night. I called Paul Gray, Michelle's husband, and learned from him basically what the police chief had told me. Someone had called him when Jamie was bitten. He and Michelle rushed fifty-seven miles from London to Middlesboro, but by the time they got there, Jamie was gone.

I heard later through the grapevine that some seventy-five people had squeezed into the Coots home or stood vigil on their porch that night. People from several counties had rushed to their home, and when he was pronounced dead, people screamed and wailed. Everyone took off to let the family be alone in their grief, and as the coroner's men hoisted Jamie out the door, snow poured from the sky.

Late Saturday night, Andrew had posted: *really needing everyones prayers tonight. I was there for the last service with him. he was like a dad to me. everyone just keep us all in your prayers. and there will be church tomorrow at 1:00 at tabernacle church of God. remember us when you pray.*

At about 6 a.m. on Sunday, Andrew posted: *as I set here this morning I try to think of what dad would have said. I miss him so bad. I will never forget how God moved on us last night together for one last time. everyone please keep all of us in your prayers. everyone remember service today at the Tabernacle at 1:00. Mark 16:18 is still forever real.*

Tributes had poured in all day Sunday on the Facebook page of the genial, bald-headed pastor who loved wearing snazzy bright-colored blazers, shirts, and suits. Jamie's Facebook page had mushroomed to 2,685 "friends" after *Snake Salvation* ran. A support page for the Coots family had 1,106 "likes" by

Sunday night. A page on www.gofundme.com with a photo of Jamie and a headline "will be used for funeral and spouce" stated that the goal was $5,500.

I found a bunch of quotes that Jamie had given me during various interviews over the past two years. We had last talked in November, which is when he'd told me of the new jobs he and Cody and Trina had gotten. He seemed so happy then. I got through to the National Geographic spokeswoman, who sent me their statement on Jamie's death. I got from Facebook another quote from Lisa Blake, a former National Geographic producer who had worked with Jamie. After gleaning more details from other posts, I filed the story at 10:00 p.m.

Soon after that, Elizabeth posted evidence that the doctrinal battle between the Trinitarian and Jesus-name folks was spilling over into guesses about Jamie's eternal destiny: *is gonna ruffle some feather here! yes I can say I love jamie coots with all my heart yes he was like a father to me I was his baby girl. I loved him dearly I can't stand to think he's gone and won't be seeing him anymore. yes we believe different he is and was a Jesus christ man till the day he died. yes I believe Jesus has a father. we didn't agree on everything. yes he was babtized acts 2:38 and I'm babtized Mathew 28:19. let's get this strait I can find both them Scriptures in the bible! no were can u find the word Jesus only and trinity in there! this babtizing war is sickening. so what if he believed different that gives u no right to cast him into hell! u ain't God! and u sure ain't Mich of a Christian to do so. I believe with all my heart I'll see jamie coots in heaven just like I believe I'll see Austin Long there. please get off your high horses before u fall off and get hurt. this man would go the extra mile for anyone. and to see some of what u all are saying is simply dis tasteful and horrible!*

Soon after that—about 11:00 p.m. his time—Andrew posted: *Arrangements for pastor Jamie Coots will be Tuesday night from 5 to 8 with funeral at 8 at creechs funeral home in middlesboro ky. interment is private. ABSOLUTELY NO MEDIA ALLOWED. if you show up with cameras you will be escorted out. please keep us in your prayers.*

This was beyond annoying, as "media" were what had gotten Andrew his fame and raised him to rock-star status from being a nobody working at IGA. And he'd messaged me saying he was not doing interviews. By the time I woke up Monday morning, my story was on the *Journal's* site. I got an email from CNN, asking for names and phone numbers. I'd offered to write about Andrew's arrest for CNN.com's Belief Blog the previous fall, but I'd balked over their absurdly low pay levels. So like the TV folks, I thought. They had not wanted to take the time and trouble to pay a writer decent money for Andrew's trial coverage. Then when a crisis erupted with Jamie's death, they had no one on the scene as an expert. Instead, they expected me to hand over my list of sources that I'd worked for more than two years to assemble. Worse still, this particular producer said that if I worked with them, I could go on the air in a few hours as a commentator. I knew she was lying because Bob Smietana had already e-mailed me to say he was going to be interviewed by CNN. When I sat down that evening to read through Facebook, I learned that Liz had had it with the media as well. At about noon she posted: *the next news media who writes or calls my phone I'm fixing to show them my bad side. sorry jamie is not going to be ur big story and pay day. leave his family alone already!*

She added: *And—the family asked us not to do interviews or release any info i have to respect his wife son and daughters wishes.*

One had to pity this poor woman, as she'd had no rest. At the end of January, her one-year-old daughter, Madlyin, spent several nights at Children's Hospital in Knoxville battling strep throat and respiratory syncytial virus. The Hamblins' feeds had been full of beseeching for prayers that the fever depart.

And in mid-January, just before Madlyin took ill, Liz had posted: *Praise report ~~~~ :o) after getting caught up on are back bills we were short on food. we prayed all day yesterday and outta the blue God blessed up with half a frig full thank u Jesus. the Lord will provide and the person who helped is a heaven sent angel and we thank u.*

The whole thing sounded odd, as I knew Andrew had just taken a job with a local snack bar operated by his friend Ronnie Daugherty. Were things that bad? They must have been, as a few weeks later, the local paper had reported that Andrew was cited by police for having no license plates, a suspended driver's license, and no vehicle registration or insurance. Apparently he lacked the money to pay for them. So, it had been a rough couple of weeks.

About an hour later the Monday after Jamie died, Liz posted: *as I turn over to mark 16:18 its still written in red. the word of God will stand forever. just because jamie is gone doesn't mean its still not real. I'm still a believer.*

The big news on her mind and that of the 124 people on writing on her feed was Westboro Baptist Church's announcement that they'd be picketing Jamie's funeral. This was a small church based in Topeka, Kansas, that had become notorious for picketing funerals of all religious groups but especially those of homosexuals and U.S. service members. Westboro had tweeted: *WBC will picket funeral of charlatan "Pastor Jamie" Coots, tomorrow, 2/18/14-7:30pm @ Creech FH, 112 S 21st, Middlesboro, KY. Isa 47:10-13.*

i hope you do come here we the people of middlesboro will run your ass off, one person responded.

This is absolutely ridiculous. You pretentious assholes better think twice. I know Middlesboro people won't put up with this, someone else tweeted.

People discussed which bikers or "good 'ole redneck boys" they could get to block Westboro from getting close to the funeral home.

I know how to scare WBC away, wrote a truck driver from western Kentucky. *Lets all go approach them and offer to hand them a nice fat rattler!!!* He added: *if they go messing with country folks in eastern Ky they will get worse than a beating, Watch the movie Next of kin.*

A nurse wrote: *Praise the Lord!!! We just heard back!!!! There are people in route to protect the Coots and the Hamblins from all these horrible people associated with the Westboro Baptist Church!!!*

Elsewhere on the internet, more media organizations were grabbing a piece of the pie. *TMZ,* the Hollywood news/scandal site, had even weighed in with an "exclusive" about there being a state law forbidding the use of reptiles during a religious service. Ralph Hood had once told me about this law, the only one of several state laws dealing with snake handling that specifically says one can't handle a reptile in church.

"So you can't even have a turtle. It's the only state law directed against a religion," he had said. "All the other state laws say you can't handle snakes anywhere. The law is blatantly unconstitutional and the [Middlesboro] police chief is on record saying he won't enforce it."

I decided to stay away, partly because of the requests over the internet for media not to show. It was a bad decision, I soon found out. The turnout may have been the biggest ever for a funeral of a serpent handler. The event brought in a collection of handlers who would not have come for anyone else. Jamie had held out to the end, stayed faithful to the signs at the cost of his own life, so anyone who was anybody in that culture was there. Ralph had known Jamie for years, so he found someone to fill in for him at the university and then drove to Middlesboro. Arriving at Creech Funeral Home, he parked himself on a pew so he could watch everyone arrive. Two reporters from the *Chattanooga Times Free Press* who were with Ralph went up and down the lines interviewing people about why they were in line. Coots's church only had twenty members, so none of the people in line belonged to his congregation. Over and over they heard stories about Jamie's kindness, his care for the poor, and the strong roots that several generations of his family had in town.

Middlesboro had never seen such a show. A group of veterans were posted outside with American flags. So were some of the local clergy, as everyone was braced for the Westboro demonstrators. I was four hundred miles away following what was happening on Facebook and Twitter. Someone was asking if Westboro had arrived.

They aren't here so far and yes the MPD are awesome they are all the way around the building, messaged a Bill and Stacey Barton. *Pretty awesome! I pray the Coots family finds some peace. Pastor Coots was a humble man and his family would do anything for anyone! God Bless them.*

At 6.15 pm I just drove by, messaged Brooke Shorter, a saleswoman at Belk's. *No protesters are out. A lot of people standing around the funeral home waiting I believe.*

God bless the Coots family, messaged Linda Thomas, a beautician. *The area lost a good man. That church group from Kansas knew better to mess with the Kentucky people.*

Another man wrote: *I'd have loved to seen the fear in their eyes when the whole town was standing there looking at them. And the veterans were there also.*

A woman added, *The Middlesboro community has been divided on opinions of Jamie's death. But there is one thing for sure about it. When the news that WBC had intentions to protest "preach" at his funeral, the community put aside their differences for the same purpose and that was to stand up and protect Jamie's service and family from the WBC Cult! Thank you everyone for that! WBC knew not to show up. After all this is a family that is use to handling snakes and Fred Phelps [Westboro's founder] and the WBC are some of the biggest snakes in the world. Once again, they have been defeated!*

Inside, the shocked family was gathered. One of them pulled out a camera and snapped a photo of Jamie lying in the casket, just after he'd been dressed. His cheeks were rouged in a way he'd never looked in real life. He had on a dark red shirt and a beige leopard-skin patterned jacket and was wearing his wedding ring. Nearby was gathered a who's who in the serpent-handling movement. Bruce Helton was the preacher. Micah was there. So was Arnold Saylor, Kentucky serpent handler Verlin Short (who had starred in a reality TV show on Animal Planet), John and Mark Brown, and many others.

Jimmy Morrow had bought a five-dollar suit at Goodwill so that he and Pam could come. The only folks missing were Harvey Payne from Jolo and Billy Summerford from Sand Mountain. Andrew was a greeter, and Ralph noticed how he seemed to be easily taking authority. The Chattanooga paper posted a photo of him outside the funeral home talking with people and wearing what looked like a bright gold polyester shirt with a shiny gold checker pattern. It was the kind of brassy shirt Jamie wore, and I later learned it was Jamie's shirt. Linda Coots had given Cody and Andrew her husband's shirts to wear. The funeral home chapel was standing room only. Media calls had come in from places like England, Australia, and Poland. The doors opened at 5:00 p.m., and half the town was lined up, waiting for a chance to pay their respects and file past Jamie's open mahogany coffin, near which was a sign asking people not to take pictures with their cell phones. Some visitors had come in their work clothes. Coal miners were still wearing their boots to pay their respects, as Jamie had once worked in the mines before he went on disability.

Linda, dressed in black, was near the coffin greeting people. Probably 99 percent of those in line had never dropped by Jamie's church on Evans Road about two miles from the funeral home, but he was known about town as a kindly man who cared for the little people. Some of the kids who were on Jamie's school bus came too.

Ralph picked up a conversation with John Brown, who told him he admired Jamie for living up to his commitments at the cost of his life. Brown hadn't mentioned Jamie's name when he lambasted *Snake Salvation* several months before at the homecoming, but the meaning had been clear. But now all was forgiven. Jamie had died with honor and integrity.

The service started with a recording of Jamie singing. A number of other people played the piano and sang, including Trina and both Codys. Bruce Helton strode up and down the aisles and preached about the Word still being the Word and the signs still being the signs. Someone had brought a blowtorch, so there was fire handling. People began to dance and stomp up and down the aisle. The praise and shouts were deafening. Others walked up to the casket to pray.

At one point Arnold Saylor stood up and said a collection needed to be taken. He passed around his black Stetson, and Short went outside, his hat in hand, to collect from the crowd there. Several thousand dollars was collected on the spot, which was pretty good for cash-strapped Holiness people. As the service lengthened to two hours and it was close to 10:00 p.m., the funeral home wanted to close things down. Most people departed, but a determined few headed over to the church to continue the service and handle snakes.

The two Chattanooga reporters came along. They had just done a huge take-out on Andrew and Jamie the month before, so the family knew them. But they were told that in no way were they to report on or take notes or photos during that service, which went on until midnight. They agreed, although Cody revealed a few days later to WBIR that snakes were handled. One reporter told me about the difference in the atmosphere with Jamie gone. Jamie had had a pastoral spirit of gentleness and openness to the world, which is why he let cameras into his church, but Cody, he mused, seemed much more hardcore, more conservative. His church might no longer be open to reporters as Jamie's was. And Andrew, he said, had been the person who had engineered the media blackout. But Liz had made it sound as though the Coots family was behind it. Either way, it was clear the shots were being called by a bunch of twenty-somethings.

Wednesday night I posted on Jamie's page an announcement about the National Geographic's special tribute to Jamie. There were good responses and a conversation between a few "friends" about Cody's preaching. *Not to be mean, but Cody screams too much. I believe he will make a good preacher if he looks back at how his daddy did it . . . and remember what his daddy told him about compassion,* said a nurse from Florida.

Nailed it, I thought. A man responded, *wisdom comes with age you have to grow and learn in the lord and no two preachers are the same.*

I had a long talk with Ralph on Thursday.

"Andrew is feeling his way and trying to survive in this tradition," he said. "They have things to hide. He's got five kids and he doesn't work except occasionally. It is not clear he can sustain a church. Cody—whether he can do it, I don't know. His church is pretty small right now."

I talked with Bob Smietana, who was remembering a conversation he had with Jamie while reporting on him and Andrew for the *Tennessean*. Jamie had been talking about all the young serpent handlers and whether their faith would endure over the long haul. The true test comes when someone dies while handling a serpent and suddenly the police and the media are at your front door.

"That's when the persecution comes," Jamie had told Bob. "We'll see what happens then." So, atop everything else Andrew was dealing with, here was this whole new level of stress. He had thought he was done with law enforcement. Maybe now he wasn't.

Thursday, he posted: *I want to thank everyone for all their prayers and support at this time in my life. always remember death is so certain it will happen to all of us one day. it pays to be ready. remember church tomorrow night. and I will be having a press conference Saturday at 3:00. thank you everyone.*

On Friday afternoon came this post: *Hope everyone is having a blessed day. Everyone please call out my name in prayer today. Really having a hard time. i just need a touch from the Master. Also everyone remember Church tonight at 7:30. come expecting a blessing.*

I e-mailed him, asking if we could just talk by phone. He dug in his heels, messaging, *tomorrow will be the only time ill be doing interviews you can come a little early if you want to.*

It's a 700-mile round trip for me, I messaged. *I'm not like these TV station reporters whose employers pay for their hotels, child care and mileage. We can talk later.*

It will probably be a long time before i will be speaking on what happened, he answered. *This has been the hardest thing in my life.*

I tried to be lighthearted. I messaged back, *I can't imagine what you must be thinking and feeling. You must feel so alone. It's just that dragging Veeka on an 8-hour road trip up one day and back another is very tough for us. Why not talk tonight on the phone after your service? . . . unless Veeka could see Payton. That might make a difference to her!*

No response. Screw it, I thought. I called Bob. What to do? Were he free, he said, he'd go. But he understood I had 120 miles farther than he did to travel, which was an extra four hours of driving. I went to sleep praying and undecided. At 5:00 a.m. I was awake. I am usually never awake at that hour, but this time I was and I was thinking that I did not want to drive 350 miles that day. But it was an absolutely gorgeous dawn. I lumbered out of bed, threw on the coffee, and dragged a protesting Veeka out of bed with the promise we'd eat breakfast at a McDonalds somewhere off I-40 and lunch at a Knoxville Starbucks. Amazingly, it took us only five and a half hours to cross the state and arrive at the door of Tabernacle Church of God.

Andrew was dressed all in black.

"How are you doing?" I asked.

"I'm here," he said flatly.

He told me about his last minutes with Jamie—how Jamie died in his arms just as Punkin died in Jamie's arms in 1998.

"Wasn't there some sort of rift between you two?" I asked. I'd heard Ralph talk about it, and Jamie refer to it, so I knew it existed. Andrew looked bewildered.

"We talked two, three times a day," he said. "Brother Jamie meant the world to me. He was just like a daddy. We didn't see eye to eye on everything. We had our disagreements and our falling-outs."

"Who's your mentor now?" I asked.

"I have me," he said. I asked him what God was telling him. "Keep on going. Don't stop," he replied. He seemed so bereft.

He went outside to make a call, and I went outside to absorb some sun. I sat on a church step, and a white pit bull ambled by and sat on my lap. I thought there would be satellite trucks out there. Not quite. Two or three other reporters eventually sauntered in, all from local media. Andrew sat forlornly on a bench in front of the pulpit. It was chilly inside, so someone turned on the heat.

"When I was depressed and lonely, I'd call him," he said of Jamie. "No one will ever know the pain. He called my children his grandkids. No one will ever know how much I miss him." His little church had elders, he added, but "I have no elder now."

I pitched the first question. Considering what had happened to Jamie, what was Andrew's position on seeking medical help if snake bitten?

His answer was vague. What did it say to the world, he asked, when someone dies an agonizing death? "There is your appointed time to die," he said. "So what does it mean to get bit and go home and swell and suffer and lose limbs when you were inside a service where God has moved on you?" Obviously he'd been doing some thinking about some of the unsolvable issues in his movement: if God is controlling the service, why such messy deaths?

"Would you seek help?" I asked.

"I don't know," he responded. Jamie had made a vow to God he'd never seek medical help, he said, "but I never made a vow that I'd never go to a doctor." He went into some detail about the first time he was bitten in July 2010. His twins had just been born; he had major reasons to keep on living; and he had been airlifted twice to two hospitals in Kentucky. His lungs kept filling up with blood, and doctors told him that unless the medications they were giving him kicked in, he wouldn't make it.

"I lay there and thought of my options," he said. "I prayed, 'Lord, if you want me to live, let me hear Jamie speak in tongues.' Two, three minutes later at the hospital, the curtain flung open, and there was Jamie speaking in tongues."

I wondered if the other reporters understood all this. Andrew went on about how he and Liz had worked out funeral arrangements if he were bitten, how he'd already chosen the funeral home and planned his wake (12:00 noon to 7:00 p.m.) and an all-night vigil and a church service the next day.

"So if you're bit and die, does that mean you're not anointed?" someone asked.

Andrew mulled that one over. "Jamie had three snakes in his hand," he said. "The one that bit him had been handled by us all." Two of the snakes had been handled to the point they were just limp, he said. And then suddenly the third one turned and bit Jamie.

"As long as I'm under the anointing of God, I won't be hurt like I was in July 2010," he said. "I know people who've been bit and walked away from it. These are puff adders, vipers—some of the most deadly snakes in the world we're handling." Adding that he had been bitten four times, he said, "I've seen Jamie go elbow deep in snakes or laid them around his neck. And then what killed him was a two-and–a-half-foot snake. Why that little bitty serpent, I'll never be able to answer. But there is God's appointed time to die."

Yes, I thought, but usually not when you're forty-two. It was clear Andrew was still working through this. We asked him to run down what happened that dreadful night one week ago. Andrew said he wasn't usually at Jamie's Saturday services, but he felt moved by God to get off from work at the store where he worked. Jamie had been handling snakes in front of the pulpit and then he flexed his hand. The snakes fell to the floor. Jamie scooped them back up.

"Dad's been bit," Cody told him. Andrew, who had also been handling a snake, put it down and accompanied Jamie as he headed to the bathroom along with Cody. Jamie was rubbing his face. "I feel like my face is on fire," he was telling them.

"He was real red," Andrew told us, "because we'd been singing and shouting." Cody offered to end the service. Jamie lifted his arms up as Andrew loosened his clothes.

"Lord, come by," Jamie said. Then, "Oh, God, no."

"He turned around and looked at me," Andrew continued, "and said, 'Sweet Jesus' calm and peaceful. Then his eyes set and he started to slump. I yelled 'Dad!' and then he fell." Andrew felt something wet and realized Jamie's bowels had loosened as happens at the moment of death.

"He died right there," Andrew said. "I was smacking him but he never opened his eyes again. I believe in the last thirty seconds of his life, Jamie knew he was dying. He was not looking at me, but past me. And then his eyes set. I believe he died standing straight up. There is no antivenin that could have saved a man that night. A serpent's fang is like a hypodermic needle. It goes in that quick."

And so Andrew was to Jamie what Jamie had been to Punkin: holding a snake-bitten man while he died within minutes. No one knew who called the medics but, "You could tell he was gone by the expression on their faces," Andrew said. Jamie's pulse was down to about one beat every thirty seconds. His body had nearly shut down. They took him to the house, changed him out of his soiled, urine-soaked clothes and laid him in his chair. Finally it was clear he was completely gone.

"Linda lost her soul mate and best friend," he said. Trina now slept with Linda to keep her company, he continued, and the other day when Trina, Linda, and Elizabeth were at Walmart shopping for containers in which to put some of Jamie's belongings, Linda broke down. Linda had been a pillar of strength before then—even handling serpents at a Wednesday morning service for Jamie.

I asked if they had raised enough money to pay expenses. Andrew didn't know, but the funeral home demanded a $1,000 down payment, which the Coots family didn't have. Andrew got his church of about fifty people to come up with that amount during one offering that Sunday morning.

After the funeral and after the late-night snake-handling service, Jamie's body remained at the church in the casket. He and Cody and Nathan Evans held vigil until dawn for "one last night with dad."

"We talked, laughed, and made jokes and tried to get prepared now that he's gone and it's just us," Andrew said. "We have to grow up." The twenty-something new leaders of the movement included the three of them and Big Cody. One of the reporters pointed out that in the National Geographic series, Jamie made it clear that he was training Little Cody to fill his shoes at some point.

"I'm worried about Cody," Andrew said. "It's like, 'boom, you're pastor.' But I'll train him."

That's interesting, I thought. An almost twenty-three-year-old with two years' experience training a twenty-one-year-old with none.

"Do you sleep much now?" I asked.

"No," said Andrew. "We're all just up and down. You don't sleep at night and you wait for his phone call."

I sat there inside the church that had become so familiar to me and wondered. There was nothing more to say. At least Andrew wasn't feeding us pat answers. We all thanked him; I taped a small segment with a local videographer and then shooed Veeka toward the car. Andrew was still talking with several folks. I was determined to get her to see Payton if that was the last thing I did. Being schlepped across the state and dragged to a press conference had been beyond boring for my daughter. And I wasn't going to ask Andrew's permission because I knew he'd think up some reason to say no. We sped back along Loop Road to the main highway, then headed north out of town. Finally I saw Frontier Road, turned off, drove a short distance, and then pulled up to the house.

It was out in the country: a two-story white wood house with a red star on the west side. A plastic snake lay on the driveway along with hopscotch markings. Confusingly, the main entry was in the back. I could see why the wildlife officers had wandered about the house, trying to find the right door. Veeka and I pounded on a downstairs door before going around the back, up some stairs, and walked inside calling for Payton. Several kids walked out to peer at us, including a teenager in a long skirt. I entered the darkened living room, which had piles of laundry about, a couch or two, and material that served as curtains flung across the windows. The dining room, which had red and white walls, was likewise messy, but I remembered they had not been there that long; they had five kids who were constantly tearing up the house and nonstop emergencies. Liz poked her head out of the kitchen to see who was there, and I waved and motioned to Payton. She said hello and returned to the kitchen, where I later learned her parents were sitting. I wasn't sure how welcome we were, so I headed to the back porch and outside with Veeka and Payton in tow, along with some other kids. Haylin padded out in a light orange dress. I remembered how her mother handled snakes the first night I met her, when Haylin was seven and a half months in utero and how the little girl's life had hung by a thread.

We went around the east side of the house, where there was a huge pile of garbage bags and a pile of aluminum cans, to where the family kept a chicken. Veeka kept shrieking when Payton showed it to her, so I got them both busy riding some scooters in the driveway. Veeka found a small bike and began practicing how to ride without training wheels. They played and shouted and ran about.

I stood by the house of the serpent handler. The warm winter afternoon sun blazed around us, lighting up the surrounding brown fields, which flowed into vistas that were beyond lovely. The nearby mountains were silent. It was perfect: the dead winter grass, the empty tree boughs, the blazing blue afternoon sky. The air was gentle, sweet, and warm.

But it was still winter.

CHAPTER TWELVE

ANDREW'S HOMECOMING

After his death, Jamie's family took over his Facebook page, posting family photos and remembrances of the beloved pastor. The main energy of the movement was clearly with Andrew, who announced in April that he'd switched his homecoming weekend from the beginning of May to Memorial Day weekend. No one else in the serpent-handling community had reserved that spot, so he was within his rights. He scheduled three guest preachers on all three days of the celebration and rented a community hall for the celebratory potluck at the end. He had also announced that his small congregation had unanimously decided to build their own church elsewhere in LaFollette and set up a website to raise funds.

I decided to attend and make a week of it by renting a cabin in Townsend, a lovely community in the mountains south of Knoxville. I invited John Morgan to come and take photographs as I didn't have many good interior shots of Andrew's church. The plan was to also take Veeka to Dollywood, a charming amusement park founded by Dolly Parton in nearby Pigeon Forge. The three of us would tromp around the mountains a bit and visit Clingmans Dome in the Great Smoky Mountains National Park a few miles away.

We arrived in Townsend on a Friday night, and the rolling hills were green beyond belief. We drove on a parkway along the Little River, which was filled with picnickers and swimmers. On Saturday, we drove to Del Rio, about eighty miles to the east, where I was attending a lunch sponsored by the local historical society. To my great surprise, Pam and Jimmy Morrow were there. We gave each other hugs, and I sat outside with them on the porch and eventually bought from him a walking stick for Veeka that had a yellow snake carved into it. She loved it. Being with them was almost like family. After all, he had painted us into his serpent-handling church painting. Just before I returned to the cabin, I called Cody. His dad had been buried at Turner Cemetery in Middlesboro, he said. Yes, the funeral expenses were paid off within two months. No, he had not done more radical things since our last conversation. He had not progressed to Red Devil as he'd meant to do. He had not seen any healings, and the church had not really grown, and yes, he and Nathan and Andrew sat by Jamie's body until 6:00 a.m. after the funeral. No, he didn't feel like being interviewed right now. Too busy.

Here I was about ninety miles—easy driving distance—from Middlesboro, and my sources were drying up on me. I remembered how something similar had happened to Dennis Covington, the author of *Salvation on Sand Mountain*. By the end of the book, the handlers were getting on his nerves. One Saturday night in December 1993, he preached a sermon in one of their churches about how Jesus had appeared to women—instead of men—after his resurrection. That one defiance infuriated his listeners: he was basically told to sit down and shut up, and he never went back after that. I understood the fatigue. At times these folks were with you, and at other times they seemed a million miles away.

We met John at the cabin and took off for the eighty-mile drive to Andrew's church. Once there, I noticed a building down the hill that may have been all of ten feet by ten feet. The door was open and a man stood inside loudly preaching to a handful of people. It was bizarre watching this miniature service happening about fifty feet from Andrew's church, where you could hear the music blaring. I took John and Veeka inside the Tabernacle, where about seventy people were gathered, including at least five photographers. I spotted Liz dressed in a floor-length black skirt with red flowers on it. Part of her hair was scrunched up in a poufy bun atop her head. A large fake pink flower was clipped to her tresses above her left ear. Several other women had similar bird's-nest poufs on their heads. The look was so 1950s retro that it was actually fetching. Following Liz was Haylin, now two and a half, looking cherubic with her red hair, clutching a baby bottle filled with apple juice, wearing an electric blue dress and white sandals on her tiny feet.

Up front, Andrew was dressed nattily in a beige vest, beige dress shirt, and black pants. Surrounded by about twenty young men, many of whom were sporting similar vest-and-suit combos, Andrew was cradling an enormous viper. His entourage was passing around fire wicks and brushing the flames against their hands. There was such a traffic jam up there that it was hard to tell who was handling and who wasn't. Sometimes the men would link arms around each others' shoulders like a football team and shuffle-dance together. Circles would form, then break and re-form as new people joined or others dropped off. Snakes were slipped from one hand to another or waved in the air. Most of their eyes were glued on Andrew, who, like a skilled dancer, set the rhythm and direction for their dance. Was there anything supernatural going on this night, I wondered, or were we seeing a law of averages that people handling snakes in church tend not to get bitten that much? Occasionally they'd take a break to pray over each other or stroke each other or make sweeping motions with their hands, as if the Holy Spirit was this invisible electric current. Nathan Evans was there in a dark orange shirt, and his wife Tiffany was among a clump of women sitting up front. I later learned they were commuting to Andrew's church—several hours each way—every weekend.

The musicians against the back wall were the best I'd heard yet, and someone was playing a mean electric guitar when I noticed that Veeka had disappeared. I headed out into the warm evening where I found her playing near a young man in a purple shirt standing in the driveway. He was Ronnie Daugherty and a deacon in Andrew's church. It was his father, Clyde Daugherty, who owned the church building, he told me. Clyde was also the man preaching that night in the makeshift church down the hill. Something about that man in the tiny church made me feel uneasy, and I wondered if he had anything to do with Andrew's decision to start a building fund.

Back inside, Andrew was pulling off his socks and shoes, dramatically sitting in front of the pulpit and holding flames to the soles of his bare feet. The photographers all scrambled to get that one. One of the photographers was Neil Brandvold, who hung out at these gatherings and who told me he'd visited Jolo last November, as there were apparently still services there. Only a handful of people attended, Neil said, but one of them was Little Cody.

Who knew why or what he was doing visiting a place that was a three-and-a-half-hour schlep away over backcountry roads. Neil rode a motorcycle and, there being no lodging in Jolo, had considered camping by the side of the road until the locals warned him he'd be held up and robbed by the local gangs of meth addicts if he did so. And that was one of the better scenarios. He finally found someone who agreed to put him up for the night.

Paul Gray was the guest preacher that night. He must have spoken for at least a half hour, but I lost track, as time seems to flow differently in these places. It was still a spiritual mosh pit up front. Then Tyler Evans, a young man dressed in a beige vest and apricot shirt shot out into the congregation like a bullet, then danced back toward the pulpit and began handling fire. Tyler, who was all of eighteen or nineteen, was the other great-grandson of Bob and Barbara Elkins. Tyler then began handling a pile of snakes and chugged down some strychnine from a jar on the pulpit. One of the women—Taylor Noe—was luxuriously handling fire, resplendent in an orange dress, her forearm bathed in flame. Her husband, Derrick, rejoiced behind her. By this time, John had climbed onto our pew and was shooting from about six feet up. Some people were nearly staggering about the stage, overcome with God, perhaps, but what I was seeing that night was the youngest generation coming into its own. Yes, there were a few thirty- and forty-year-olds in the mix, but the energy belonged to the twenty-somethings led by Andrew.

On Sunday, I had something else to do in the morning, so it was late in the afternoon by the time we got to LaFollette. We missed the service, but the potluck had just begun, which was followed by a pie-in-the-face contest. I struck up a conversation with forty-year-old Derek Abrams, a supervisor at a wire fabrication plant in Kentucky. He'd been handling snakes for years and once handled a cobra at Jamie's church.

"We feel the anointing come on us," he said. "The Lord tells me when to do it, how to do it, and when to hand it back."

How did the anointing come? I asked him.

"Elders taught me how to pray the Word and get ahold of the anointing of God by prayer, fasting, and weeping," he said. Then he added that his eighteen-year-old son, Andrew, handled two copperheads for the first time at the homecoming. In fact, it was his father who had handed a tangle of serpents to him.

I sought out the young man. Andrew had been praying for a sign. The young man told me, "I said, 'Lord, if it's your will, let my dad bring it to me.'

There's no feeling like that on Earth—knowing you're holding death in your hands and it won't do anything to you. I thought, 'Lord, I can't do this,' but I knew the Lord was in it and it'd be all right."

Then I flagged down Joshua Daniels, a tall guy from Williamsburg, Kentucky, with a sparse brown beard and an outlaw tattoo on his left arm. He worked in yard maintenance and had spent some time in jail during his thirty-six years. He didn't say why he was locked up, but "I'd drink 100 proof vodka and chase it with 80 proof," he told me of his former life. His wife then walked up. "I've handled before," she said. "It was at home. The Spirit moved on me." Her husband cut back in. "I wanted to get into the boxes last night," he confessed. "God will tell you, and He'll give you the okay. I didn't feel the okay to get in the boxes."

I ran into Michelle Gray, one of my favorites in this group. She told me her fourteen-year-old daughter, Madison, had just started handling. They even had a date: Friday, April 25. The girl had picked up a northern copperhead. Michelle beckoned her daughter to come by, and an earnest young woman wearing a long denim skirt appeared at my side. She'd swept her hair up in a bun and wore green sandals and a blue T-shirt.

"It was like a burst of feeling; overwhelming and exciting," she said. "Once I knew there was no harm in it, I wasn't scared."

I picked up from Michelle that a lot of the newer folks had followed them to Andrew's church and that while Cody was very old school up in Middlesboro, Andrew was much more accepting of sinful folks. "They call this the 'land of misfits' church," Michelle remarked. "People with a past come to Andrew's." That fit in with what I'd picked up elsewhere—that Andrew's acceptance of a variety of personalities, his noninsistence on dressing or acting a certain way, his noncompliance with the "Jesus only" doctrines of other serpent-handling churches, and even his own obvious faults, such as smoking, actually endeared him to a populace with very imperfect lives.

Michelle also dropped another interesting tidbit: she and Paul had decided that while they'd tough out a bite from a copperhead or cottonmouth, they'd head for the hospital if bitten by a rattler. Many of the deaths—those of Jamie, Mack, Melinda, and Punkin—had come from rattlers. It was unclear where God was in all the deaths, but the Grays weren't going to take chances. Plus, she had a pacemaker. And if they lost status in Holiness circles because of it, so be it. Not that this family was at all wimpy when it came to snakebite. The Gray home had been a hospital ward of sorts for at least seven snakebite victims over the years, she told me. In fact, there was a science to how you handled it all.

"Make sure they're sitting up, pray over them, and make them comfortable," she said. If a finger's been bitten, "put the elbow into ice water for fifteen minutes, then pull it out," she said. "Not the finger, though. If you get ice on the bite, you get large black blisters. You want the blood to hyper-circulate so as to get the venom out of the joints. If it stays in the joints, it locks them. Even if it hurts, you have to flex your arm. And don't pop any black blisters."

As I was talking with this kindhearted woman, someone pulled up with the Hamblin kids in the car, and Payton jumped out. Veeka went to greet him, but like small boys everywhere, he was squishy about girls, so Veeka ended up following him around the playground.

I expected a quiet week after that, but on Monday, Facebook lit up again. Little Cody had been bitten by a canebrake while he was cleaning their cages, and calls for prayer were going out. About twenty people, including Andrew and Nathan Evans, rushed to his house, where Cody had retired to tough it out. Andrew and Nathan kept Cody walking, moving, and drinking water and Gatorade to flush out his system and then tried to get him to rest and sleep.

We were at Dollywood that Monday, and as is often my luck on these things, I'd chosen to take some time off from the internet that day. Earlier, I'd seen this from Andrew: *Thank God for another beautiful day. I thank him for the wonderful homecoming we had. But I really need everyone's prayers today. I haven't been this hurt in a very long time. I remember now why I keep my guard up and don't open up to people. Glad to know that Jesus is the one person that will never leave nor forsake me. Hope everyone is having a blessed day.*

I wondered what he was referring to. It wasn't until later that day that I discovered what had happened to Cody. By Tuesday, his pain was gone, and he was starting to eat. On Wednesday, John and Veeka and I were heading up north to spend some time with Andrew. I was beyond grouchy, as accounts of Cody's snakebite adventure were on TV, in the Lexington paper, in the Associated Press, and elsewhere. Cody had made room in his schedule to do interviews with them, but he'd been too busy to talk with me the previous Saturday. This whole serpent-handling business was definitely burning me out.

Andrew met us at the church. Yes, they were still on food stamps, he said. National Geographic had paid him $1,500 per episode, he added, but the money disappeared fast because church members were continually asking him for loans. No, he didn't have a job at this point.

This frustrated me to no end, as two years before, I'd given him the name of an agent in Hollywood who could have arranged a much better deal or at least gotten him the $5,000 per episode that Jamie received. I asked more about his past and was told that his mother was a meth addict. He wouldn't speak about his dad, so he was raised by his grandparents in a church open to Pentecostal practices. His maternal grandfather was the one who suggested he get ordained, which he did at the age of eighteen at a nondenominational church on Tennessee Avenue in LaFollette. I asked about when his major snake bites had been and learned he'd been bitten in March by a copperhead at a revival.

"My finger swelled a little bit," he said, "but I stayed at that service. I preached forty-five minutes and the service went for two and a half hours. My finger swelled to the base of the hand—it was the middle finger on my right hand. My joints got sore and my elbow swelled, but I never got sick. I came home and ate two double cheeseburgers." His first bite was the one in July 2010 that nearly killed him and got him airlifted twice to hospitals in Kentucky. Then he was bitten that August on the back of his head by a four-foot cottonmouth.

"The Lord instructed me on what to do and there was no harm," he said about that. He listed the species he'd handled: a puff adder, a Gaboon viper, eastern and western diamondback rattlers, pygmy rattlers, copperheads, and cottonmouths of various types. The bite at that first New Year's Eve service I visited was just a nip, he said. So was another bite he got the following Good Friday.

"Up there I feel joy unspeakable and full of glory," he said about snake handling at his pulpit. "It's the most powerful thing, being one on one with God." But closer to Earth, "Jamie and Melinda's bites were from rattlers," he said. "That was the first time either had been bit by one. Since Jamie died, I've offered a rattler to no one. I'm very more cautious." He took issue with signs posted in places like Sand Mountain and Jolo disavowing responsibility on the part of the church if someone were bitten. "I am the shepherd and I am responsible for what happens in this building," he said.

I asked him more about what it was like to be in a reality show, and he confirmed what he'd hinted at before about the excruciating process. The producers had wanted to film him and Liz having a confrontation; he nixed that. They wanted him and Jamie to argue about baptism; Andrew deep-sixed that. It was obvious the producers were tearing out their hair trying to get dramatic footage. At one point, he said, Liz was trying to get the five kids ready for a 1:00 p.m. shooting, and the camera crew was trying to get them to hurry. Finally, she refused to budge any further. "You signed a contract," the National Geographic folks reminded them, but Liz had walked out on more than one scene if she felt she was being pushed around.

"They wanted me to do stuff I don't ordinarily do," he said. The Texas trip: "We were nervous and stressed. We didn't ordinarily do that. People asked me, 'Do you snake hunt that much?' I don't. This year I've snake hunted four times. That will last us through the summer. We don't have an exciting life. We wanted to show that we were normal people. We swim, we go out to eat. It isn't a life revolved around snakes."

Things weren't going well until National Geographic brought in a second producer who treated them with more respect, he said. I'd never been able to worm out of the National Geographic's press office what really went on behind the scenes, but it sounded like they found the filming very hard going and swore off doing the series again. Eventually Andrew said he had to leave, but instead of heading back toward Knoxville, I asked John if he'd mind if we took a detour to McCloud Mountain, an overlook about six miles out of LaFollette. I needed to clear my head, plus I wanted to see the restaurant perched up there. We drove up a steep hill and climbed out, walking over to a wood-paneled deck overlooking Powell Valley. Nearby was a thirty-foot-tall, green metal cross bolted to a rock on the edge of the cliff. Below us somewhere among the large farms with red roofs and white siding was the house where Andrew and Liz lived with their kids. Trucks moving along Route 63 towards Kentucky. Clinch Mountain, House Mountain, and the far-off Smokies to the south all shimmered in the late afternoon light. Norris Lake glistened in the distance behind green hills. The sky showed a palette of smoky blues, grey, periwinkle, and whites, but thunder rumbled in the distance. There was a smell of rain in the air, and I put on a jacket.

The next day, there was more Facebook chatter about Cody feeling ill. Of the eighty-six comments posted on the Coots family page, several criticized him for not going to a doctor. *Maybe the Lord wants him to think of his wife and 2 babies he's leaving behind if something happens to him,* one woman wrote. *The Lord blessed him with his beautiful family and to give it all up over a stubborn snakebite showdown is just plain irresponsible and i do not see how the Lord would want him to do that. I respect their belief and what they believe but it's not always about yourself.*

Katrina snapped back: *He is 21 years old. He don't want to go to a doctor. Please be respectful god has moved the worst part is over.*

That same day, I'd gotten a phone call from the University of Alaska. I'd been applying for jobs all over the country, and this was an endowed chair with the journalism department for a one-year residency in Fairbanks. The salary was quite generous, and I was dying to get out of western Tennessee any way I could. We were at a pool near the cabin where we were staying when the call came in offering me the job. I told John my days in Tennessee were now numbered. Veeka and I returned to Jackson, and I was too taken up with getting my house on the market to pay much attention to what was happening in the eastern part of the state.

When I eventually checked in on June 6, Liz posted a photo of herself in a long black skirt with red and yellow flowers and a long-sleeved red blouse holding a cardboard sign: "Baby Hamblin #6." It pointed to her tummy. Payton and the twins were standing by her with their hands on her stomach. That post got 245 Likes. But something seemed wrong. On June 9, Liz posted: *Does anyone know what the symptoms are to depression? Please inbox me.*

Also on June 9: *Please pray for me don't know how much more crap I can take!* Later that day: *OK people just because I ask abt depression doesn't me i separated my self for god. fyi I'm going threw a lot and Jesus is what I need . . .*

This seemed to be a bit early for postpartum depression. For a woman who constantly seemed to be in her husband's shadow, flashes of Liz's personality occasionally came out online. She loved pretty clothing and often posted selections from the Apostolic Clothing Company, which had a site showing modest dresses, long skirts, and long-sleeved blouses. Only five feet tall, Liz no doubt perused specialty catalogues, and even though she apparently didn't have two pennies to rub together, she had dreams of what she wanted.

On June 10, Liz had posted: *Joys gonna come in the morning.* Later: *One way or the other I've got to make it.*

On June 11: *So hurt and heart broken </3.* This included a smiley face shedding a tear.

Later that day: *Just wants to say thank you to all the prayers everyone has said God has moved big time.*

On June 12, she posted: *Baby is fine I'm 7 weeks are lil peanut is healthy and looking good so blessed.*

But later that day, Andrew dropped the boom: *It is with a heavy heart and I so deeply regret to inform the world that we were put out of our church building today. My mind is racing with millions of thoughts and the pain of all this is almost unbearable. I ask everyone to please pray for all of us during this painful time. So as of right now we have nowhere to have church at and I will inform everyone when something changes. And everyone please keep me in your prayers as well.*

I wasn't horribly surprised at the news, as I'd sensed at the homecoming that something was up. I got a text from one of my sources saying that the landlord wanted to start his own church there. Linda Spoon posted: *We were put out because the man that owned the church said to go. Snakes were not mention. He is one of those off again and on again preachers, the church was doing good so he decided he wanted it back. It is a shame what people do in the name of the* LORD.

But that was nothing compared to the message that Liz posted on June 18: *For a preacher/pastor to divorce his wife without just cause there is something going on behind closed doors. . . . . . with that being said Andrew Hamblin and I are getting a divorce. no I do not won't to but he's the one taking and doing this to his family who has stood behind him threw everything he's ever went threw. so to inform u all this way but its no secret. I love him with all my heart and has begged to him not to do this but its in his hands. he knows he has preached against divorce . . . . so for me and my kids I'll take care of us. pray me cause I'm gonna need it.*

CHAPTER THIRTEEN

THE SUMMER
OF THEIR
DISCONTENT

By the time I had logged onto Facebook, Liz had gotten 194 comments.

I am so sorry to hear this, a woman from South Carolina wrote her. *I was a devout fan of you guys on the show and I would've never have thought this could happen to y'all. Kick and scream and don't go down without a fight. If there is no just cause then the law should require a year of separation first. I pray God will restore your relationship a thousand times stronger than before.*

Liz replied: *That's what I'll look into cause I will not give up in gonna fight for my marriage. . . . . I love him with all my heart and I won't allow this. I've gave him 7 years and five beautiful babys. And one on the way.*

Rose Mary Hamblin from Jacksboro posted: *Im going to say this. I know that he is my family but I dont approve of this. u have supported him thru the troubles that yall have had with those snakes and others that I won't say anything bout but he need to stop thinking like all the other Hamblin do and grow up to be a man that his papaw showed him to be. If his papaw was still alive today he would be very unhappy with him rite now. Liz u r still family no matter what.*

After a few people chastised Liz for airing out her concerns so publicly, her aunt spoke up. *Liz is only doing what she has been taught to do, ask prayer warriors to call out to the Lord on her "Family's behalf,"* Jo Carr Ray wrote. *The people who have made comments that this shouldn't be on face book, may I ask you what would you like to see on face book? If this upsets you, I have a suggestion, hit your delete key, and keep your opinions to yourself, she doesn't need that right now or ever. If you can't say something kind, don't say anything at all.*

And of course there were detractors.

If half these people knew the whole story they wouldn't be posting on here taking up for you, said Jessica Bledsoe.

Amen jessica let's throw it out there if you won't me to tell why we fight, Liz responded.

Liz just use wisdom about what u post is all im saying I love you and am praying for you, said Josh Lowery, Jessica's fiancé. I'd seen photos on Facebook of him and Andrew baptizing Jessica in May, along with photos of Andrew, under which Josh had inscribed "my pastor and best friend." On May 3, he'd posted a photo of Elizabeth praying over a sick woman at the church. *This is a woman of great strength,* Josh had written. *And what a help to the people she is, she stands behind the Man of God and is content to stay in the shadows, she is a virtuous woman and a pillar in the church, many times she is overlooked as we lift up our pastor but I just want you to know you are appreciated and loved very much God bless you First Lady.*

Liz responded: *Thanks everyone please just pray he takes time to think about this. to me I love him with all my heart. please just pray he thinks this threw.*

Leaving you with 6 kids to raise. . . . what a man, said one woman.

I've been through a divorce and it's horrible! Especially for the kids, said another.

People I have begged and begged him not to do this but he has his mind made up, Liz wrote. *I'm praying he will think about this. I even asked if we could seperate for a while but he said no.*

Josh chimed back in: *Oh be careful little fingers what you type for the father up above is looking down in love oh be careful little fingers what you type.*

As I could see the church members start to bicker with each other, I felt heartsick. There had been warnings. I'd heard church members say that Liz wasn't pastor's wife material, that she neglected the kids and would wander off during services, leaving Andrew to go in search of her. Just before her announcement, she had posted a large poster on Andrew's page that showed two wedding rings with words that read: "If people put as much work into their marriage as they will have to into a divorce, more people would be happily married."

People were starting to turn to Andrew's page and leave posts there.

Please do not leave your family, whatever the problems, the Lord will get you through, one person told him. *So many people are watching you, the Lord is using you to do his work. If you give in now all your work will be in vain and the evil ones will be happy, the Lord will be in tears. Stay in the Lord's army.*

But Andrew was silent. Later that evening or early the morning of June 19, Liz posted: *Please everyone let's keep the comments on here positive. never meant to offend anyone with my status. it will be removed. he is going threw a lot and so am I so pray for the both of us. thanks everyone.*

That very day, a Knoxville TV station ran a story about Andrew being evicted from the church. It was a curious story, as Andrew refused comment, and Clyde Daugherty refused to go on camera, obligating WBIR to use old videos. They showed Andrew's name taken off the church sign and a lock put on the door. Daugherty said he charged $267 in rent for the place, but he no longer wanted serpent handling on the property. He also thought Andrew was "focused too much on the wrong things, like attention from the media and the TV show, instead of the word of God." Curiously, however, he offered to sell Andrew the building for $67,000, which Andrew turned down.

On Saturday morning, June 21, Liz posted a pathetic request: *Needing some were to go to church. . . . please if you know of any places that would welcome me with open arms and be nice to me please let me know.*

She got more than fifty suggestions and invitations. But on Sunday morning she wasn't in church. Instead, she posted a photo of herself staring straight at the camera, unsmiling, with shorn hair. It was her declaration of independence from the Holiness movement, which decreed that a woman's hair be kept long. Her sister, Chastity Carroll, had just gotten married, and Liz was in the family photo, hair shorn, unsmiling.

One woman asked, *So do u not follow holiness anymore?????* Several people (all of them texting on a Sunday morning) trashed the writer for criticizing Elizabeth, including this person from Bell County: *Don't let anyone bring you down religiously over your hair. Long hair doesn't make anyone a better Christian than short hair. I know many good Holiness women who cut their hair. You are wonderful and beautiful. Keep on keeping on!*

Liz then posted: *I'm not praying right now.* A few dozen comments followed, plus reams of advice and remarks like this from one woman: *The sadness on your face speaks volumes. It's not about hair. It's not about any of that. Whether you cut it or not, that's your own belief and decision. But your pain and hurt is all over your face. I'm sorry you are hurting.*

This latest rift between Liz and Andrew was the worst that had happened yet in a marriage that was already quite stormy. This time, neither were backing down, and Liz was airing her side via Facebook. Once again I realized how this was a generation that didn't see privacy as a great need. They continually emoted on Facebook, Twitter, Snapchat—basically everywhere.

On Monday, June 23, a woman posted: *Just a thought. Has anyone actually spoken to Andrew Hamblin in the last week. I know he is not posting anything but if his own good friends don't know where he is, shouldn't someone contact the sheriff. I'm making no judgements but I would be out of my mind with worry if no one has spoken to him. Such a sad situation.*

Two days later, Liz posted a little smiley face shedding a tear and these words: *Things just keep getting worse.*

During that week, Veeka and I were in Oregon on vacation, so it wasn't until June 28 that I saw that Chastity Carroll had posted a frantic prayer request for her sister, who was in an ICU in Knoxville. Someone then posted that an ambulance had come by at 7:00 a.m. and taken her to the LaFollette hospital and that she'd then been transferred to Knoxville. She and the baby were said to be "all right."

Glenna Daugherty, Clyde's daughter-in-law, chimed in to say Andrew had called them to ask what was going on, so he was obviously not living at home.

Just talked to someone! Everyone please pray for her it's not good, a woman posted.

A man posted, *Oh my goodness that poor woman! Hoping and praying that she and the baby are doing okay. Nobody should have to go through what she is dealing with right now and no matter what her husband is feeling, he should be there to support his wife, his children and their baby.*

It was not difficult to figure out what had happened. Liz had been posting desperate comments on her feed such as this: *Do you ever just want to pack up and leave out of the blue without saying anything to anyone like just leave and start a new life?* She also lifted a quote from a Facebook page titled "She's a Homewrecker" that said: *Hypocrites: Those who preach to try to convince everyone and themselves, that they are a good person, while being evil on a daily basis.*

I started e-mailing my sources, trying to figure out what was up. It never failed that a crisis always arose in this neck of the woods when I was on vacation. The "homewrecker" post alerted me that another woman was involved. Searching about on Facebook, I found the cuckolded husband, who the day before had posted: *The pain in my stomach this morning is almost unbareable. I wish I had the money to get my kids and I as far away from this place as possible for a few days! Away from everything! The pain, this big empty house . . the constant reminder . . . I'm begging for prayers today . . . begging that the Lord will help me.* This was Derrick Noe, one of the men who had been dancing in front of the church at Andrew's homecoming. His wife, Taylor, had been the woman handling fire. He was posting copious requests for prayer, plus having this conversation:

Derrick Noe: *Better run as far as he can run. Thats a fact.*

Linda LSpoon: *He is not running, takes two people to have done what they did. pray for both and live for God. I hate what has happened but satan has had a field day in this situation.*

Derrick Noe: *Takes two absolutely. but u cant defend one. That kind of stuff causes men to kill one another. Ive seen it time and time again. He is no pastor. A wolf in sheeps clothing. Both of them are pathedic in my book. They'll get exactly whats coming to them both.*

Linda L Spoon: *I am not defending neither one. I love them both but if we are living for God we have to show our love for people and pray for all there is no hate in my heart for people just what they did both of them and what they have put the others thru especially you and liz.*

Derrick Noe: *It'll take God because I get sick even looking at him. Im sorry . . . im just human.*

Linda L Spoon: *I know you should have never been this hurt by him but they did not think about their partners or the children Iam so sorry.*

Another poster said: *He's let the fame and spot [light] get to him. Should've never done that TV Show. Now he thinks his poop don't stink. Not much of a pastor if you ask me.*

Derrick Noe: *Hes a coward. If someone talks to him,* PLEASE *tell him Id like to meet with him. This is not about snakes, it's about having three somes and sleeping with as many women as you can decieve!" My rant is over. Sorry everyone. Im too good for this. Dont even need to waste my time. They'll lift their eyes in hell if they dont repent of their wicked ways and* RECONCILE *with their mates or remain unmarried. Its the* BOOK. *Not an opinion.*

Jeremey Henegar: *1 Timothy 4:1-2 KJV Now the Spirit speaketh expressly, that in the latter times some shall depart from the faith, giving heed to seducing spirits, and doctrines of devils; Speaking lies in hypocrisy; having their conscience seared with a hot iron.*

A pastor posted: *Just be the man you are and the man that God created you to be and the rest is tooken care of remember.*

I also noticed that Liz had posted a photo from the National Association for Gun Rights; it showed a woman with a rifle and the words: "Because a restraining order is just a piece of paper."

Someone posted: *So what are you trying to say?*

Liz: *That some people better watch there back.*

She then posted: *Lord I still trust you.*

Also on June 26, she wrote: *Please stop what your doing and get down and pray for me.* She got 156 likes and 70 comments. How must it feel to have this enormous online cheering section? It was obviously addictive. I came across another post from Derrick: *Might as well . . . after all I've been through. my mom with cancer, my wife leaving me and the babies and running off with a preacher . . . I at least deserve a Super man CAPE! lol. might as well try to laugh . . . helps the pain . . .*

I clicked over to Taylor's page. She was an attractive woman with dark brown hair, and she had two small children. I noticed she'd dropped her married name and was going by Taylor Elaine, using her middle name. There was obviously something going on as people were offering to pray for her about something serious. Liz Hamblin had been posting on Taylor's page as recently as June 3, so these revelations were fairly new. Taylor had also posted several glamorous-looking photos of herself on her Facebook page, plus an announcement that she'd lost weight recently. Andrew, meanwhile, had switched his page to a "support for Andrew Hamblin and his family" page from the previous fall. Otherwise, he had dropped off the social media map. But the young man who had built his empire through Facebook was not going to be let off that easily. On July 2, Liz—now publicly the wronged wife—posted a photo of a woman crying and the words: "Have you ever missed someone so much that even the thought of them made you burst into tears?"

A woman responded: *yep lots of times im going to pray that god will give him a hell of whoppen and sister im so sorry you are hurting it ant right but that's how the devil [works].*

Liz: *I've never went threw anything like this in my whole life . . . i just keep telling myself everything happens for a reason.*

A man posted: *u r crazy to hold on to someone who wants someone else, move on.*

A woman responded: *U are rude and no she is not crazy. She loves him and I hope you never have to travel in those foot steps.*

The man shot back: *well I tell the truth, ive been there, I gave up and moved on and came out ahead, did Andrew not leave her? why wait on a loss cause? im not a church man but ive lived a 39 year old life and I know once someone leaves u for someone else the don't stop. im not rude, im honest. it takes 2 to tango and once a man smells a doe in heat, unless it's a real man, that buck will follow his nose.*

Another man said: *I don't know the details, . . and it's none of my business, . . but if he did leave Liz for another woman, . . his little "pajama party" will be short lived, . . pastor or not, . . you don't blow off your pregnant wife and 5 kids and not expect God to chastise you, . . I love Liz and Andrew BOTH, . . and I'm praying for their family, . . I hope these rumors are wrong, . . if their right, ... Andrew, . . please do the right thing and come home . . .*

Yes, Andrew, I thought, please come home. By this time, I was on my way home from Oregon and dumbfounded by this turn of events. Why hadn't Andrew even hinted during our marathon interview on May 28 that he was so near the breaking point? In all my contacts with him, I'd been beyond impressed with how he'd weathered so many reversals and trials with good humor and grace. Rereading the Facebook postings of the previous month, I noticed he had posted nothing after the announcement about losing the church. That must have sent him over the edge. Although he had already located property to build a new church on, Andrew had nowhere near the finances for such a venture, and he knew it. And now that he'd lost his building, there was nowhere he could go. There wasn't a landlord in the entire county who would let him rent a place while allowing poisonous snakes inside. No insurance company would insure it. And if Andrew held meetings in a private home, the TWRA folks would be at his door in nothing flat, charging him with endangering children. His own home wasn't zoned for church services, and I figured Campbell County officials wouldn't give him a variance in a million years. Andrew had gotten off earlier because the TWRA folks had gone on church property where Andrew had some constitutional protections. But this time he was cornered. He had to have snakes to keep the crowds coming. "It is the one thing that defines them and makes them unique," Ralph Hood had told me when I first interviewed him. "If you took away the serpents and they did everything else, no one would do a story on them. They'd just be another Protestant evangelical group." Andrew had five children, no college degree or Bible school certificate, no job, and now no church. I wondered if the eviction alone had been the final straw or whether there was yet something else.

Liz soon posted: *gods dealing with him already . . . just keep a praying.* I looked at Derrick Noe's page with its many veiled comments. People told him to keep his head up and hang in there. A few called him a "Pentecostal stud muffin." By this time, the secular world had noticed what was going on. A website called *topix.com* that has forums for cities all over the country had a number of postings under Andrew's name in the LaFollette section by early July.

One person posted: *His wife took a bunce of meds and tried to kill herself she's over knoxville in the hospitol.*

Said another person: *I was completely* STUNNED *when I found out that he was cheating in his wife!! Ive always said that he needs to get off his rear and get a job. I work everyday, and he's no better than me. If you have five kids and one on the way you should be working!! I always thought they were great people. I would have* NEVER *thought Andrew would do this to his wife and kids. He's 23, probably never experienced life. But that's no excuse to jump into bed withoa woman in your congregation! . . . In my opinion, god shut the doors on Andrew's church because of his fornication. I'm still stunned! He has a great wife. My heart breaks for her. She has stood behind Andrew all the way, and he walks off and leaves her like she's a piece of trash. He needs a good dose of reality. I know the members of the church are shocked. They had so much in Andrew. The devil is trying to destroy them.*

And on and on the conversation went, with more details about Taylor's marriage, whether or not she was pregnant by Andrew, and so on. So much for Andrew ever having a hope of ministering in this community again.

On July 9, Elizabeth posted: *Does anyone know if I could do anything about a women who is friends with my hubbys girlfriend writing me making threats that she works for dcs [Department of Children's Services] and she was going to see to it that my kids are removed from my home. . . . . that she works with surprise visits / has pull. . . . . and my kids would be took. . . . . I mean I don't think she's allowed to write this stuff to me . . . so of you know anything that would help please let me know. . . . .*

This was raising the separation to a whole new level of viciousness. If Andrew had anything to do with this, it was not the Andrew I knew. I was beginning to wonder whether I knew him very well. Liz received posts with prayers, legal advice, ideas for getting Andrew put in jail, and rants all evening from North Carolina, Louisiana, Ohio, Maine, Florida, and many more states. There were 187 replies in about three hours.

Meanwhile, packing boxes were all over my house, but I was on the phone with Michelle Gray one Friday evening. She had just messaged me on Facebook that she and Paul were taking over Andrew's church. I knew I had to call her. I asked about Liz's hospital stay, and she told me that Liz had swallowed a bottle of Phenergan, an antinausea med. She was in despair about Andrew, and what saved her as she was fading off was the thought of her children being raised by someone else. So she called the ambulance.

"When we heard about it, we jumped in the Blazer and drove down to her," Michelle said. They extracted a promise from Liz to never pull such a stunt again. I asked her when everything started to unravel.

"At the homecoming, we found out he was cheating," she said. "We knew something was wrong." After Andrew had a pie put into his face at the reception, she said, Taylor and another woman cleaned him up in a way that seemed overly intimate. "That was so embarrassing," she said. I just listened. I'd seen the food fight as well but had not picked up on any of the currents running underneath.

When I asked about the Tabernacle, she said that Clyde Daugherty had offered the church to Paul, and the Grays decided to take it on with the condition they could do what had to be done to clean it up morally. Plus, they had to fit the services in with Paul's job at the Laurel County Detention Center in Kentucky. Andrew had made off with about $4,000 from the building fund, she said, leaving them with almost no funds to get the Tabernacle back on its feet. But it would be a job; one of the young men in the church had recently slept with Liz, she said, so "it's left on our lap to sort through and fix this. Paul's bold and you know I am. There are two things in the Holiness movement you will notice: people committing adultery and people turning gay."

I asked more questions. "Liz cheated on him once—but it was one time—it was nothing like this," she said, adding that it was back in 2011. I remembered Andrew telling me of his own suicide attempt that summer while being separated from Liz. The picture was coming into focus.

"I think [Andrew's attitude change] started the middle of that show," she mused. "He changed. It was like he got an ego. Things started mattering less and less as long as he was getting the attention. Andrew doesn't want to work. He always said the church is his job. He had in his head because he pastors a church two nights a week, people were supposed to hand stuff over to him. His grandparents were good people. His mom was a drug head—but she didn't raise him. His grandparents did."

Even at this point, Liz would still take him back, she said. But he would have to work. Meanwhile, Liz was so destitute that she was having a hard time coming up with the money to pay the air conditioning bill for that big house. I told Michelle that Liz had thousands of Facebook friends who would gladly help her out financially. But she had to ask. And why did Andrew snap? I wondered.

"He wasn't getting the attention he thought he needed," she said. I also learned there had been tensions among church members who had appeared on *Snake Salvation* and who expected Andrew to pay them for their time. When he didn't, they left. I half-pitied Andrew. The backbiting and sniping from people with bit parts must have been unendurable. On July 14, Elizabeth posted a message asking if anyone knew of a good, affordable, local divorce lawyer.

Meanwhile, Derrick Noe told me he filed for divorce in early July. He'd changed his profile picture to one of him wearing a short-sleeved T-shirt and shorts—a get-up that a Holiness man would not wear. I saw that someone on his feed had asked if he'd "laid everything down" and gone to talk with his wife.

He responded: *She hasnt spoke to me in a month . . and committed adultery on me. I have no desire to talk now.* A few days earlier he had posted: *People crack me up! Your long hair, long skirts and long sleeves doesn't give you a free pass to GOSSIP, BACKBITE and whatever else. I'm so over with worrying about the opinions of people who live a DOUBLE standard! Not in the mood today for people who have feet that are quick to run to mischief!*

He got 231 likes on that one. He added: *Those people running their mouth about whats going on in my family. If ppl dont know facts, they need to mind their business. Because of the GARBAGE that I have seen for YEARS in those churches, I have NO desire to go back! Too many liars, hypocrits, ppl.*

He got many replies, the best of which was from someone in Corbin, Kentucky: *AMEN BROTHER . . . i don't care to say it i was in the die hardest, strictest, hell fire and brim stone snake handling fire breathing holiness churches for 13 years and there are some of the best clean living kind hearted loving Godly ppl that ever walked this earth and i love them as much today as i did then . . . at the same time ive seen the other side of so called holiness. ive seen them wear there long sleeve shirts buttoned to the neck and the sisters wearing the long sleeve shirts and skirts to there ankles and there hair to there waist. and the prophet and the preacher handle a big black rattler on Saturday night and Monday morning the preacher leave his wife and the prophet walk away from her husband and babies and run off together . . . many sinners today just laugh when you try to witness to* them and say something like *man you ppl ant know better than we are the way alot of you live . . . so many sinners have seen so much sin in the church and Gods ppl that they are discouraged and don't want any part of it.* LORD HELP US ALL.

On July 19, Liz posted: *It hurts so bad to look at all our pictures are memory's. hearing my babies ask when is my daddy coming home. I feel like my life has been distroyed. I feel empty inside. I feel broken. having to go to doctors appointments by myself. I feel like I'm never going to be happy again. I feel lost and alone.* On July 20, she posted: *When u pray please pray for Andrew he really needs it.*

Two days before that, I'd packed the car completely full with a grumpy cat in the front seat. The last things I had done that afternoon were to take my daughter to a swimming lesson and then to the local theater, where she was acting in a short play. By 7:00 p.m., we were saying good-bye to our lovely four-bedroom home. I set off on the highway toward Dyersburg. It had been a cloudy, rainy day, but as we approached the Mississippi River just after 8:00 p.m., the sun burst out. Light flooded the bridge and the surrounding countryside like a benediction. And with that, we left Tennessee.

CHAPTER FOURTEEN

DESOLATION

The 5,700-mile trip from Tennessee to Alaska via Seattle took a month. Once we arrived at the home of my parents in Seattle, I had to fly to Montreal in early August for a journalism educators conference—and to present my paper about serpent handlers and Facebook. There, someone stole my laptop out of my satchel as it was slung across the back of my chair in a hotel restaurant. I'd carelessly left the zipper open, never dreaming that someone would be brazen enough to reach in there, grab the laptop, and sprint off through the lobby of the downtown Sheraton. The ensuing mess—the filing of a police report, the dealings with my insurance company, and the two days it took to buy another laptop in Seattle and download all my info from the hard drive I had thankfully remembered to bring along—soaked up time and energy. Some of my notes on the drama in LaFollette got lost in the theft as well. The ensuing trip along the Alaska-Canada Highway and getting settled in Fairbanks insured that it wasn't until early September that I was able to figure out what was happening in East Tennessee.

Not much had changed other than that the Tabernacle Church seemed to be doing well under the Grays. But the vitriol between Elizabeth and Andrew had become the Hatfields vs. the McCoys. Because too many people were posting an assortment of junk on her Elizabeth Hamblin Facebook page, she'd created a new page under her maiden name, Elizabeth Carroll.

On September 2, she posted: *It takes a real peace of S### for me to call and say ur daughters has two diapers and is running out of milk and for u to reply back and say call someone and have them run u to town. well hello I don't have money to buy diapers and u reply back neither do I. I don't know what to tell u to do ! I've never in my life hated someone has much as I hate him!!!!!!*

She got fifty replies fairly quickly, including: *I am so sickened by him he preached Holiness dressed Holiness who does he think he is to not work?* a woman posted. *what saddens me is God gave him so many gifts to preach sing play instruments God gave him a sweet wife beautiful as u are beautiful kids and he gets tested by the devil and gives in throws his whole life away God will ask of him to explain someday and he will have to answer hang in there sweetpea im a prayin every day.*

A man posted: *He never worked provided before but had $ for cigs, snakes. And while I'm @ it I'll just put it all out thier!! Lol he accused me and another* MARRIED *woman of fooling around which wasn't true at all . . and stopped talking to me* NOW *look. I was raised holiness and I was taught if you to lazy to work for your family would be to lazy to take care of the house of God . . remember God don't like ugly . . a man that don't work let him not eat!! Hope everything works out Liz.*

Liz: *All he's gave me for 3 months is 40 $ dollars. . . . but yet his whore runs him around and he sets and smokes all day!!!!!*

There were a few more comments, then someone messaged her to say she was bringing diapers over.

Thank god for her, Liz posted, *and you cause I don't know what I'd do. I don't see how he can just dump his responsabilitys off on other people and sleep at night ! But who am I kidding he done it before he ran off.*

A woman posted: *Let's hope the girl he is with can't have babies.*

Yea well she can, Liz responded. *he doesn't use pertection and she done got two by two diff men. shell be popping them out next!*

From what I could discern from other chatter, Andrew was staying in Clairfield, a town in a rural area between LaFollette and Middlesboro. He was keeping the twins during the week while Payton and the girls were staying with Liz. Because of rumors of one of the younger men in the church taking up with her, Liz posted: *to the idiots that's saying I'm living with someone I want u to know I don't live with anyone but my kids!*

A friend asked, *Don't ya just love ppl that talk about something they know nothing about.*

Liz replied: *Girl people are pushing my button today's lol . . . Ask anyone who knows me or comes around. I sit here from Monday to Friday go to church with my kids come back home sometimes go to moms on sat back home Sunday morning and back to church again. then the same thing over. I don't live with anyone and go to church and shout over anything . . . I set on the front seat at church and go to the bath room . . .*

Then on September 17, she posted: *Does anyone is the lafollette area have there own business that they could hire me for work. . . . I don't care if its just cleaning toilets. anything will be fine. just no heavey lifting.*

A day later, she announced she'd signed up with Families First, a state health program that gives out cash payments if the parent agrees to work or volunteer a certain number of hours per week, plus follow a "personal responsibility plan" that insures the recipient is keeping her children in school and up on their immunizations. The worst part, she said, was leaving her daughters in daycare. She got a pile of return messages, many of them congratulating her and others condemning Andrew for not paying child support. *It's a big change,* she wrote, *but I'll look back on it and be proud of myself.*

On October 3, Paul and Michelle Gray dropped a bombshell: *ok so I really wanted to do this a little more in person but because some people work for the news paper, the tv brodcast and the radio all at the same time and can spread private info and add to it the make it lies and gossip wich really upset me here goes. we are moving. its not something we really want so bad to do but the economy is bad, my health is getting worse by the day, and the winters are getting so brutal and with the type of heat in our house it would be impossible. so please, say a prayer for the first time in a long time our little group feels like we are walkin thru fire so don't judge us u don't know what we are truly enduring.*

What? I began looking at posts by members of the Gray family, who appeared to be about to take—or in the process of taking—a six-hundred-mile journey to northern Florida. When nineteen-year-old Jonathan Gray posted something that same day about moving, Linda Spoon had caustically commented, *That's a long way from our church, don't you think?*

Jonathan replied, *Yes it is but our mother need serenity. She will find peace in Florida.*

With the Grays leaving, there went Andrew's last mentors and any hope of him returning to that church. I didn't really know Linda Spoon, but I knew it was time to get to the bottom of what was going on, so I got her on the phone on October 7. She told me that church members learned on Facebook that the Grays were leaving. They had not had church for several weeks, she said, adding that Paul was spending some of that time traveling to Florida to job hunt and find a house. The last they heard was the mysterious Facebook message, and later they learned that Paul had left the key to the church on the pulpit.

"They didn't tell nobody they were leaving," she said, adding that Michelle had suffered another serious seizure recently. "He promised over and over again he'd never leave unless God was through with him." Only five members, including herself, were left. My heart went out to this retired nurse who found herself in charge.

"We're going to have church Friday night and vote to see whether to keep it open," she said. "Andrew is trying to help. But no one wants him. He's doing nothing."

Not working?

"No," she said. "Andrew came back and repented," she added. "He prayed and he was getting help. I guess Paul called him up with some stuff and Andrew quit coming. He was tempted above what he could tolerate. We compared him to King David and Bathsheba."

All indications were that they'd close the church as there was no pastor, no money to pay the next month's rent, and increasingly, no members. Even the snakes were gone.

I asked her to post their decision on Facebook about staying open, and then unexpectedly she gave me Andrew's phone number. He wanted to talk with me, she said.

The next day I called him at a home with a landline because he said he no longer had a cell phone.

"I've seen better days," he told me. "It seems like since November of last year, nothing has let up. It's been like going through a hurricane. We went through the court stuff; when we got over that, the police started pulling me over for all sorts of reasons. Then Jamie died. In March, things kept on getting worse. The homecoming was fair and done me some good. I was begging for help. It *seemed* like I had the perfect home, marriage and church. I had the biggest serpent-handling church since Jolo. I then said that I need prayer; things were eating at me. People said 'You're the pastor. We are the ones who need help.' Then when the church was taken from us, it was like I threw my hands up."

I asked him to clarify the bit about the police pulling him over, as the local paper had made a big deal of Andrew's two arrests, one in January and the other a month later.

"After we won [in court], we had some sheriff's deputy friends who said I'd better watch out; the county police was out for me," he said. "They'd follow me when I would take Payton to school. I was pulled over twice for the same thing. The first time, the man was rude. I'd gotten a van from Ronnie, but Ronnie had not given me the title. They pulled me over because there was no tag on it. I told the police I had just gotten the title. They also did it the Saturday after Jamie had died. We had no groceries. I was tired, worn out, and depressed. The officer didn't even read me my rights. He just took me to jail."

I refrained from mentioning that he was actually cited for having neither a driver's license nor car registration. I guessed he had confused the title with the registration as one very rarely carries a title in a car. He was in the process of getting his license, he said. I asked him where he now lived, and he'd moved back to a family home in Clairfield, the tiny community in which he'd grown up.

I brought Andrew back to the homecoming and how happy he had seemed then.

"It was a classic homecoming," he said. "I have no pictures from it. The homecoming was when things were at their peak. When there were snakes in my hands, all my problems vanished. Then Clyde called. It was on a Thursday. He called Ronnie, and Ronnie called me furious. I said to calm down. Then Ronnie said we can have church there this weekend and then we have to get out. It was like my world just crumbled."

Then followed a revival weekend he had to lead in Ohio; then it was back to LaFollette, where there was constant arguments with Liz. "I said, I am done," he remembered, "and not going back to church. I hated everybody and everything. I am done. The rest was a downward spiral until I crashed. I tried to go back on the fifth anniversary of my picking up my first serpent," which was August 3. "I tried going up to my grandpa's church. I started getting a little help and my grandpa's church . . . I backslid. I was an alcoholic. I tried to go back to church. Either churches would look at me like I had a disease. Or churches that were Holiness and serpent handling told me I was not welcome. But I started missing the feeling of taking up serpents and the fire. I went back to the Tabernacle. I raised my hands and did a little shouting."

A few members of the church were kind to him, he said. And a handful of people made the effort to try to get his new phone number and call him. But others—including those whom he had pastored through their hard times—weren't so accepting.

"Those that have shouted and spoken in tongues and told me their deepest darkest secrets—they said, no he can't ever come back," Andrew said. "I said, 'Y'uns have come to me and I counseled you in love, and not one time did I tell you not to go back into church.' I'd tell them to dust themselves off. But they were the ones who turned around and stoned me. I had preachers come to me who had cheated on their wives. They'd never had no one to talk to. I had compassion. People came to me who'd committed homosexual acts, and now they treat me like the scum of the earth."

He then switched to his vast knowledge of serpent-handling history. "It's like history repeating himself with Carl Porter," he said, referring to the late pastor of a snake-handling church in northwest Georgia. "He got a divorce, then tried to remarry his wife. He died ashamed, disgraced. He is buried right near the church. When he died, no one cared. I do not want to die like that. I want to renew my reputation. I am miserable."

I asked him where his flock had scattered to.

"Other churches," he said. "I told them, 'You are all satisfied and happy. I guess I will sit at my house and look at my videos, won't I? I won't step inside a church house now.'"

He returned to his high school haunts and tried to forget how the last five years of his life had been flushed away.

"I started drinking heavily," he said. "I'd drive one-lane roads up here seventy to eighty miles per hour. Sometimes I'd sit and scream and cry. I'd scream for Jamie: 'Why did you leave me? Why did you die?' Jamie was my rock. When things got hard at home, I called Jamie. He'd say, 'Son, I'm here.' I'd sit in the snake room and cry, and he would hold me.

"I near beat a boy with a baseball bat one night. I had a mouth like a sailor. I do not even remember the month of July. That is how drunk I got. That was the shape I was in. It's hard having nowhere to go to church." He deactivated his Facebook account because of the constant criticism he was getting.

"No one gave Andrew time to say yes, I did wrong. Everyone said I had deserted Liz and my five children," he said. "Actually, my twins live with me Sundays through Fridays, and the other kids come on the weekend. I was getting harassed by people who knew nothing about me. So for two months, I disappeared off the face of this Earth. Over the summer, the gentle humble man everyone knew went out the door."

Was there any warning about burnout? I asked him. He returned to his memories of Jamie's death. "God moved on me and instructed me to go that Saturday night. I held him in my arms as he died. When he died, his last words were to *me*. When he died, the whole world said, 'We have Andrew.' It was like everyone was sitting in the back while I was driving the train. But the train was going off the tracks."

I asked him if there was any hope that he and Liz would reconcile.

"I'd say no," was his answer. "I went and got another woman. When I fell, I fell hard. When I called things off with that woman, I begged Liz to forgive me. I know what I did, and I can admit to what I did. But there are people who did the same thing I did, before I did it and after I stopped doing it."

I wondered if he meant Liz. Tennessee law forbids a couple to divorce while the wife is pregnant, he said, so everything remained up in the air. When he and Liz met, he added, he was playing for bluegrass and country bands. "Liz, she was a redneck backwoods girl. I took her out from that lifestyle. She didn't know how to survive. I made the doctor's appointments. I went and got the food stamps. I drove because she never got her license. She didn't know how to survive on her own. It was always Andrew. She stayed hid behind me. If people called, she didn't want to talk to them. On *Snake Salvation*, there was only two times she was on the show. She kept to herself."

They were mismatched, I thought. Who would have known? They were both from the same part of Tennessee, the same culture. Once they had slept together, the die was cast. "We were both fifteen-year-olds when she got pregnant," he said. "I married her when I was eighteen years old. I was head over heels for her. I would have walked through fire with a water gun. But that didn't seem to be that's what she wanted. She got pregnant with the twins at eighteen. She never really had a chance to get out."

They had no marriage counseling, he said, and there were times when the marriage was good. "It was repetitive—I'd get so hurt—when we dated there were things that happened. In our marriage, things happened. I don't want to live my life miserable."

I asked him how much Jamie knew of this.

"When things like that would happen, Jamie'd say, 'Son, either you forgive her and go on with your life. Or you've got every right to biblically divorce her, but you can't remarry nor preach or pastor.' Jamie and I didn't see everything eye to eye. Liz and I have both committed adultery. I didn't do a thing until I backslid, and then I committed adultery. The things she's done since March, I have a right to put her away. There was stuff going on before I left home. It was an attention thing."

Well, that's a no-brainer, I thought. Even I could see two years ago that Liz craved attention from a husband who was already bored with her. Or who had quietly given up on the marriage but was sticking it out as long as there were other things—the church, the reality show, and Jamie's helpful presence—as escape valves. Once all those supports were removed, Andrew was out the door.

After Liz's suicide attempt, he was going to try to reconcile, and they spent the night together July 1, he told me. That didn't fix things, and judging by the gossip I was reading on Facebook, Liz was with the other man only a few days later.

"Liz is a pretty woman," Andrew mused. "I've always had a thing for women with long hair. I thought they were the most gorgeous women ever. To have five kids—she has a beautiful body—hardly any stretch marks. What happened? She was tired of the same old Andrew. She thought: 'I am stuck here with five kids.' Some boys come along and give her a little bit of attention. And what happens?"

I asked what could he have done differently.

"There were times I put church members before her; I put snakes before her," he said. "Not one time in eight years have I physically hit her. The first month of my marriage, she spit in my face. I wanted to hit her but I punched the wall. She had every snake-handling woman's dream: a husband who could preach, take up serpents, five beautiful children, a four-bedroom, two-story, two-bath home. The love life was there, but she never felt like it. Jamie always taught us, 'happy wife, happy life.' You take care of your wife and don't just jump on her to breed a baby. That is what we were taught."

From time to time he drove to the Cootses' church. Once, "I had been drinking and wanted to go to Middlesboro," he said. "I wanted to hear Greg Coots sing 'God Understands.' I put on a long-sleeved shirt and went in. Bruce Helton was preaching. Linda came back and hugged me. I stop by Middlesboro every so often and say I miss them. I miss pulling snakes out of boxes with my hands. Cody has told me, 'I talked with some of the elders, but I have got to pray before you come to church again.' But I always preached the church is for the sinners and backsliders. There is a cold hard side to snake handlers. At one time, I was like those. When I was a humble, loving pastor, it brought serpent handling to the twenty-first century. I don't want people to see this side of snake handlers. If people knew the dark secrets of snake-handling churches, they'd never believe in God."

He did try to return to his church twice, he said, but the leaders there were split on whether he should be there. Once, he said, he showed up at the church alone, lay down next to the altar, and cried. What really set him off was how Liz—in her passion to get rid of anything that reminded her of Andrew—had given his snake boxes to Jeremey Henegar, the man she had taken up with.

"I would have blown his brains out over those boxes," Andrew said. "Some were Jamie's boxes. One Cody gave me when Jamie died. Jamie paid $200 for that box to be made—you'd pack big rattlers in it. There are two snakes engraved on both sides of the box. Jeremey had a box I'd given Ronnie. When the church shut down I'd taken the boxes to the house. He even had a box I'd given Liz once."

I asked about Taylor. "In the three months we were together, Taylor was better to me as a person than I had in eight years [with Liz]," he said. "Two days after I did something with Taylor, I called up Liz and said I am sleeping with Taylor Noe. That day Facebook went crazy. She had every right to be furious, but why did she have to air my sins on Facebook when I never did the same to her?"

Because you said you wanted a divorce, I thought. Our two-and-a-half-hour conversation touched on many things that evening, such as his conversations with Jamie about divorce and his realizing that simply telling people they're going to hell if they remarry was not the answer. "They don't know what it's like until they're put in that situation," he said. "I used to be dead set against divorce. Now I look back on the things I told people about staying together. Now I think, what if these people really need to separate?"

He had a point, I thought. The one smart thing he'd done during this whole miserable time was step away from Facebook. Facebook helped make him; it also broke him. Then again, Facebook was a public confessional with this crowd. The man who had a one-night stand with Liz earlier that summer hadn't stopped apologizing for it on his feed.

When I asked Andrew how he was paying his bills, he announced he'd come up with a bootlegging business. Campbell County was a "limited" county where some liquor was sold, and Claiborne County, where he now lived, was completely dry. He'd get liquor from points in Kentucky and Virginia and import it in. "I did a lot of bootlegging over the summer," he said. "I had a good little thing running in this holler. I was going to get a business license and open a bar up here. I ran some Jack Daniels and Jim Bean and sell it and moonshine—I ran moonshine like you would not believe. My daddy was an alcoholic; my grandfather was, too. I came from a long line of alcoholics."

Nothing like alcohol to dull the pain, I thought. I asked, "Are you called to be a pastor?"

"I miss being a pastor," he said. "I loved being a pastor. I loved fire being handled and serpents being handled. But I also loved evangelizing and helping people all over the world. I'd love to travel. I still mourn over the death of Jamie Coots. I think of him every day. It's been thirty-four weeks. In my house there is that picture of him in a blue vest at the altar holding a canebrake. I finally got the nerve to go to his grave a few weeks ago and lay there and cried. People don't understand what it's like to go through this. I lost two people including Randy Wolford, who helped me. Were it not for Randy sending me two reporters, *Snake Salvation* would not have happened. Then to lose Jamie was unfathomable. And now to be outcast."

I reminded him of another fallen pastor I'd covered. In 1988, when Jimmy Swaggart was about to confess to the world about his sexual sins, I flew to Baton Rouge to see the event live. Tons of TV stations covered it, and twenty-five years later, the memory was fresh. Despite his tears in front of the TV cameras, he was defrocked by the Assemblies of God because he apparently never repented. After all, three years later, police caught him propositioning a prostitute in California.

"I was the Jimmy Swaggart of snake handling," Andrew mused. "One night I was drinking, and I got on YouTube and watched Jimmy Swaggart. I wondered: is that what I need to do? I hold onto my rays of sunshine. I have hope I will stand under the anointing of God with five rattlers or dance across the stage with copperheads. Because I don't want to die like this as the once-great man of God who stood for the signs and then backslid and left his wife and committed adultery and died on a highway and went to hell. I want to do what Carl Porter could not do. I want to be able to come back."

Until then, "My videos and my pictures, that's all I've got," he said. When I told him about John Morgan's photos of the homecoming, he eagerly asked for copies. I could not imagine a sadder fate: at the age of twenty-three, he was relegated to watching movies of his past great moments. I looked up his address on Google Maps, which had a 360-degree view of the block of Highway 90 on which he lived. Surrounded by low, green hills and freshly mowed grass, I narrowed down his home to a simple brick cottage with a porch and carport. The only thing that made it stand out were two white lintels over the porch and under the roof.

The chatter from his wife did not let up. On October 11, Liz posted: *I really don't see how someone who has no job can offord a brand new car! A beautiful brick house! There ciggs! Cable and phone. . . . I mean really lol someones making money somewhere! But yet your pregnant wife has to bum trips to town. . . . .*

But then on Friday morning, October 17: *How long does a person half to be missing before you can file a missing person report???* Andrew had been gone for two days, she added, and no one had talked with him.

She got a pile of comments about how long to wait and how to file a missing persons report. Andrew had no wheels, she said. He had wrecked his van while drunk.

He may be laid up in another hotel, was one sardonic comment. *At some point you have to stop trying to constantly save him. He has to learn on his own.*

Liz finally wrote: *I never in my entire life I would be going threw this: / I thought it would easier but to be honest it gets worse every day.*

Then two days later, a Sunday, she posted: *Please if anyone hears from Andrew hamblin let me know. he came home yesterday and I woke up this morning to a letter saying he was leaving. . . . . he had my phone when i went to sleep and when I went [through] the history the only thing on there he looked up was suicide! Please if you see him or know were he is let us know.*

Following were seventy-nine comments, including: *If you report that to the police, they will automatically start a search, Liz,* a woman wrote. *They will consider him a risk to himself. I would really go ahead and report it NOW before something happens. This sounds like a cry for help to me.*

Said another: *Did the letter say he was going to harm himself?*

Liz: *All the letter really said was that he loved me and the kids and to take care of them.*

Numerous posters told her to call the police. I realized that what her family and friends could not do, the Greek chorus on her Facebook page could do: provide her with encouragement and comfort. Liz was addicted to these invisible friends even if it meant spilling all her secrets to them. Eventually she did call police, then posted Andrew's note, which read: "Liz, if your reading this, then you've found that I am gone. You will never know how much hurt I have caused. I am a failure in every way. There is nothing I could do to ever fix this and tonight I have realized that. I would like to thank you for some thing. One last wonderful evening with you and our babies, that's all I wanted and you gave me that. please don't go into a panic and begin to go off and cause everyone to get [unintelligible] and scared. I just can't handle the pain and hurt of [unintelligible] of being. . . . . . on us. And most of all, be happy. Find someone that can be the man and husband to you that you deserve. There is no way I can allow myself to hurt you any longer. Maybe one day I'll be remembered for what I used to be and not for what I've become. Tell our babies every day that they're Daddy loves them. And Liz, I want you to know something. I will always love you to. More than you will ever know. Please forgive me."

He had signed the letter, "Love with all my heart, Andrew." The word "all" was underlined three times.

But at about 12:30 a.m. on October 20, she wrote that Andrew was with Taylor: *Update! Andrew is fine. but I'm most certainly done with him. until he can get away from her his life is gonna be hell! I'm not putting my kids threw this anymore to be hurt! Please pray for his soul!*

Again, a stack of comments showed up on her feed, telling her not to stand for such treatment, to put her foot down and to stand up for her rights along with a pile of digs against Andrew and Taylor. I was amazed to see how many people across the country were up at that point.

One woman posted: *Funny how people can be glad a grown man acting like a little boy is ok! Did he get a job? Did he give sister Liz rent money? Did he buy his babies diapers and food and making sure Liz is treated like a queen. . . . . NO! He hid like a coward to get everyone to worry about him!!! Ignore his sneaky behind. Liz is being put thru hell and I'm sorry, that none of you can see that. She is expecting a baby, doesn't deserve to cry a single tear. She should be pampered and not worry about anything.*

Liz replied: *I'm filing for divorce and going on. I'm not gonna be someone's second choice! I've been threw enough and so has my kids. if he only new what he's putting threw. he told them last night he was gonna start being a better dad. . . . they wake up and he's gone once again . . .*

After one poster made a remark about Andrew's girlfriend, Liz wrote, *Well she just said she was pregnant! Happy for them they deserve each other!*

I messaged her at about 2:30 a.m. her time to say: *She actually called you? Oh Lord.* Liz replied: *No threw messages. but I would love to see her face to face!*

A red flag went up in my mind about what she had said. Were she and Taylor talking with each other? But I was too sleepy to process the thought. The following day, I sent Andrew copies of the homecoming pictures that John took. I closed the letter with: *Don't stay in the place of Jimmy Swaggart, my friend.* That same day, I got a message from one of my contacts: *Every time I think the wheels have come completely off this story,* he wrote, *it goes to the next level.*

I—and the rest of the world as it turned out—would hear more of this background correspondence between the wife and the mistress a few days later. For months, the person operating the *Snake Salvation* fan page on Facebook had been asking around about Andrew and Liz. On October 23, I got a message from the same friend at 1:16 a.m. his time.

Have you read the Snake Salvation page this evening?? It's smoking, he wrote. It was just after 9:00 p.m. my time, and when I checked the page, I saw a headline proclaiming: *This is Andrew's New Flame Taylor, She Will Be Making some First Hand Comments Tonight, We are in for a big treat!!!*

Sure enough, there was a long essay from Taylor describing a lengthy affair Liz had in 2011, how Andrew had suffered through it and taken her back, how their marriage had been rocky from then on, how she had constantly criticized him even when his star was climbing in the secular world. Jamie's death in February was bad enough, she wrote, but in March, "Liz sent picture of her private areas to a deacon of the church." So that is what Andrew was hinting at, I thought. Things came to a head in June, she wrote, when Andrew went to speak at a church in Ohio, then stopped back in Berea, Kentucky, for a week.

Andrew left Liz alone with all the kids for a week? I wondered. When he got home, Taylor said, the couple had a knock-down, drag-out fight, in which she punched him, causing Andrew to walk out. *At this point Andrew and I had not been together,* she wrote. *That following week was the first time we had a kind of relations.* But Liz was committing adultery as well, she said, adding that over the summer Andrew had borne his share of the childcare and bills. *What Andrew and I did was wrong and sin,* Taylor concluded. *Never have we tried to deny that! And we have say by all summer long and watched people degrade us and put us down. Not saying a word . . .*

But I am so sick of Liz and people pitying her when they do not know the whole story.

My friend contacted me again. *I just read that train wreck on the Snake Salvation page,* he messaged. *Unbelievable. This is not going to end well.*

Sure enough, the general public was listening in on this one. *I'm just here for the hillbilly snake show,* one man posted. *But the backwoods soap opera isn't bad either.*

This stuff is better than any reality show ever, a woman posted.

Another man posted: *you wanna share some popcorn and watch this hot mess together?* Most appeared to be locals from Kentucky and eastern Tennessee, although there were posts from a man in Jackson, Missouri, a woman in Guntersville, Alabama, and a songwriter in Nashville.

Taylor then posted a photo of herself and Andrew standing on an overlook near Gatlinburg. Andrew had a sickly smile on his face. Taylor had her arms partly around him. He had his hands in his pockets.

Liz's friends and relatives had lengthy rebuttals posted just under Taylor's essay calling her a liar, among the more printable names. Then Jeremey himself weighed in.

Best get some facts straight, he wrote. *Yes what I done was wrong truly was and there was no justification there . . . But what about when I wasn't seeing Liz and you all kept accusing me of it and Andrew saying oh im not with Taylor and you all were still seeing each other. . . . . Im a failure for what I've done. . . . . But don't you dare spread one more lie. . . . If Andrew wanted to be with Liz he could of been, he would just come in say oh im sorry . . .*

I kept numbly thinking that things could not get much worse for this group, but the next day they did. Starcasm.net, a gossip web site, ran a two-part exposé on the whole mess, complete with private messages between Liz and Taylor that dripped with poison and foul language. Taylor was accusing Liz of cheating on Andrew before she entered the picture. *We did wrong,* she concluded, *but she's not the perfect little holiness woman everyone thinks she is.*

No matter what she did, wrote a commentator whose name was hidden by Starcasm, *how could you go to bed with you preacher when you had a husband and two kids? Did you think you and him would live happily ever after and she would be gone forever? No. They have five kids together and if he works, he will pay bookoos in child support to her for the next 18 years. They will have to talk forever, they will always have five links. You will never be a mother to those kids. He will never be able to preach under Gods calling again. Would you not agree that it would be much better for the kids if they were able to work out their family for those kids, rather than him having an easy out with you?*

Taylor responded, *That's the point!!! She won't let him come back BECAUSE of her boyfriend and him believing the new baby is his. I'm not trying to be a mother to them. They have a mother and we was backslid and the church was gone before we ever done anything so throw your stones again.*

I'm not throwing stones, I'm telling you as someone who has been the other woman, was the answer. *It is a very hard road. He has children with his wife, which is even harder. And you are ruining their lives by being there for him.*

Taylor doggedly kept on insisting Liz had cheated on Andrew and that his efforts at reconciliation had not worked. The site included screen grabs of text messages each had posted on the fan page arguing who was right and wrong and which woman Andrew actually preferred. It sounded like several people had been jumping in and out of each other's beds for some time. There was page after page of Taylor and Elizabeth in a digital hair-pulling contest with friends on each side chiming in. It was entertaining in a sick sort of way.

But near the end, someone posted a message for Andrew referring back to one of the reality show episodes in which Andrew got to meet Ricky Skaggs in Nashville: *Please someone make sure Andrew sees this. Andrew, I am reminded once again of Ricky Skaggs' comment to you: "God didn't call you to be famous, he called you to be faithful." I know Ricky was talking about faithful to God's work but when I saw the photo of you & Taylor together today, I was reminded of that statement and felt it applied to your wife & children as well. Love in Christ.*

I thought I was the only reporter following the pitiful aftermath, but with this exposé, it was clear I was not alone. The writer mockingly portrayed the story as something that "is sure to be optioned for the big screen (or at least a Lifetime movie) by year's end," making Andrew's nightmare complete. Not only was his church gone, his marriage in tatters, and his ministry ruined for the foreseeable future, but people in several states were laughing at him.

One person posted, *I don't know where these people live, but wherever it is, the school system sucks!*

Well Andrew is from Lafollette, which is in TN, but only like 40 miles away from me, wrote a woman in southeast Kentucky. *And yes school system does suck, you'll be lucky to make it through 9th grade without dropping out around here. As bad as I hate to say this, but their drama is typical for this area. Uneducated "Christians" that have 15 welfare kids are always in a middle of some kind of argument cussing up a storm. But then shout and ask God for forgiveness. Bunch of morons.*

Fortunately, none of the usual media seemed to be following this spectacle or if they were, they were staying in the shadows like me. It was one thing to cover an attractive young man who was an underdog in every way but who had overcome many obstacles to become a star. But what happens if the star falls?

CHAPTER FIFTEEN

NOVEMBER MOON

Dusk was falling fast over the hills north of Fairbanks when I called Michelle Gray. There had been so much criticism of her and Paul simply pulling out of the Tabernacle with no notice and fleeing to Florida that I wanted to know her side of the story. I had a hard time believing anything evil of this couple, and I knew that things had to have been rough for them to have fled as they did.

Michelle's voice was very soft as she was very weak and on oxygen. She was continuing to have problems with her heart, and in October she collapsed at home in Kentucky and was rushed via helicopter to a hospital in Lexington. It was her second hospital visit in a very short while. During her first visit—while having heart surgery in Louisville—she was told that if she didn't get a transplant in two years, she would be dead. With two leaky valves and a hole in her heart, she had had a pacemaker installed and had endured one heart attack and two strokes before the age of thirty-nine, her age at the time we talked. One of their reasons for moving to the Tallahassee area, she said, was to be close to the University of Florida Health Shands Transplant Center in Gainesville, which specializes in heart transplants. I was amazed at this woman's toughness. Along with all her heart ailments, she had ovarian cancer at the age of eighteen but managed to give birth to four children after that.

"We were working ourselves to death to keep the church going," she told me. It was a 180-mile round trip to LaFollette from their home in Kentucky and the cost of gas alone for two of those trips each week was draining their meager funds. Plus the church members themselves were wounded and turning on each other.

"People were so Andrew, Andrew, Andrew," she said. "His reputation flooded the place. We felt like we were beating our heads against the wall. There was drama, drama, drama, drama, drama. There's drama in every church but this was ridiculous."

Paul had laid down the law that Andrew couldn't preach or even hang out at the front of the church, but one weekend when they were gone, Andrew showed up and sang and played the guitar, which infuriated them to no end. I remembered Andrew mentioning this as his way of saying he wished to repent, but obviously that message didn't reach the Grays. Michelle was more impressed with Jeremey, who confessed his sins to her and Paul and who stayed off the pulpit platform so as not to cause any division. Because he seemed contrite, they allowed him to be in church—a decision that brought them endless grief from Andrew's friends.

"Jeremey would help with the kids and clean the house so she could rest some," Michelle said. "In July is when they did it [slept together]. They sat and talked with us, and they both felt horrible. They told us they liked each other, but they weren't going to make that mistake again."

By September, Michelle had decided she could not take one more Kentucky winter, and her mother in Florida wanted the Grays to move close by. Paul drove down to Florida to job hunt and look for a house. One of his relatives unwisely announced the family's plans on Facebook.

"When I told the church we were leaving, Linda Spoon got on us," she said. "Taylor Noe called us white trash. We were so discouraged by how people acted. People showed their true colors."

I wondered why they were surprised at the rage they received. Paul and Michelle were the last vestige of hope this church had. Paul never said an official good-bye, she said. She had been planning to drive to LaFollette and privately meet with people, but couldn't take the stress of more confrontation.

"If my health would not have been so bad, we would have hung on and fought it out," she said. "We had put our heart and soul into this, but to say what they said . . . I was going to go down there but after this thing on Facebook . . . instead of loving and supporting us, they screamed at us. All that mattered to them was keeping that church open, even though you can't get anyone to come to it. People would ask if Andrew was still there."

I asked Michelle if she believed the rumors about Liz and the supposed photos she'd sent out in March.

"Not as far as I can swing it," she said, adding that when Liz had her electricity cut off for two weeks, Andrew did not help her. Then Michelle dropped a bomb: the home in the country that Liz and Andrew had moved into a year before was gone. They fell behind on rent payments, and for some reason the owner—who Andrew had told everyone had given them the house outright—was forcing them to leave.

That lovely home. Why hadn't Liz let on that she was losing it?

And so the Grays had called Clyde to say they were leaving, and he told them to leave the key on the pulpit. She thought the building might be sold. All that go there now are ghosts and memories.

"I don't get on Facebook anymore," she said. "I get so angry."

I asked her if they felt taking on the church had been a mistake.

"It was more than what we could do," she said. "I almost think it was not God's will for us to be there. If it is His will, it will prosper and grow."

I said to Michelle that it had been almost three years to the day when Andrew and Liz started up their tiny congregation. Since then, the world got to hear about serpent handling, a valuable court battle was won, and maybe somewhere in there, souls were saved. But now two of the most famous serpent handlers were dead, and the house of the serpent handler was now empty.

"Andrew has ruined so many lives," she said sadly. "He destroyed and hurt so many people in so many ways that he won't even know. We probably will never know why it happened. He handled serpents but if he was so perfect, why did he fall from grace?"

I had to go teach a night class, so I bid Michelle good-bye, hoping she could get better. Andrew wasn't known by his most recent failure, I thought. He was one of the most unusual young men I've ever met—whom a lot of journalists have ever met—and I believe the Bible said something about the gifts and calling of God are irrevocable. A few hours later as my daughter and I were walking home through the snow, we spotted a luminous glow behind the trees. "The moon," I told her. "The orange moon."

And up it rose into the northern sky, a brilliant orb with its seas and craters plainly visible. The snow and the hills around us glistened with pale light—a moment of beauty in a world of winter. The apartment we returned to was warm in spite of the freezing temperatures, which was more than Liz was going to have. On November 22, she announced she was being evicted for failure to pay rent. *What?* I messaged her, saying that Andrew had said the house was given to them. No, she responded, they had had to pay $400 a month in rent ever since they got it. *It must kill you to leave such a lovely place,* I messaged her.

Its horrible, she responded. *my child has to move schools and everything plus its much harder living at an apartment with kids. people complain if there to loud. I dread it. plus getting someone to help me move. I'm not sapose to be doing anything. so this is gonna be rough and stressful.* She added that she was on a HUD waiting list, but nothing was moving.

On December 8, a new "Andrew Hamblin" page appeared on Facebook with a photo of Andrew preaching on the courthouse steps the year before. Then a more recent photo showed a much more rotund Andrew.

Gained a lol weight ole buddy, a friend messaged him. *Glad to see you back.* But there were no postings on the page. Then on December 28, Derrick Noe posted: *I never hardly post ANYTHING about what I go through in my personal life, but I need good praying people to please pray for a need I have. After everything I've been through, I pretty much lost everything I had . . . a five bedroom home, vehicles, ect. . . . I need a vehicle in the worst way and I need the Lord to move quickly. My job, going to church, meeting the needs for my baby, it all depends on having a good vehicle. I know the Lord will surely move! Its just truly sad how the one who tries to do right and didn't make the awful decisions, is the one who constantly seems to get the worst of it . . .*

That same day, Liz posted a curious message on her page: *Always thought if I had a problem with someone I went to them not facebook. . . . . so therefore face your problems not facebook them.*

Noticing the seventy-five-plus "likes" below that post, I figured something was up and I'd better listen in. Sure enough, Liz's good friend Tabitha Bennett posted: *Some people lying about housing to get a hud house and bless someone with it then evict them because they have no money and cant get hud to pay the bills for them and claim to be a Christian when they lie to the government that is fraud and pass judgment on you some one that is doing the best she can with what she has well shame on Betty Hastings and to making post about you is no kind of Christian I would want to be she will reap what she sowed and keep your head up God has a great plan for u liz we love you and the babies.*

Suddenly, Betty herself let loose with several insults: *You stupid slut you all I did was tell them the truth. Did she think I was going to lie for her. No way. I just sent them proof of everything. I didn't bless them with. They told a few lies along the way. I even heard that they said I gave it to them. How stupid.*

Elizabeth Marie Hamblin: *Calling someone a slut isnt of God.*

Betty Hastings: *You god despising hick you. Tell some more lies.*

Elizabeth Marie Hamblin: *Lies???*

Clearly I had to find out more. I looked up Betty Hastings on Facebook and learned she lived in Pleasant Prairie, Wisconsin, but was from Red Bay, Alabama. She was a retired civil service worker and currently worked for H&R Block. So that was the mysterious woman who gave them the house, I thought. Betty then sent a few more insulting posts.

Finally, Liz responded, *Having someone approch us saying they wanted to help us get a bigger place knowing that we had no income and it says right on my lease paper that I have says self employed. plus saying the extra bed room was for ypu incase someone from hud was to ever come to our home you wouldnt get into trouble . ypur not even sapose to be renting that house. and u are ! You visited are home twice and never stayed you went to the hotel. you wrote in the eviction notice it was so u would have somewhere to stay when you visited. lieing to hud can get you into big trouble. and come court time they will see all this plus the rude statuses you have made abt me. thsnk god for screen shot.*

Then Tabitha chimed in: *I was at church with you Andrew stood in the pulpit and said he wanted to give honor were honor was due and he told the whole church you blessed them with that house and you never stood and said you didn't so don't lie all I wish you would do is leave liz alone you are going to reap what you sowed God for bid leave her alone she is trying to get out of your house but it takes a while for hud to come and check the house so they can get a better place for her kids.*

Betty Hastings fought back: *You people are just so stupid. First of all you wouldn't pay, then somebody [took] a hammer to the heat pump and air conditioner and tore that up. I saw my mistake right away, I have wished thousands of times that I had not tried to help you. You got to Learn the hard way. You and Andrew had those kids and it is your responsibility to take care of them. HUDs requirements are that a tenant be current with the current landlord with no damages and that the landlord must be given a 30 dat notice. Thank goodness that I made copies of it all too.*

Wow Betty Hastings a girl is in labor and u gonna kick her out, a friend of Liz's messaged. *Plus she has small children this is no my business but don't you live outta state do you need the house? Ever heard pay it forward. She might not can pay but u knew that.*

Betty Hastings: *You are mad because I told the truth.*

Elizabeth: *Good cause your gonna need anything to help you out frauding the goverment and lieing is a major no no in the state of tn. I know my babies are my responsibility. I never said they werent. so please leave my kids out of this. they are innocent!*

Liz's friends chastised Betty for several minutes until the older woman finally blew up. *Why didn't they just get out,* she wrote. *I have been trying to get them out. I have not received any rent plus I am 72 years old and having to make the mortgage payment. It cost me $3500.00 to get the heat pump and air conditioner replaced. You'd say something too if you had put up with what I had to put up with.*

A man chimed in to say he too was at the church when Betty was introduced, and it was announced she was giving the Hamblins a home.

I've been trying long before this to try to get her to move out, Betty responded. *I just turned it all over to a lawyer.*

Liz responded: *Betty I never said anything abt you! You added ME the other day then started making statuses abt Me! Fyi I have been looking for a place I want to move out. im not wanting your place and im not wanting to stay there for free. I did like you ask and signed up on hud and started getting welfare. like you told me in my eviction notice plus threw in there that the reason I wouldnt sign up for welfare was because I was afraid id half to turn in money people gave to me. I did everything you asked!*

Part of me sympathized with this woman who may have had good intentions at one time, but the rest of me was horrified at the timing. At this point, Liz was about one month from delivery. What insanity was it to force someone—who had obviously been abandoned by her husband—to move out of her home? Further posts revealed that what little money Liz got—maybe $220 a month—went toward paying rent and that she had paid as recently as October. Another poster said what I was thinking.

People these days don't have a heart for no one, a woman wrote. *This girl is in the hospital in labor having a baby and some one on here bashing on her wanting money for tent, Wheres your live at lady? Seems its in the almighty dollar, Betty Hastings want you get after that god forsaken those half grown husband of hers, he lives there also until he took off with his lady friend, he is also to blame for rent money, sorry to put my two cents in but my bible tells me if you see your brother, also means sister too, in need and close up your bowels of compassion against them the* LOVE *of the father is not in you, this girl has no where to go at this time and plus in the hospital having a baby, woman you are* HELL *bound, Liz God is putting to a test, you will come out on top, keep trusting God, sorry I seen this and thought I would throw God's word in, God hates greedy people.*

The drama wasn't over yet, though. On December 30, a long post came on the TaylorNAndrew site: *This is Andrew posting this. Tonight I went to a house meeting at Sam and Sylvia Wilson's house and I have prayed threw and got back a hold of what I needed. I failed so many people and hurt people beyond all reason but most of all I had failed God. I turned my back on the one that had been so good to me and he had never left me but I left him. I'm posting this on here simply because I do not have a Facebook of my own and don't plan on getting one anytime soon.*

I'm writing this to ask anyone and everyone that reads this to please forgive me. I will not go into detail of everything I've done because God has wiped my slate clean tonight ans cast everything as far as the east is from the west. But I'm begging everyone that reads this post to please forgive me. And please pray for me as I have a long long road ahead to get back as close to God as I once was.

If I'm welcome to come to your church, not to preach or take over or do anything like that, but just welcome to come and get help and be a help let me know. I know I'm gonna get a lot of negative feedback, some say I can never get back but I'm so thankful I'll one day stand before a just and true God and not man.

Just wanted to share this. But please everyone and anyone that reads this please forgive me.

Love everyone with all my heart.

He got 148 likes and seventy-eight responses, many of them inviting him and Taylor to their churches from as far away as Middleton, Ohio, and Newnan, Georgia, and nearly all saying they wouldn't judge him.

He responded: *Anywhere that I am welcome at please just post your churches service times and dates. As I read all this comments tears fill my eyes just to know that so many are praying for me. I'm a nothing in this flesh but that that dwells within is a something and I say look out cause all I have time for is Jesus!!!!*

The responses were a rainbow of religion in Appalachia:

Layton hill holiness in London ky has is on Tuesday & Saturday @ 7:00pm your more then welcome to attend! May god bless you!

Big fork is having church tomorrow!

God is the second chance giver I pray that u can come back into the fullness of God and Taylor I pray for u as well.

GOD truly is a forgiving God! I know that for myself people may not but God does. Just hang in there and keep on keeping on u can't go to heaven for no one else but urself. All sins are forgiven except for blasphemy, so just hang on to him and he'll hang on to u! Love ya bro.

We're having New Year's Eve service starting at 9 we'd. Night hope you all can come.

Bro Glenn collins is having church tonight at smokey church message me for direction, he has it on Tuesday and Saturday night.

It's at Hal's fork at Jerry Hollands on bob fork.

Revival Tabernacle is in revival with Scott Smith from georgia and the message last night was about God doing a work on us internally if you need God to help you, you need to be at RT tonight at 730.

Deliverance church is having a watch night service tomorrow night. It starts at 8. All is welcome.

Then John Saylor from Crab Orchard, Kentucky, burst in: *What about your family where are they your wife and children. all the people in the world can say they forgive you but God?????? Shame on all the churches that open thier arm to a man that has left his wife and kids for another woman call him brother he has committed a willful sin he needs to go home to his family.*

Andrew then posted an hour later: *Ok so as of right now I'm gonna be going to church in Barbourville at Glenn Collins church it being the Lords will. I can't wait!!!! I just want to be able to get help and be a help. If your in the area and know where it is come on out I'd love to see something move on the people to help me go another mile.*

A few hours later, Elizabeth, who had obviously seen or heard of Andrew's posts, wrote: *You can NOT be shacked up living with someone and still be married and live right!!! Im not perfect but please if youve had 8 months to file for a divorce and to scared to cause of back warrents and afraid youll half to get a JOB and pay child support. uhhh makes me sick. and all you who are praising him I really hope your telling to get the sin and trash out of his life before he runs his arm in a snake box!*

She got 192 likes by the time I logged in a few hours later, plus 154 comments, most of them sympathetic to her and very unhappy with Andrew. A sample:

Does he realize he has to make things right, a man named Gary wondered. *Can't believe how people invited them as a couple to church.*

Amen gary I couldnt either, Liz responded. *He has preached so much against fornication / adultry and turned right around and thats what hes living. If he wants to live right then go file for a divorce .it would look alot better . . .*

A woman messaged: *And sometimes you just brush the dust off of your feet and leave them with their reprobate mind!*

Liz responded: *Hes not a sinner hes praying. wrong is wrong. andrew would make people sit the front bench when they confessed or told they had sinned. and thats just cuss / mess up, let alone someone leave there pregnant wife for her friend.*

As Christians, we have to forgive, wrote another woman. *But, you don't have to give them liberties inside your church. That is asking for trouble.*

Liz said, *I want to see him do good. I would never want to see someone die lost. I know God is everything to andrew when hes in. but I do know when hes praying hes snake crazy I dont want to see him end up hurt or killed. he has 6 kids that need there father. im just stating he needs to leave her alone get his divorce. and then go on.*

What followed was a theological discussion by several people about whether someone like Andrew could hope to pastor again. Then Liz—who had been in the hospital recently for pregnancy complications—dropped this bombshell: *He showed up at the hosital the other night they had gave me sleeping meds so I could rest I woke up to andrew laying behind me in the bed trying to hold my hand I had to tell him to move. im sorry yes hes with her they live together. we got into at the hospital cause he asked had I filed for divorce. I did have an appointment to but he asked me not to ask for child support cause he would end up in jail. . . . . the nurse heard us arguing and andrew left she came straight in and got down and was balling her eyes out and prayed for me. sorry but hes been working under the table. its not going to kill him to help with money for the kids. but I wish him nothing but the best in life I want him to do good.*

Once people read this, the comments turned venomous.

People do need to pray for Andrews soul, one man wrote. *Hell is a horrible place for anyone to have to go to for eternity.*

Liz you deserve child support and so do the babies, a woman wrote. *There is not a thing wrong with him that he cannot go get a real job and take care of his responsibilities. You need to do what is right and not what he has asked you to do. If you don't think it's right and you don't want to then that's a different story but follow your heart.*

Said another woman: *Andrew is a coward . . . stand up like a man . . . Andrew, turn yourself in for your warrants . . . grow a set of man balls and take responsibility for your children . . . your mama did not raise you right!!!!! Shame on you and shame on her!!!!! Elizabeth, let the police know where he is, he needs to sit in jail and think about his actions. . . . what a big scam artist he is. . . . JERK!!!!!!*

Derrick also posted that day: *I heard the good news that Andrew Hamblin and Taylor Noe are going to church together. I pray for mercy, that they make things right with folks, and that he goes back home to his little wife and babies. . . . Hebrews 13:4—Marriage is honourable in all, and the bed undefiled: but whoremongers and adulterers God will judge.*

Much later that day, Andrew posted: *Just got home from a WONDERFUL church service, with WONDERFUL people, still blessed by a WONDERFUL God. Really got a lot help tonight. And for all the ones who think I am lying or trying to deceive and be a hypocrite this is what you need to do:* 1. *Quit texting EVERY one,* 2. *Quit calling EVERY one,* 3. *DEFINITELY turn off your Facebook and get down on your knees and pray and ask God and I guarantee if you think Andrew Hamblin is a liar and still living in fornication and adultery and everything else you'll get the answer you need. Thankful to know where I stand with my Lord and savior Jesus Christ.*

Trying to fall asleep that night, I clicked onto a new TaylorNAndrew site and an accidental press of the button showed me several dozen photos cached there when she was still married. So many of them were of her and Derrick: rapturously happy photos of them with the two kids; her in the hospital after giving birth to their little girl in January 2012; them ministering together; a portrait of the family on one of Derrick's album covers, singing together and apparently happy. There was a shot of Christmas in the interior of their home, which looked as nice as anything I'd ever owned. This was a successful couple with a growing worship ministry. Derrick had won some kind of award for his singing. They were going places. It hit me how obscene this whole spectacle was and how many lives had been seriously damaged by this episode. Taylor's son, whom she brought into the marriage, had lost a father. The little girl was being traded back and forth between both parents. And then there were the Hamblin children. What must Payton be thinking? He was clearly old enough to understand something of what was going on. Because his mom had to move again, he was getting pulled out of his school, for starters. The whole tragedy of it just got to me.

On December 31, Andrew posted: *So thankful to be getting to start a new year back on track with Jesus. 2014 has been literally the worst year of my life from losing Jamie to losing my church then backsliding and doing things I never thought I'd ever do to losing my papaw that raised me. But I see the sun starting to shine again in 2015. I'm gonna do everything in my power this year to make sure my beautiful children are taken care of and most of all live EVERY day like it's my last and know that I've been giving a second chance with God and nothing can stop me now. Hope everyone had a blessed New years and please keep praying for me.*

CHAPTER SIXTEEN

A BIRTH

• •

Cold weather had descended on eastern Tennessee by the second week of January. Only eleven days from delivery, Elizabeth was having to search for housing. *Going monday to try and get an apartment for me and the kids in Jellico,* she posted January 10. *were do I go to exactly? Please say a prayer that we get it.*

Several people warned her that Jellico, a town twenty-four miles northwest of LaFollette, was a dive.

All the places in lafollette has done dened me, she wrote. *so jellico is my last option. My sis lives in jellico so she would be able to help.*

She then posted a photo of herself in a long white skirt and short-sleeved red blouse gazing down on her bulging stomach. *Its sad I cant get my kids father to watch them for a couple of days so I can get an apartment or try and get some help,* she wrote. *and I get threatned of him just keeping my kids cause I cant provide for them! (but yet he calls himself a man of God. I need prayer in the worst way. He doesnt even keep them on his days hes sapose to. I alwayd have my babies with me anc I get told im a bad mom.*

She got 113 likes.

Thank u everyone, she wrote. *I really need it. here it is dayton will be born in* II *days k being evicted and my lights go off prob monday.*

People began posting comments about Andrew being "trash" and a "scam artist."

I have tried really hard not to get on a bashing Andrew jag but you really need to get to a lawyer or the courthouse in the worst way and nail his butt to the wall, a Virginia woman wrote. *don't think it over or think twice just get madder than you've ever been and do it. I mean who in the name of God does he think he is?? I'm telling you from experience it's* HARD AS HECK *but there are lawyers out there who will take you Pro Bono but you have to look for them and you sit down and tell them the entire story of what's happened to you . . .*

Many others chimed in, advising Elizabeth to get legal help. All the invective did not go unchallenged. Later that Saturday evening, TaylorNAndrew posted: *People really need to learn the* TRUTH *about things before the begin to sling slanderous and harassing comments around. Really need everyone's prayers. But one thing is for sure. The real* TRUTH *will stand when the world is burning down.*

Elizabeth shot back on her feed: *I find it very funny that I put a status on her abt my ex then he texts out of the blue saying he doesnt have time for mine and everyone on my facebooks garbage then seen were andrew had liked a post that someone had wrote that not everything you read on facebook it true. hmmmm? Awful funny lol. lets just say im not a liar. im having to move he wouldnt not keep his girls so I can get me a place! He helped make them he could help watch them for a few days. but its no biggy. ive done it this far by myself. why would he want to help now? People crack me up. althought im not praying I want to thank the Lord above for moving already for me. its gonna be a hard couple of days and gonna take alot of work but were going to have a place till I can get on my feet! :")* *thank you everyone that has prayed and please keep a praying.*

Two days later, TaylorNAndrew posted: *Andrew here. . . . . I really desperately need everyone's prayers today. Today I'm having to [take] drastic measures just to see my children. Months ago DCS set an agreement that my twin boys were to live with me and attend school where I live to until today they have and then DCS set the agreement that I was to get my daughter's and oldest son* EVERY *weekend which has also been done till now. But now because I will not revolve my life around my ex's life she is taking them and not letting me have them back. she has lied to everyone saying she is raising the children alone, I may have left her but I did not leave my children. I have sent my twin boys to preschool 2 minutes from where I live everyday since school started, and I have gotten my girls and*

Payton every weekend since the agreement was put in. But now she wants to get mad and try to take them from me, I think not. Really need everyone's prayers. If you have something negative to say you will be deleted and blocked, this daddy is done with the threats and lies. He got forty-two likes and thirteen comments.

Elizabeth did not stay silent long: *To everyone who is friends with my ex lol the reason andrew is not getting his kids back as of right now is because they live with his mother!!!! Not him! Sorry she did not help me make them he did! He never wants to keep my girls! aka his girls to. as for the dcs agreement he also signed when he ran off with his whore! That he would make sure my bills were paid garbage took off to keep a roof over my kids head and he has not!!!! My oldest came back yesterday and stayed he had not got any rest cause him his sister and baby sister had to sleep on a couch. when I asked were did daddy sleep. he replyed in the bed with taylor! That there are only one bed in the house! No my kids are not going back. end of story period. andrew aslso stated to the social workers months ago when asked if his mom was to be given a drug test would she pass it his reply was. I do not no. ! Cause she met her and she said she looked like someone on drugs! Now I dont care who I make mad but my babies are not living like shit anymore!* She got 138 likes and sixty-four comments.

Where does her 2 babies sleep, a Knoxville woman asked.

Prob on the couch to, Liz answered. *my kids sleep in the bed with me. or if we fall asleep on the couch im right there with them [on] it ! Plus them saying there not sleeping together that there just friend and him going to church? Wow.*

He needs to be playing that banjo and saving tips for diapers, wrote a man from Detroit.

He's going to end up in jail, Liz wrote. *he has back warrentts for failure to appears!* From there followed a discussion of whether the state of Tennessee jails for child support arrears and how to get Andrew to pay up.

Liz doesnt have to file for child support because she receives assistance, a Knoxville woman wrote. *The state will automatically go after him. They are probably looking 4 him now. Liz, if u wanted to be dirty you could call the law and tell them where he is and that he has FTA against him. Like someone else said, let him sit in jail and see how long his chic stays with him! She would go back to Ky fast. Lol.*

Elizabeth chimed in with, *Everyone pray for him and pray he straightens up for his babys! They love him to death. I know for a fact they do! but stop casting them aside. why should I let them go back if its every week I didnt stay with daddy I stay with mamaw!!!! Sorry im trying to be the best parent I know how and do whats right. im 38 weeks I have a one year old a two year old twin four year olds and a 7 year old. there my life. they need there parents to raise them not someone else. its hard taking care of thrm. yes I know. but stop sending them down the road before they even get to his house. gezzzz if he didnt want em he should have tried to of pervented it. and needs to be going something right to get himself fixed! . (and before some smartelic replys) im having my tubes tied next week after dayton is born.*

She added: *I would lay my life down for them. but I dont understand how he would want someone to keep his kids 24/7 when even himself told on nation tv that she didnt even raise him his granny and papaw did.im in no way downing his mom she has been a very good grandmother / motherin law. she brings me the kids and pocks them up when andrew is sapose to have them. so please no one take it that im degrading her .im just saying they need to live with him like they were sapos to. I just cant stand the fact ive let it go on this far.*

I learned privately from Elizabeth that she was moving her kids into her mother's two-bedroom trailer and that she was trying to raise money to buy a friend's trailer for $8,000. But the state Department of Children's Services was threatening to take her kids away because two bedrooms were not enough for six kids. The agency was demanding she have a home with at least three bedrooms, including a separate room for boys and girls. I sent her some funds.

By the time I logged on the morning of January 21, she was posting every stage of her labor through Facebook, and at 12:19 p.m., Dayton was born at a Knoxville hospital. Congratulations were pouring in from many of her approximately 3,300 friends. Hundreds of well-wishers from Indiana to Arkansas to North Dakota were congratulating her for surviving the worst year of her life. She posted a photo of herself wearing what looked like either a black bra or sun dress underneath a sheet and holding her tiny child. Her hair had an attractive cut, and she looked radiant. Tiffany Carroll Hill, the sister who posted the original birth announcement complete with a photo of the newly born Dayton, got 502 likes. Tiffany also posted a picture of an ID bracelet normally reserved for the father of the child. She was wearing it.

Elizabeth also posted screen grabs of her conversation with Andrew. *You'll half to come over and sign the birth certificate. He's here,* she messaged about her seven-pound, eight-ounce child at about 2:30 p.m. She included a photo. Andrew asked what his name was, which seemed strange in that Liz had been calling the child "Dayton" on her feed for many months.

Dayton Isaiah Hamblin, she messaged back. *He's got huge feet and long fingers. And lots of hair.*

He's pretty, Andrew replied. *Wish I could have been there but oh well I guess, right? Right.*

Nineteen and a half inches, she messaged. *Tiff was here with me.* Then: *Are you coming to see him? There doing my tubal in the morning and his circumcision.*

Andrew: *No, I told you if I wasn't allowed over there, I wasn't coming at all. I guess I'll see him when I finally see my other children.*

Liz: *OK then just asking. If I new that I wouldn't have even sent you pics but he's healthy and fine.*

Andrew: *Good, glad your boyfriend was there.*

Liz: *Tiff and Christian [actually Christin Marie Stanfill] was here with me. I do not have a boyfriend so please just stop texting me.*

Andrew: *Well, tell my babies I love and miss them.*

He had not a word of tenderness for her after hours of labor and a pregnancy so filled with tension and sadness that she nearly delivered the child two months early. Elizabeth posted more screen shots from another part of their conversation. It picked up with Andrew's message: *he can't pray. He's a reprobate. With yours and his newborn apparently, I wasn't even allowed over there.*

Liz: *I told you all youns could be here.*

Andrew: *You never told me THAT. You taking my kids from me and letting him be there is my problem.*

So Andrew didn't want to drive to a hospital where his wife was delivering a child he thought was not his own. But the woman he had thought was such a dimwitted wife had outwitted him on the social media end. The spectacle of her suffering over the past nine months had gotten everyone's respect. She had 111 comments by the time I checked in near midnight Alaska time.

Yup, said a woman from Pineville, Kentucky. *Piece of shit right there.*

That's sorry as hell, said an Alabama woman. *He should of had his ass there. Just proves everything he showed on TV was all fake and he deserves a place in hell.*

The woman from Kentucky chimed back in: *I'm sorry I just can't stand pos [piece of shit] ppl like him! He should be thankful for another blessing! I burried my babygirl who was stillborn at 29 weeks 4 days and it just hurts and makes me angry to see ppl like him not give a shit!!*

Elizabeth: *Hes saying I wouldnt let him here! I told him and his family they was welcome to come over. and my sister and friend was here for daytons birth.* She included a screen shot of a message she'd sent to one of his family members as proof.

A woman from LaFollette posted: *Oh my god Liz, how can a father not wanna be their for their childs birth? An to beat it all in the messages after u sent him a picture all he said was he's pretty, an more worried bout what his last name was?! #1 dead beat I've ever seen or heard about! Doll, u shoulda carried on out the Carroll tradition and gave that handsome lil feller your last name. He doesn't deserve to even get to sign the birth certificate or see the child.*

It was too bad, I thought, that they could not see Andrew's despair beneath the nastiness of his posts.

Elizabeth posted one more thing online: *Daytons binkie aunt tabby made.* She got 130 likes quickly.

A woman from Virginia: *That is adorable!!*

A man from Berea, Kentucky: *A snake!*

A woman from Los Angeles: *Taken them up early.*

And there, in two shades of velveteen green with large black eyes, a tiny red felt forked tongue with a pacifier attached, was a serpent.

But Elizabeth was not allowed to rest for long, as she had to move her family of seven the following week into a two-bedroom trailer along with her mother and stepfather. Her Facebook entries for the next month were about an upcoming child custody hearing between her and Andrew who, she said, wanted joint custody.

Unnoticed was another broken marriage, Nathan and Tiffany Evans, he being the great-great grandson of Bob and Barbara Elkins, and she being the young woman from an Assembly of God church who left it all to marry him. They separated that January. It was a marriage buttressed by a close-knit Holiness community and Jamie's caring mentorship. Once Jamie died and after Andrew's apostasy, Nathan's wife would later say her husband "lost his love of Christ." The marriage faltered, and she and their daughter fled Virginia for South Carolina, where she got a job as a Zumba fitness instructor.

Then on February 15, about a dozen members of Jamie's church posted a video of a gathering by his gravesite in a wooded setting. It had been a year since he died. Placing snake boxes on both sites of the grave marker, they danced and sang while handling snakes, which appeared listless because of the cold weather. Although it was a sunny afternoon, everyone was bundled up against the cold. Little Cody was dressed in a black trench coat that nearly reached to his ankles, and he was hopping up and down, shouting, "Praise you God, thank you God!"

Music was blaring from somewhere, and a woman loudly wailed in tongues interspersed with praises to God. I looked closer. Yes, that was Linda, Jamie's widow, who was wearing a long, white coat. Katrina was in a green overcoat with her long hair piled into a huge bun. Big Cody stood silently by the grave in a green coat and trademark overalls.

"He's in a better place!" bellowed Little Cody "and I ain't crying for him. I'm happy. We're supposed to rejoice when they leave this world. " In the closing frames of the video, a woman in an orange top was weeping while she clutched a rattlesnake. She wiped away the tears from her face with the snake.

On February 23, Derrick posted a picture of himself arm in arm with his new girlfriend, Kayla Jean. He had 1,373 friends at this point.

Bub shes a 10000000000000 *times prettier then the last one shes beautiful,* Elizabeth wrote. *you all are perfect.*

Thanks friend! I think so too, he replied, *and I trust her with all of my heart. That means the world when you can do that! We are gonna come out better sis. God works all things out for our good.*

CHAPTER SEVENTEEN

GUNSHOTS

* *

It was a sunny Sunday afternoon in northeastern Tennessee on March 15, and a lot of people were outside playing and relaxing. Then a message ripped across Facebook from Tiffany Carroll Hill: *If anyone sees Andrew Hamblin please call the cops!!! He went to my mothers house were my sister Elizabeth Marie Hamblin is staying and shot my moms house up! He is on the run and is armed!*

Several shocked comments followed, and then Tiffany responded: *No one is hurt but my moms house got shot! The cops are looking for him cause he took off after he done that.*

People chimed in with more comments, including locals who were hearing about it on police scanners.

Was all the kids there, asked Kasi Powers.

Yes, Tiffany responded, *everyone was outside letting the kids play and he just pulled up and started shooting.*

Elizabeth began posting more. *To let everyone know we are all ok today,* she wrote. *we took the kids to the park and as we was coming threw jellico we stopped at the red light well acros on the other side someone kept honking and waving. well as we passed it was andrew and he had pointed a gun. so we took off and got back to my mommas on white oak. . . . ten mins later andrew came flying up the road*

*and stopped at the end of the driveway and held a gun out the window and shot.
me jeremey and the kids was outside. he shot one time in the air and shot again
at jermemy while my kids and me was ten foot away. . . . . no was hurt but the
bullett did go threw moms trailor and missed dayton by only a coupel of feet. then
he left. . . . . . please keep a praying till hes found.*

The shocked comments poured in. Elizabeth's sister posted photos of the
bullet holes. By late afternoon, the local network affiliates were on the story.

*He just lost his chance of getting custody from you that proves he is unfit right
there,* said a man from North Carolina.

A woman said: *I hope you called the police and filed a report, not only has he
walked out on his wife and children, this is attempted murder, he needs to be locked
up, he's not paying support anyway so you won't lose anything, and at least he
won't have any visitation rights! If he owns any property the courts can seize it
and sell it or give it to you to sell, he's a NUT!*

Elizabeth: *yes it went threw and got stuck in my closet they found the bullet.*

Another man: *I'm late here but did anyone call police? Its a felony to shoot in
occupied dwelling, if it hit trailer there should be physical evidence!*

The North Carolina man posted again: *He is miserable is what he is because
he is running from the calling of God thats a miserable place I pray he does like the
prodical son and comes to himself! Praying for yall Liz hang in there sis!*

More comments rained in, and so many people promised prayers that one
Alabama man sent out this unhappy post: *The adults don't need prayer they
need to stop acting foolish! This has turned very serious, it is obvious Andrew has
lost it, this could become very tragic, you see it everyday! Jeremy n Liz for the kids
sake need to chill out and he needs to keep his butt away till Andrew gets his head
straight or stays locked up. No matter who started this or who cheated on who first,
the fact is all of the adults don't need prayer they need to act like adults, put the
kids welfare first!*

I had been out all day, and by the time I logged in at 6:45 p.m. Alaska time,
Andrew had turned himself in. When I had first called up Liz's page, she had
3,375 friends. Within two hours, she had gained fifteen more. Meanwhile,
the Campbell County Sheriff's Office had charged Andrew with aggravated
assault and six counts of felony reckless endangerment and jailed him on a
$200,000 bond. WATE-TV showed a photo of an unsmiling Andrew dressed
in orange prison garb and looking very overweight.

The TV station also added that Andrew had fired once in the air but had
fired a second time at Jeremey, missing him but sending the bullet through

three walls in the trailer until it lodged in a closet. The reporter interviewed Angel Brotherton, Elizabeth's mother, about how the children reacted.

"Terrified," she replied. "Actually, they don't understand what's going on at all. All I know is they kept asking as the police was there, 'Why did daddy do this?' I hope he has to get help. I do, and maybe Andrew could straighten back up and be Andrew again. That's what Andrew needs to do is grow up, get a life, and be a dad."

The trial was set for that Thursday, but on Tuesday, as if nothing had happened, Taylor posted an open letter on her site. *To everyone who enjoys relaying everything I post on my FB to Derrick Noe,* she began. *Would you please courteously let him know what this says, even screenshot it and send it to him. That would be great. I am* SICK *and* TIRED *of getting lied on and about while Derrick goes around looking like he is the risen Jesus Christ himself. I am so sick of* FAKE *christian people taking up for him when they don't have enough of* GOD *to take 5 seconds to pray about a person or situation and let the* REAL GENUINE HOLY GHOST *show them what is* TRULY *rooted in their evil and deceitful hearts.*

Then followed several lengthy paragraphs alleging years of mental, physical, and emotional abuse. Their ministry as traveling music ministers, she wrote, had a whole other side.

When I would come into your churches and try to help you it was because I was looking for help too!! I was seeking help from God by doing everything I possibly could to please him, because I needed him to help me, she wrote. *I needed him to move for me and my babies. I needed devine deliverance . . . But* NO ONE *saw it.*

Finally, she concluded, she had to get out. *I want* MY STORY *to be heard. I left him in the wrong way,* she said. *There is better ways to do it . . . Bit if* YOU *are being done this way . . . Please get out!! No one diserves this . . . No one should go through the* HELL *I went through on a daily basis. And no. I wasn't the perfect wife. But I in no way deserved the* YEARS *of torture I went through under this man.*

She received 209 likes and about 125 comments within thirty-six hours (by the time I saw it on the evening of March 18). Many comments were from women who said their marriages had been abusive.

She responded: *I just want everyone to know I am thankful for the support!! I didnt put this on here to draw suppprt . . . But thats what I got and I am thankful for it. He is texting me* AMD *calling me now threatening to sue me and everything else. Begging me to take it off . . . But I won't.* I AM NOT AFRAID *to use the* VOICE HE TOOK *from me all those years ago!*

I wondered how to square Taylor's account of the past four years with what other people had told me about her lying in wait for Andrew the previous spring. I wanted to contact Derrick for his side of the story, but he had inexplicably unfriended me about two months before.

As one man commented on her feed: *I am NOT saying Taylor should have left the marriage the way she did either BUT without upholding how she did it, I UNDERSTAND how easily she was drawn. When you have been beaten down to the point she was, no self esteem left, thinking you are the ugliest, fattest person on the earth and not worthy of air and someone comes along (yes married or unmarried) and tells you TOTALLY different, you just FALL to pieces in their direction.*

Thursday was Andrew's court hearing. WATE-TV showed up, pointing out that it was the only media outlet to cover the proceeding. It was a huge change from some sixteen months earlier, when Andrew was at the same courthouse surrounded by cameras. After a dramatic press conference on the courthouse steps surrounded by followers in red, he had entered a packed courtroom full of supporters. This time, he was dressed in a dark green prison uniform. A photo on the station's website showed him looking unhappily over his left shoulder at the spectators.

One thing that came out during the hearing was Andrew's murderous feelings toward Jeremey Henegar.

"When she was in the hospital, he come up and asked where I was, and people said that I was not there," Jeremey testified. "And he said that if I was there, that he would gut me."

Elizabeth, who took the stand wearing a dark blue dress and a light blue sweater, got to debate with Mark Hatmaker, Andrew's attorney, who was clearly trying to prove the kids weren't in any danger.

"Andrew didn't intend to hit anybody except Jeremey, did he?" he asked her.

"Just Jeremey," she said.

"That's the only person that was put in danger, wasn't it?"

"Well his kids was outside," she said.

"I was outside," Hatmaker said, tapping his chest.

"You weren't there," Elizabeth retorted.

Andrew headed back to jail and Elizabeth, satisfied that she was in no immediate danger, posted the following on April 2: *Wants to take time and thank God for what he's done for me. . . . . my first place after getting married was a two bed room lil house that was literally falling apart. it had no heat and air. and*

I can remember in the winter at night the wind would blow and I'd half to reach up and hold the window shut from were it was broke. and I remember waking up a many [of] times with my whole arm num from falling asleep from holding it up. so we moved are matress in the living room and lived like that for 3 months while pregnant with the twins. then the Lord blessed us with an apartment. I loved it. but we lost it. Then blessed with another and it was to small for all of us. moved to a house then God blessed us with an even bigger then lost it cause I couldn't afford it so I moved me and six kids in with my mom. but now I have great news!!!! My mom is giving me her trailer!!!! Me and my babies now have a place. We no longer half to worry if we're going to be kicked out!!!! God has been so good to me even when I'm so unworthy of it. I really can't thank him enough.

She got 400 likes and a myriad of comments. The trailer was where she had grown up in the hill country north of LaFollette.

Not to be outdone, Taylor dropped this small bomb on Good Friday, April 3: *This month has been the longest and hardest month of my life. I am over it. I need this new baby to hurry up and get here . . . I need the man I love more then anything in the whole world to come home and hold me. And I need Derrick Noe to be long gone. He threatened me again this evening. And I have taken out a new EPO on him. I am tired of all this crap. My children and I don't deserve it. New wife . . . I hope you understand that he is going to hurt you . . . I promise he will. Its just a matter of time. I am sorry you were so blinded you couldn't see it. Please pray for me people.*

Judging by the surprised remarks on her feed, no one else knew about this baby.

On April 21: *The kids found out today they are getting a "Little Sister"!! It's a GIRL!! Andrew and I are beyond excited!*

Then on May 29, she announced she was into her forty-first week.

On May 31: *As of right now I have 35 hours to go into labor by myself!!!!! A few hundred Jumping jacks, A thousand squats, and a run around the world sounds like a plan?? Anybody in?? LOL.*

At dawn on June 2, she said she was being induced. Then later that morning: *Introducing Miss Bailee Alexis!! June 2nd @ 10:29! 8 pounds 13 ounces and 21 1/2 inches long!!*

She got seventy-six comments, but not one mention of Andrew, unless one counted Dakota Seiber's laconic observation: *Looks just like her daddy.*

To which Melissa Hamilton Evans, the great granddaughter of Bob and Barbara Elkins, replied: *She looks like you.*

Meanwhile, back in West Virginia at the home of Vicie Haywood, "Old Yeller," the snake whose bite had killed her son Mack Wolford, had been kept alive and was used in worship services. On May 27, 2015, three years to the day that Mack perished, the snake died.

On June 30, Elizabeth posted: *It has been exactly one year and two days to the day that i tried to comet suicide. i want to thank the lord for the mercy he showed me that day. i just want to encourage anyone who is fighting this. that [even] tho life is not going as u planned and you may be going threw something that no ones else understands that suicide should never b the option. i myself felt like i was just taking the easy way out and twenty mins after i relized it was not. so just hold on and ride out your storm it will get better. im living proof.*

In July, I was moving back to the lower 48 from Alaska and in transit much of the month, so I lost track of a lot of the chitchat. I noticed Taylor posting messages about ironing Andrew's shirts plus a pathetic post from Elizabeth mentioning her text to Little Cody's wife, Brittany, asking if she could attend their church.

He said no, Brittany answered. When Elizabeth posted this on her page, about fifty people expressed their disgust at Cody. But Cody was having his own trials. He had been bitten in the ear and face by a rattlesnake; the bite was serious, and it was clear to Cody that he was afraid to die, unwilling to die, or both. Unlike his father, Cody allowed himself to be taken to a local hospital, which had him airlifted to the University of Tennessee Medical Center in Knoxville.

Then on July 31, the *Knoxville News Sentinel,* which had produced minimal coverage of Andrew to date, reported that Andrew had pled guilty to one count of aggravated assault and seven counts of felony reckless endangerment and had been ordered to serve 150 days of a six-year sentence behind bars with the rest spent on probation. Because he'd already served 134 days, he was eligible to be released soon. On August 12, the Campbell County Sheriff's Department said Andrew had been released.

From what I could tell from various posts, Elizabeth didn't have regular access to a cell phone, much less Facebook. On August 25, she wrote: *i cant get on here much. just when family visits i steel there phone for a few lol.* Then on September 15, one of Elizabeth's friends posted: *Everyone if they would say a prayer for Elizabeth Marie Hamblin!!! It takes a dirty person to do what has been done!!!*

Several people responded, including Linda Spoon. *Anyone that puts their own LUST above the love of their children is doing nothing but taking up space on this earth,* she wrote. *Liz is a good mother you said you would go away and leave her alone. You are a lying liar i believe those are your words.*

Elizabeth wrote: *thank u everyone. im ok for now. cant realy explain whats going on just yet. but please pray hard for me this coming up monday.*

Later: *thank you everyone for the prayers the judge granted me and andrews mom to have joint custody till oct 22 due to not having a lawyor in time. please keep praying that the lawyor im talking to will be able to do the court date sooner. . . . . andrews mom isnt trying to keep or take them me and her are on very good terms.*

On September 21, someone asked Liz: *What is Andrew doing now?*

Liz: *Getting married today!*

Wow I really thought he was sold out to god, the man wrote.

Liz: *i just wish him the best.*

After some more dialogue, a woman from Knoxville asked: *Why would the judge not grant you full custody? Just don't understand why his mom would get part custody.*

Elizabeth replied: *andrews lawyor was sending my papers to the wrong house there fore i missed court last month and she stated she had been raising my kids. which isnt true. she does keep them on the weekends tho. thats why im having to get a lawyer.*

A woman from Indiana said: *You should have had a lawyer the whole time sweetie. You think you know people but you really dont. Keep a record of everything.*

A paralegal from California asked: *So Andrew didn't get any custody himself?*

Liz: *no cause of the shooting. he can have supervised visits with his mom.*

She also revealed she was going after Andrew for child support. Then a woman from Pacific Palisades, California, posted: *Get in touch with NatGeo, I am sure that rise to fame did not help with Andrews ego. They should help you because they helped make it happen. I am sure they won't but it infuriates me that reality shows insist on making a mockery out of people's lives and destroy so many in it's path. You guys were totally fine before the show.*

Good luck with that, I thought. All my efforts to contact the National Geographic folks for any comment—other than immediately after Jamie's funeral—had gone unanswered.

Later that day, a renamed Taylor Elaine Hamblin posted, *Got Married,* with a photo of her and Andrew seated cheek to cheek in a car. She received eighty-seven likes and many congratulations.

Then on September 29, another boyfriend from London, Kentucky, posted a note on Liz's feed saying he was "in relationship" with her. This was no great shock in that she'd been dating various people. I looked at his feed and saw he had short brown hair and brown eyes, a Playboy bunny earring in his right ear, a baseball cap that he never seemed to remove, and a chain necklace, plus the beginnings of a mustache. At least he had a job at a local pizza place. He had four kids and was quite recently divorced. Judging from the birth date of the first child, he had been married close to ten years.

Reams of encouragement poured onto her feed from her Facebook friends. But the would-be boyfriend had been posting love notes to his now ex-wife on Facebook only six months before, so it was obvious something had gone wrong very fast. I looked on the feed of the ex-wife, and along with countless videos about ways to style long hair, pleas to keep local coal mines open, and links to songs by Reba McIntire and Jimmy Rose were posts such as this: *being single is better than being lied to, cheated on and disrespected.* Her words sounded hauntingly like Liz's feed during the summer of 2014.

On October 14, Liz posted: *After a year of waiting i never thought love would come my way. . . . but God sure did surprise and bless me with the most amazing man and 4 wonderful babies that feel like my own. fairytales really do happen cause I've finally found mine.*

After several comments and 171 likes: *Lol its exactly five boys and five girls,* she added.

A woman from Berea, Kentucky, posted: *That's awesome as long as he works and provides for you and treats you good and those babies.*

Not surprisingly, on October 17, a Saturday, Elizabeth posted a photo of her wearing a ring. She got sixty-seven replies and 242 likes.

I don't know you personally but you've not been divorced a short time with very traumatic ending, a woman messaged her. *I wouldn't rush things but hopefully at least he won't be a psycho snake handler! Congrats & God bless.*

Elizabeth's reply: *He believes in snake handling just as much as I do. . . . . . . He was raised in it. But thanks.*

There was one naysayer: DONT DO IT *!* posted Arnold Saylor, the serpent handler from Indiana, who was at one of Andrew's court hearings two years before. Maybe he was onto something, because by the end of November, Elizabeth was sadly posting on her feed that the relationship had ended.

CHAPTER EIGHTEEN

THE FULL
HOUSE

●　●

Meanwhile, Andrew had decided he was ready for a comeback.

Had a fabulous weekend, he wrote on October 25. *Had a great time at big fork last night with great fellowship, a fabulous meeting, and wonderful food. Then we had a wonderful Sunday and we thank God for brothers Virgil Gibson and Gary Long for baptizing us on this cloudy Sunday but it was wonderful. Then we had an amazing service at Redbird tonight, so thankful for redbird church and all they've done for us, they will never know what they mean to us. Now headed home for something to eat then bed time lol. Hope everyone had a blessed day. Pray for us and we will pray for y'all.*

On October 30, Elizabeth posted*: Guess who got full custody of my babies? ME!!!!! Lord I can't thank you enough for letting court go as good as it did.* She got 483 likes. She added: *Thanks everyone there daddy does get to see them every weekend so everything worked out I lifted the band on him not taking them alone and now he gets to take them unsupervised so it worked out for him.*

Thus began a Facebook battle between Liz with her relatives versus Taylor and Andrew. Taylor fired the opening salvo. *Well it's Day 3 of thankfulness and I haven't even done the first one,* she wrote at the beginning of November, *so I guess I have to make up for them today. So, today I am thankful for My husband. He is the most wonderful man I have ever met and I couldn't thank God for him enough. The second thing I am thankful for is how hard my husband works to provide for his family! I am more proud of him then he will ever know and appreciate every hour he works for us, so we can have the things we need and want! Third, I am grateful for my children and how each of them are their own little person.* After naming all three, she concluded with, *I am thankful for my* FAMILY. *My life couldn't be any more complete than it is right now!!!:)*

Meanwhile, Andrew was posting: *I love it when the spirit of the Lord wakes me up of the morning, teaching me and blessing me. I can't even begin to thank God for all he's done for me and mine. He's brought me a long, long way. Hope everyone has a blessed Sunday. I'm standing on the cornerstone, I shall not be moved. #determined #feelingblessed.*

In response, Tiffany Carroll Hill posted: *Im sorry but I can't keep my mouth shut on this one. Im so glad that he's working and providing for his new family cause that's what he should be doing but why isn't he helping my sister provide and take care of the 6 kids that he helped bring into this world? If it wasn't for my sister, mother, grandma and other family members helping out those kids would have absolutely nothing. We was the ones that made sure they had school clothes, shoes, back packs, electricity and water . . . Where was he at when they needed those things? Or how about making sure his son made it to his dentist appointment? I was the one that took him. His kids haven't even got a phone call on their birthdays. Only one to help out any on his side of the family is Andrews mom. Which Liz is very thankful for. Those kids need their dad in their life. Step up and take care of the other ones!*

What made things doubly interesting was a November 14 Facebook post by a Corbin, Kentucky, car dealer showing Andrew and Taylor, along with a baby carrier, standing in front of a Nissan Quest minivan along with congratulations for their purchase. The vehicle was probably used, but it still implied that the couple had some financial resources. By the end of December, Elizabeth was realizing that help from Andrew was not on the way. *Shout out to all those parents who starts a family then leaves them to go raise there whores kids,* she wrote on December 21. *fyi in years to come your children are gonna realize what a peace of s@?? you truely r. guys like u need to fixed ! just sayin.*

Soon after the beginning of 2016, she posted: *i wont to thank my aunt and uncle for my new stove and frig. im glad i have family members that goes the extra mile to help me and the kids.*

Meanwhile, I'd been e-mailing Ralph Hood, who told me the serpent-handling churches in Sand Mountain and Marshall were doing well. I asked him about Little Cody's decision to seek medical help the previous summer for his snakebite. I could understand Cody's dilemma. His father had not been dead two years, and there was no one else to support his wife and two kids, not to mention his mom.

"It caused some tension because his father died for refusing treatment," Ralph said. "He lost some stature." The unwritten code was that you trusted God to heal you. Cody had toughed out bad bites before, including the one he had gotten on the reality show, so clearly he was having a major battle with his faith.

"He's not a good pastor," Ralph said of Little Cody. "He is very authoritarian. Little Cody doesn't have the skills or wisdom like his dad had. People aren't reacting well to that."

I asked about their view of Andrew.

"They don't want Hamblin or his people at the church," he said. "Andrew has set it [the movement] back one hundred years."

On April 25, Elizabeth posted a "feeling heartbroken" emoticon and posted the following: *Please someone screen shot this status and send it to my kids dad! Your kids are missing you and hasn't talked to you in months. . . . . . I'd write him myself but they have me blocked. . . . . . I know you have a life but my god you have six little ones that need you in there life to. . . . sorry to rant and rave but I'm fed up with this. my kids think I'm keeping them from you. . . . they don't understand why you don't come around. fed up with my kids crying every dang night over you.*

She got a bunch of sympathetic responses, including several from people who had access to Andrew and Taylor's Facebook page and could message them or could take a screen shot of Liz's post, post it as a photo, and then tag Andrew.

Just pray for Payton, she messaged. *Once again he's asking for him.*

One Knoxville man, whose Facebook groups ranged from animal rights to Confederate causes, decided to address Andrew openly. *Listen buddy,* he wrote, *if you see this you need to know your messing these kids up ESPECIALLY the older ones. My mom and dad divorced when I was about seven or eight and dad picked his new old lady over me and my sisters. I didn't see him again for about fifteen years. I always wondered what I did too make my dad not love me I blamed myself and it really f-ed me up for years. I quit school was drinking and raising hell and now I look back and think alot of shit that I did and went thru was because*

I couldn't understand why daddy didn't love me anymore. GET YOUR ASS OVER THERE AND BE A DAD! *Their mom mite not be your wife anymore but they will always be your youngins. Get you shit together because nobody is gonna suffer like these kids.* I KNOW!

However, most of the people trying to post to Andrew and Taylor's page messaged Liz back a day later, saying their page had disappeared off Facebook.

On June 28, Liz posted: *Today makes two years that I tried to commit suicide. . . . I'm so thankful that the Lord had mercy on me that day.*

But life was clearly miserable for her. She was living in a rural area north of LaFollette without a car and with no one to mow grass or take the garbage to the local dump. By this time, Donald Trump was the clear front-runner for the Republican presidential nomination, and all sorts of people around the country were asking what kind of person would vote for him. In mid-July, I read a column about a new book on Appalachia's poor white residents and how J. D. Vance, in *Hillbilly Elegy: A Memoir of a Family and Culture in Crisis*, had described these folks to a T. The columnist, Rod Dreher, had interviewed Vance, who explained that Trump was the only political candidate in ages who understood these peoples' struggles.

"What many don't understand is how truly desperate these places are, and we're not talking about small enclaves or a few towns—we're talking about multiple states where a significant chunk of the white working class struggles to get by," Vance said in the interview. "Heroin addiction is rampant."

Well, no kidding. East Tennessee was a haven for meth users, and other parts of Appalachia were much the same. As for jobs, there weren't many. For most of the people I knew on Facebook, a job at Walmart was the best they were ever going to get. None of them lived in large cities with easy access to education. That's why Tennessee, ranked forty-third in the nation for its share of residents who had completed college, announced in 2014 a plan to offer free community college to all state residents. It was the first state in the country to do so.

"The average kid will live in multiple homes over the course of her life," Vance told Dreher, "experience a constant cycle of growing close to a 'stepdad' only to see him walk out on the family, know multiple drug users personally, maybe live in a foster home for a bit (or at least in the home of an unofficial foster like an aunt or grandparent), watch friends and family get arrested, and on and on. And on top of that is the economic struggle, from the factories shuttering their doors to the Main Streets with nothing but cash-for-gold stores and pawn shops."

I thought of the children involved in the lives of Andrew and Liz and Taylor and Derrick. Taylor had brought to the union children from three relationships. Had Liz's engagement to the Kentucky man worked out, they would have had ten children between them. I was aware of so many other couples who had kids from multiple marriages or liaisons to the point that one could truthfully say they were related to half the town.

On Sept. 11, Linda Spoon posted a twenty-seven-minute video of Andrew preaching in a Knoxville church. It was clearly a Holiness congregation, as all the men were in long-sleeved shirts and the furnishings were minimal. Andrew, who was wearing dark pants and a long-sleeved white shirt, was wailing away, gesturing with a portable microphone and waving a Bible.

"I've come to tell you that the gifts and the signs are still working in the church today," he shouted. "I've come to tell you that there's still a Holy Ghost! I've come to tell you there's still prophecy! There's still miracles! There's still healing!" And so on.

People were shouting, "Hey, c'mon," to his every phrase. I finally figured out he was preaching on Mark 16. He talked on and on about healing, tongues, and other gifts, striding back and forth, occasionally dancing a few steps. But he didn't mention snakes. That was not going to sell with this crowd.

I spotted what looked like Taylor in a long skirt sitting a few rows back with two kids. The blond-haired girl on her lap looked to be about the age Bailee would be.

The comments on Linda's page were withering.

There for sure is a Holy Ghost and He don't have it!!!! wrote one man.

He's a mess, chimed in a woman from Berea, Kentucky. None of our churches will have him. *So he's going around places that don't have good understanding and that accepts him.*

I think people are more mad at what he's still doing by not seeing his kids, Elizabeth wrote. *I don't have anything against him. we have all fell short . . . I just wish he would realize that his kids needs him in there life's to. I saw her three kids there and he helps raise hers but has forgot about his. :(*

I checked Derrick Noe's page, as he had married his girlfriend, Kayla, sometime back. She was now several months pregnant with a boy. He and Andrew and Taylor had all recovered—in a fashion—from the devastation of the past two years. Only Elizabeth was left holding the bag. I called Michelle Gray. Her health was no better, which made it necessary for her to stay close to the Mayo Clinic's Florida campus in Jacksonville, about a three-hour drive away.

She and her family desperately missed Kentucky, but she wondered, "Did we really want all that drama again?" Florida still didn't feel like home and they weren't attending church. None of the ones near their home felt right. I asked her if she missed the serpent-handling scene further north.

"I miss it so much," she said. "The church was the only place where I felt I could be myself." Yet, even that terrain was destroyed. "Nearly everyone we know has backslid," she said, listing several affairs and divorces. "What Andrew didn't tear down and kill, Jamie's death finished off."

I got a similar report from Linda Spoon.

"Everyone is scattered," she said. "Some in church, some not. I go every once in a while but not like I used to. It just done something to everybody. Just about the whole congregation has gone down the wrong road."

She said Andrew and Taylor were somewhere near London, Kentucky, where Taylor's family lives. She'd called around to various state offices that enforced child support, but nothing happened. She guessed Andrew was about $9,000 in arrears.

"They know where he lives, but he just ignores the letters," Linda said. "I don't know what they are waiting on. They told me and Liz he'd pay or go to jail. If he goes to jail, the state picks up the bill. Everyone knows what's going on. They know he ran off and left his kids. We don't understand why nothing happens."

How odd, I thought. There was a time when Andrew felt he couldn't drive anywhere without a state trooper on his tail, and now the state couldn't seem to figure out where he was. Didn't his parole officer keep tabs on his whereabouts?

As for Elizabeth, "She has no water or no electricity right now," Linda told me. "She has to carry water from her grandmother's house next door. She takes the kids over there and bathes them. She doesn't have a phone any more. Oh honey, she's in bad shape.

The house of the serpent handler was dark and cold.

Then I heard from Ralph that neither Little Cody nor Big Cody was running the Middlesboro church at present. The grandfather—Gregory Coots—was overseeing it on a temporary basis.

"He does not have the flexibility to handle those things and the church rebelled," he said of Little Cody. "He is convinced Katrina can't get double married. Katrina will remarry at one point, and the notion that Little Cody could impose on his sister won't work."

I told him the latest about Andrew and Liz, and he mentioned the names of other handlers who had likewise dumped their spouses.

"Once they leave, they get another woman and more kids, and they take care of that family," he said. "He'll start his own thing, but once he's above the radar, the state will come down on him."

He had recently been at homecomings in Marshall and Sand Mountain, and both places were doing well, he said, compared to the devastation farther north.

"It is hub churches with key families," he said, "that continue the tradition."

I reached Linda Coots, who said that Little Cody's snakebite had put him on life support at one point and in the hospital for two weeks. There had been some hearing and memory loss, not to mention the damage to his faith.

"When he got back to church, he was worried about being responsible for everyone," she said. "Now that he'd been bitten, he didn't want others going through this." So Cody, who back in 2012 was thinking up ways to quaff Red Devil and do other daring exploits for his God, hadn't been back to church in over a year. After Jamie died, other serpent-handling pastors had volunteered to fill in, she said, on the condition that Cody not let in TV cameras. Cody had promised one pastor that he'd banish the media. But an MTV crew had approached him; in fact, they were there the night he was bitten, she said, and Cody had concluded the snakebite was God's punishment for breaking his promise.

So there, I thought, goes the last chance of any media being allowed into that church. Why did this culture hate reporters to the point that they associated coverage with a divine curse? Then Linda told me a funny anecdote about Cody getting his tongue pierced. The act shocked Linda, but she decided to say nothing.

"I fell on my knees and told God he has to sing and that could mess him up big time," she said. "Cody's tongue was so sore the next day, he couldn't eat. The thing kept on falling out. I figured he's like his daddy; anything that comes between him and eating, he'll get rid of it." Eventually, that's what happened, "so God took care of it."

Cody took a job at a furniture rental store in town. The church was still having three services a week, but only fifteen people could be counted on to show up.

"It's like going to a dead church," Linda mourned. As for Katrina, she'd been all ready to register for a nursing program at a local college, she added, but Jamie's death had made it necessary for her to work. Now twenty-five, she was still working at Walmart.

All this brought back memories of an interview I'd once done for a Christian magazine with Bob Sorge, a Kansas City-area evangelist. We'd talked of how suffering can break people or transform them.

"There are casualties," he told me. "Satan is gambling he can turn you into a casualty, and God is testing you to see if you will become a spiritual giant."

All I was seeing were casualties.

I reached out to Liz and arranged a time when I could call her at her grandmother's home next door where there was a land line. It was Nov. 1; two years since I'd heard Andrew's side of the story. I had yet to hear hers.

She began by denying she'd sent out any risqué photos of herself prior to the divorce and admitted she and Jeremey had been sexually involved more than once but only after Andrew had left her for Taylor. What I found fascinating is how Andrew kept on coming back to her in the months after that.

"The week before the whole shooting," she said, "Andrew had come to my mom's and said he was not with Taylor." They were even sleeping together, so Elizabeth harbored a tiny hope that maybe even at this late date, the union could be saved.

"I was served my divorce papers on Valentine's Day, and we were seeing each other after that," she said. "He said let's just get divorced and still see each other but if it's meant to be, it would be." Then she happened to go by Andrew's place in Clairfield—the same place where I'd phoned him—and saw Taylor's car there. All hope died. Then she and Jeremey arranged to go on an outing on a warm Sunday afternoon in March.

"The reason the whole shooting happened is that Andrew was jealous I was with Jeremey," she said. When she found out two days later that Taylor was seven months pregnant, "That kind of killed me," she said. "I thought he'd wanted to work things out, but he was just a player. I think she buys him. Andrew has always been about money. They pay for him to have new clothes, new shoes, everything."

But this time, there was no venomous back-and-forth on Facebook.

"Taylor wrote me while Andrew was in jail," she said, "and apologized and said she couldn't help falling in love with him and that Andrew treated her so good. I told her she could have him, that everything happens for a reason. Taylor added me on Facebook the day before she had Bailee—we told each other we were sorry for what's happened in the past." That didn't last long, as Liz was eventually blocked from their page as were others who were her Facebook friends.

Liz had never gotten a driver's license, so could not drive. Although she was willing to work, she had three preschool children at home, three older ones who arrived home in the mid-afternoon and no public transport. "I am stuck between a rock and a hard spot," she said, so her sisters and other relatives, Linda Spoon, and Andrew's mother were helping her pay the bills.

At that point, she added, Andrew had missed four court dates, probably figuring that if he didn't show, he wouldn't have to pay child support. She was due $709 a month, and he was at least $2,000 in arrears, she said, but to date, she had only gotten $400. Then she added a fascinating rumor: one of Andrew's now-deceased grandfathers had had a church in Clairfield, and Andrew might start up a new congregation there.

As we talked for almost two hours, I realized that I was dealing with a different person from the woman who was almost too shy to talk with me when I first dropped by her place more than four years before. Now twenty five and a half, she was articulate and confident, honest about her own failings, but amazingly free of bitterness after a very difficult and public slog. To be in a two-bedroom trailer in the middle of nowhere with six kids, on food stamps, dependent on your friends and family to keep the heat on and the water running, with your ex-husband on the lam and not even to have a car, would be dire straits for anyone. Fortunately, she had a new boyfriend.

I also talked with her grandmother, Pearl Carr, about Payton. He had not answered the letter Veeka had sent him. Now nine years old, he was not doing well at school and making few friends. He had been six when his father left; a horrible age to lose a parent. The other children had been too young to realize what was going on, but Payton had seen it all. These days, Pearl stated, the child never got to see his dad.

"Payton loves Andrew with all his heart," she said. She added that the twins were doing better but, "They are angry kids with each other and with other children."

Meanwhile, where was the famed serpent handler himself? I knew Taylor's maiden name and her father's business, so I did a number of internet searches, made some phone calls, and left lots of messages. I pretty much figured out where her family home was, down to the street number. I found on Google Maps a pretty place on a country road with white paint, black shutters, and a red door. It had stepping stones across neatly cut grass to the front door, a chimney, and what looked like a deck out back with a barbecue grill. If that was truly the new house of the serpent handler, Andrew had clearly moved up.

I got an e-mail within a few hours from Taylor, who was clearly nettled that I had called her father's business.

"We do not talk to anyone outside of our immediate circle," she wrote. "I'm sorry if this is not what you wanted to hear, but we do not wish to correspond with anyone with ties to Elizabeth. We enjoy our drama free life and would like to keep it that way."

I reminded her that reporters never take sides, that Andrew and I had always related well, and that it was a conversation with me nearly five years before that had started it all. She would let him know that I was trying to reach him, she responded, but if the topic wandered past fact-checking, "that will be the last contact we have with you. Once again, I do not want to come across rash, you just need to understand what we have had to go through thinking we could trust people, and it coming back to bite us."

I never heard back and several weeks passed. In the closing days of 2016, Liz announced she was engaged to an Adam Hensley, a man eight years older than her who had three children of his own. Three months later, she would marry him and move to his home in Ewing, Va., 46 miles north of LaFollette. Meanwhile, Andrew was coming out of the shadows. His Facebook account magically awoke and the people who had wanted nothing to do with him were leaving endearing messages on his feed. Linda Coots, Little Cody Coots, Arnold Saylor and others were wishing him well. The following summer, he would show up at their homecoming and happily handle snakes.

Most amazing was that he had started services at Rock Creek Freewill Baptist, his grandfather's church on the main street going through Clairfield, next door to the elementary school. Judging from the photos someone had sent me, it was bigger than the place he had in LaFollette, and the sturdily built sanctuary was only 15 years old. The interior had a maroon-pinkish carpet, yellow walls and upholstered pews. There were microphones, a sound system and a place for a band. Andrew could not have done much better if he had tried. There were maybe two dozen people in the congregation, but once Andrew decides to publicize the place, he will have a full house.

His Facebook feed showed many selfies of a grinning Andrew and Taylor and a shot of the newly minted family of five: Taylor with her first two kids and Andrew balancing a cherubic Bailee on his left arm.

"That is the dark side of that tradition," Ralph had told me. "They just continue preaching and start all over again."

I had heard that Andrew had gotten the church, which he renamed Rock Creek House of Prayer, on the condition there'd be no snakes involved, but I imagined that prohibition wouldn't be followed for long. For on Dec. 25, he chose to proclaim a holiday wish on a serpent handlers forum on Facebook.

Merry Christmas to all of my serpent handling brothers and sisters. . . . love and miss everyone of yall. Love, bro. Andrew, it said.

He was facing away from the camera and in his left hand, arching and twisting, a rattlesnake reached for the sky.

Coda

By the summer of 2017, Cody Coots had returned to pastor his father's church. No doubt frustrated by her brother's obduracy concerning her ability to remarry, Katrina had moved out of her parents' home and left the Full Gospel Tabernacle in Jesus Name. On August 30, while driving back home from her new church with a female friend, she got into an accident with another car on a rain-slicked highway near Pineville, north of Middlesboro. Both women died instantly. Katrina was 26.

The Coots family refused to allow Elizabeth Hamblin, now Elizabeth Hensley, to attend Katrina's funeral on September 4. However, Andrew Hamblin was listed as a "special brother" to Katrina in her obituary. Later that month, I visited Elizabeth and Adam Hensley and their combined family of nine children in their Ewing, Virginia, home, which was atop a hill with a view of the mountains and woods. For the first time in several years, Elizabeth appeared happy and at peace. She too had a full house.

APPENDIX ONE
RESEARCH METHODS

Researching a book that's heavily based on social media feeds, in this case Facebook, is tougher than it might seem. One has to be constantly monitoring peoples' conversations, as important material will often disappear into the pipeline or the author will think better of the post and remove it a few hours later. I'm grateful to the many people who sent me material that I missed, and what you read in this book is the result of hundreds of hours simply spent checking in on peoples' conversations.

Facebook can also be used for academic purposes. In the fall of 2013, I had enrolled in the University of Memphis's MA program in journalism. I commuted to Memphis twice a week taking overloads of four graduate courses per term, meaning that while I was zipping back and forth across Tennessee to cover Andrew's court appearances, I was juggling papers on media entrepreneurship, ethics, website construction, and research methods. It was the latter course, taught by the journalism department's venerable and soon-to-retire Rick Fischer, that showed me how to put together an academic paper.

The first way to obtain data, I learned, was by from personal interviews. No problem there: that's all a reporter does. I listed the six churches in Jolo, LaFollette, Del Rio, Marshall, Sand Mountain, and Middlesboro as locales for site visits, then conducted at least one hundred interviews, although many were multiple interviews of the same persons. The Appalachian culture, I pointed out in one of my papers, is highly personal, and great emphasis is placed on face-to-face interaction. Phone interviews do not work as well. I listed Pentecostal and "signs following" terms in an appendix. It was tough to explain why people handled snakes, as many interviewees were reluctant to give complex reasons for why they did so. Most said it was something they felt God led them to do or that it was stated in the Bible; therefore they had no choice but to follow it. Sentences like "I believe it's right," "I believe it's the Word," and "because the Bible says so" were sprinkled throughout a paper I prepared for a religion and media conference in Boulder the month before Jamie died. Noting how fascinated these academics were with my photos from a recent New Year's Eve, I realized there was a lot of interest in this project.

The second research method was a content analysis of Jamie's and Andrew's Facebook pages. I had to put together a data codebook by which I listed codes that corresponded with various characteristics: age, occupation, education level, and other details. It was very difficult to get personal details off of many people's Facebook profiles because of privacy settings, but I managed to discern a few trends from the thirty-seven people I surveyed. Their average was 39.7. Women slightly outnumbered men. Most respondents were white, only two were black, and no one belonged to other ethnic groups. The vast majority were married with children. The largest number (fifteen) were from Tennessee, followed by Kentucky (seven). Only one was from West Virginia—an odd finding in that it is the only Appalachian state where serpent handling is completely legal. Georgia, Missouri, and Alabama were runners-up with two each. Other states included California, Illinois, and Pennsylvania, and overseas visitors included Scotland and the Netherlands. Education-wise, one-quarter had bachelor's degrees. The rest had a high-school diploma or had attended a community college or business college.

A SurveyMonkey questionnaire that I drew up was far more helpful. I posted requests on the Facebook walls of Jamie, Andrew, and Liz, asking for responses. I also sent personal messages to various people who posted on those pages, asking them to fill out the survey. Those who responded ranged from a devout EMT in Texas and an elderly moonshiner in Kentucky to an agnostic college student in Cincinnati and a middle-aged atheist medical professional from Guam. It got sixty-six responses—not as many as I wanted but not bad considering none of the respondents personally knew me. Also, it was difficult to get people to fill out surveys about something as unusual as serpent handling. A graduate student from a university elsewhere in Tennessee had contacted me earlier in the year, telling of her fruitless efforts to survey people at "signs following" services for her master's thesis. Most people gave her the cold shoulder. I figured that a survey through Facebook might feel more anonymous and safe.

Sixty-nine percent of the respondents were female and more than one-third were in the thirty-five-to-forty-four age category. Some 35.8 percent of the respondents were from Tennessee—no surprise there. Some 26.4

percent were from Kentucky. Georgia, Alabama, and Virginia (but not West Virginia) were runners-up. All this data squared up with what the content analysis showed.

The SurveyMonkey data made it clear how much these preachers owed National Geographic, for almost 54 percent of the respondents said they learned of these serpent handlers through *Snake Salvation*. After all, Andrew had about a thousand Facebook followers before the series ran. This jumped up to five thousand by the end of the series. One-third of the SurveyMonkey respondents agreed that Mark 16:17–18 meant that believers should pick up snakes in church. That was a large percentage, considering that every mainline Pentecostal group has condemned the practice. When asked whether watching the show got one interested in actually handling these reptiles, 77 percent said "no," 20 percent said "yes," and two souls (the remaining 3 percent) directly credited the Hamblin/Coots' social media presence with their decision to recently start handling snakes. Not a huge trend, but the 20 percent plus the 3 percent constituted nearly one-quarter of all respondents approving such a controversial and deadly practice. I had no previous data on public attitudes about serpent handling. But a lot of positive pieces about young serpent handlers had run from 2012 to 2014 in publications ranging from the *Tennessean* and the *Chattanooga Times Free Press* to *Buzzfeed*. And an organization like National Geographic would not have outlaid significant money for a sixteen-part reality show unless producers thought there was a lot of interest in the photogenic handlers.

Both Jamie and Andrew had said their reason for appearing on *Snake Salvation* was to spread the Gospel. When I asked on SurveyMonkey whether anyone had actually become a Christian through the show, one person, a Kentucky woman in her late thirties or early forties, said "yes." Eighty percent were already believers. When asked if Jamie Coots's February 15, 2014, death from a rattlesnake bite affected their opinion of whether snake handling should be legal, close to 8 percent said the death turned them against the practice; 9 percent said it made them more certain the practice should continue; and 83 percent said it didn't affect their views one way or another.

When asked whether serpent handling should be made illegal, only 10 percent answered "yes." Twenty percent said watching the show made them want to visit a serpent-handling church, and 63 percent said that following and/or reading about both men on Facebook made them more sympathetic to the movement. This proved—to me at any rate—that social media, especially Facebook, had created a sympathetic audience for a fringe religious movement. Now, 13 percent said reading about these men made them *less* sympathetic, but that 63 percent figure said volumes about what posting updates, family photos, pictures of various poisonous serpents, and lots of Bible verses on one's Facebook page will do in a relatively short span of time.

APPENDIX TWO
WHERE TO FIND SERPENT-HANDLING CHURCHES
MENTIONED IN THE BOOK

JOLO, WEST VIRGINIA—CHURCH OF THE LORD JESUS: This historic congregation was once the most famous serpent-handling church, possibly because of its openness to the media. Bob and Barbara Elkins started house meetings in the late 1940s and founded the actual church in 1956. It is located in isolated McDowell County in the southernmost tip of the state. The church got reams of publicity in 1961 when Columbia Gaye Chafin Hagerman, Barbara's daughter, died of snakebite in 1961 while handling serpents in church. She refused medical treatment. The West Virginia state legislature nearly passed a law two years later making the handling of poisonous snakes a misdemeanor, but the Elkins family themselves testified against it and the law was never passed. The church was closed down around 2014 and, when I contacted its pastor, Harvey Payne, in early 2017, he had no plans to open it. If that ever changes, homecomings are every Labor Day weekend.

The Church of the Lord Jesus in Jolo, West Virginia, as of September 2011.

Directions: Find Interstate 81, which runs through western Virginia and from there, locate I-77 going north to Bluefield. There are two ways from Bluefield. The first is to take State Route 460 through Virginia (a very nice road) all the way to Grundy, which is close to the Kentucky state line. Grundy is also the location of the nearest hotels. (I recommend the Comfort Inn.) From Grundy, take Route 83 about twenty-five miles over the state line into West Virginia. It's a very pretty drive. Just after the state line, the road winds steeply down to Jolo, which is unincorporated. At the Marathon gas station, turn right on Route 635 and go about two miles. The church will be on your left. Or from Bluefield, take Route 52 west to Iaeger (about a ninety-minute drive), then turn south on Route 80. Continue to Bradshaw, then head right on Route 83. That takes you to Jolo in about two miles. Take a left on Route 635, and the church is two miles down the road to your left. The roads in this isolated corner of West Virginia are very good (thanks to the late Senator Robert Byrd).

MARSHALL, NORTH CAROLINA—HOUSE OF PRAYER IN THE NAME OF JESUS CHRIST: This church is in far western North Carolina not far from the Tennessee state line. John Brown is the pastor, and the

The House of Prayer in the Name of Jesus Christ in Marshall, North Carolina, pastored by John Brown.

church's annual homecoming is each second weekend in September. This church was remodeled and is quite lovely with inlaid wood floors inside, a veranda with benches at the front of the church, and a small porch in the back. Services are at 7:30 p.m. Saturdays.

Directions: From I-40 (near Knoxville), take exit 432A which will put you on Route 2570 heading east. Drive about twenty-one miles through some very pretty scenery to Hot Springs, North Carolina. Continue for another ten miles through town, over the river and up a mountain, then down, then up another mountain (passing the little community of Walnut at the top), and then head down the mountain to a red light. That is Lower Brush Creek Road. A school is on the left. If you go straight, you'll eventually end up in Mars Hill. Instead, take a right on Lower Brush, and follow it less than a mile until you get to Ledford and Crane Road. Take a left, go one-quarter mile to the house with a red roof. Around the bend on the right is the driveway to the church. One can get there from Hot Springs in about twenty to twenty-five minutes.

MIDDLESBORO, KENTUCKY—FULL GOSPEL TABERNACLE IN JESUS' NAME: Jamie Coots was the pastor of this church, which was heavily featured in the fall 2013 National Geographic Channel reality series *Snake*

The Full Gospel Tabernacle in Jesus' Name Church in Middlesboro, Kentucky, founded by the Coots family.

Salvation. Since Jamie's death by snakebite in February 2014, it's had several pastors, including his son, Cody, who is currently at the helm. Homecomings are usually the second weekend of August, and weekly services are 7:30 p.m. Wednesdays, 7:00 p.m. Saturdays, and 1:00 p.m. Sundays.

Directions: From 1-75 north of Knoxville, drive thirty-three miles and take exit 134, which puts you on Route 63 going through LaFollette. Drive another thirty miles toward Cumberland Gap National Park (a beautiful place worth a day's visit), then turn north and west on Rt. 25E and go through the tunnel. The tunnel puts you at the fringes of downtown Middlesboro. Take a left on Cumberland Ave., then another left on South 21st Street. This turns into Evans Drive. Stay to the right and don't take Holmes Road, which forks off to the left. After crossing some railroad tracks, go over three small hills (barely a mile), and at the end of the third one (more like a bump), you'll see the church on your left. It is very easy to miss if you're driving at night.

NEWPORT, TENNESSEE—EDWINA CHURCH OF GOD IN JESUS CHRIST'S NAME: This is pastored by Jimmy Morrow, who is a veteran in this movement. If you come by, ask to see his American primitive paintings (mostly of church scenes and Christian themes) and his serpent

The Edwina Church of God in Jesus Christ's Name in Newport, Tennessee, pastored by Jimmy Morrow.

handler dolls. He's an amazing artist. Services are 7:00 p.m. Fridays and 1:00 p.m. Sundays. Its homecoming is every second weekend in June.

Directions: From Knoxville, head east on I-40 and take exit 440. At the bottom of the ramp, turn left, go under the underpass, and take the second road (Picnic) to the right. There is a church sign posted there. Go about three hundred feet, then turn left onto Bloom Drive. Go one-quarter mile, and the church will be on your left at 1751 Bloom Drive.

SAND MOUNTAIN, ALABAMA—ROCK HOUSE HOLINESS CHURCH: The pastor, Billy Summerford, lives next to the church and is friendly. Homecomings are every Father's Day weekend. This was the church made famous in the 1995 book *Salvation on Sand Mountain.*

Pastored by Billy Summerford, Rock House Holiness Church is on Sand Mountain in northeastern Alabama. Photo by John Morgan.

Directions: From Huntsville, Alabama, head east (a little over an hour) to Scottsboro. Get on Veterans Drive and cross the river (going east). Drive 4.3 miles on Route 35 past the bridge going uphill. You will pass the Washington Park viewpoint over the Tennessee River, which is worth stopping for. Once up the mountain at a crossroads named Section, take a right on Route 43, a.k.a. Main Street South. Drive south for 5.7 miles. In the middle of this, at the 3.4-mile mark, you will go through a stop sign in Macedonia, which one can't really call a town. Continue south on 43 for another mile or so until you get to Rt. 415. Take a right. Drive 0.7 miles through one intersection and then down a long road—through a corn field—that dead ends at the church. There is no sign, but you can guess the locale from the parked cars in front and the light yellow building. Services are 7:00 p.m. Fridays and 6:00 p.m. Sundays.

CLAIRFIELD, TENNESSEE—ROCK CREEK HOUSE OF PRAYER: This is Andrew Hamblin's new church. Don't expect snake boxes there, as the author does not know whether the bylaws allow serpent handling at the place once pastored by his grandfather, Jimmy Bowman.

The Rock Creek House of Prayer in Clairfield, Tennessee, is a few steps away from an elementary school and a volunteer fire department.

Directions: From Knoxville, take I-75 north to exit 134, then take Routes 25w/63 about six miles east to downtown LaFollette. That's where 25w splits off to the left from 63 and heads up into the hills. Drive about 16 miles north up a wooded, winding road until you reach Highway 90, a rural route heading east. (You can also drive further north on I-75 to the Jellico turnoff at exit

160, then head south on 25w about eight miles to Highway 90). For the first three miles, Highway 90 winds up a mountain with steep drop-offs (and no guard rails) on your right until you reach a Smokies Market at the top. Drive another 11 miles east on 90 until you reach the tiny hamlet of Clairfield, marked by a post office on the left and a NAPA Auto Parts store on the right. Look for the elementary school at 6360 Highway 90 (on the right) where it intersects with Tracey Branch Road (to the left) just before a big hill. About 300 yards to the east of the school on the right are two white buildings with blue roofs. The larger one with the blue railings is the church. Bowman's grave is in the back. To get there, exit onto a gravel driveway alongside the highway that crosses the railroad tracks. Do not confuse it with the Missionary Baptist church next door. If you continue 20 miles further east on 90 (which changes to Highway 74 when you cross the Kentucky state line), you end up in Middlesboro.

BIBLIOGRAPHY

Barrouquere, Brett, and Travis Loller. "Memo to Serpent-Handling Pastor: What's OK in Ky. Isn't Cool in Tenn." Associated Press, February 14, 2013, published in *Knoxville News Sentinel*. https://www.knoxnews.com/news/2013/feb/14/memo-to-serpent-handling-pastor-whats-ok-in-ky/.

Braden, Beth. "Remaining Reptiles in Hamblin Case Euthanized for Parasite." *LaFollette (TN) Press,* January 20, 2014. http://www.lafollettepress.com/content/remaining-reptiles-hamblin-case-euthanized-parasite.

———. "Snake Citation: Charges Against Preacher May Spark Religious War with Serpent-Handling Congregation." *LaFollette (TN) Press,* November 15, 2013. http://www.lafollettepress.com/content/snake-citation.

Breed, Allen G. "Custody Fight for Snake Handlers' Orphans Pits Faith Against Safety." Associated Press, December 13, 1998, published in the *Los Angeles Times*. http://articles.latimes.com/1998/dec/13/news/mn-53450.

Brown, Fred, and Jeanne McDonald. *The Serpent Handlers: Three Families and Their Faith.* Winston-Salem, NC: John F. Blair, 2000.

Burnett, John. "Serpent Experts Try to Demystify Pentecostal Serpent Handling." National Public Radio, October 18, 2013. http://www.npr.org/2013/10/18/236997513/serpent-experts-try-to-demystify- pentecostal-snake-handling.

Coots, Jamie. "The Constitution Protects My Snake-Handling: It's an Exotic Religious Practice, Yes, but No Less Deserving of Protection." *Wall Street Journal,* October 3, 2013. http://online.wsj.com/news/articles/SB10001424052702303796404579101831593270054.

Covington, Dennis. *Salvation on Sand Mountain: Snake Handling and Redemption in Southern Appalachia.* 2009. Reprint, Cambridge, MA: Da Capo Press, 2009.

"Dead Pastor Violated Law." *TMZ,* February 17, 2014. http://www.tmz.com/2014/02/17/jamie-coots-snake-salvation-pastor-jamie-coots-kentucky-law-rattlesnake/.

De Choisy, Gemma. "Pastor Andrew Hamblin Would Rather Die or Go to Jail Rather Than Give Up Handling Snakes." *Buzzfeed.com,* January 3, 2014. https://www.buzzfeed.com/gemmadechoisy/pastor-andrew-hamblin-would-rather-go-to-jail-or-die-than-gi?utm_term=.eg7Oxbnb0#.bdrv8RgRX

Dreher, Rod. "Trump: Tribune of Poor, White People." *American Conservative,* July 22, 2016. http://www.theamericanconservative.com/dreher/trump-us-politics-poor-whites/.

Duin, Julia. "In West Virginia, Snake Handling Is Still Considered a Sign of Faith." *Washington Post Magazine,* November 13, 2011, 18–22.

———. (2012, April 7). "Reviving Faith by 'Taking Up Serpents': For a New Generation of Internet-Savvy Pentecostals, a Century-Old Practice Provides 'Anointing.'" *Wall Street Journal,* C3.

———. "Rev. Jamie Coots, Co-Star of 'Snake Salvation,' Dies after Rattlesnake Bite." *Wall Street Journal,* Speakeasy blog, February 17, 2015. http://blogs.wsj .com/speakeasy/2014/02/17/rev-jamie-coots-co-star-of-snake-salvation-dies -after-snakebite/.

———. "Serpent-Handling Pastor Profiled Earlier in Washington Post Dies of Rattlesnake Bite." *Washington Post,* May 29, 2012, C1. Also available online at http://www.washingtonpost.com/lifestyle/style/serpent-handling-pastor -profiled-earlier-in-washington-post-dies-from-rattlesnake- bite/2012/05/29 /gJQAJef5zU_story.html.

Estep, Bill. "Months after Snake-Handling Pastor's Death, His Son Recovering from Snake Bite." *Lexington Herald-Leader,* May 27, 2014. http://www.kentucky .com/2014/05/27/3261690/months-after-snake-handling-preachers.html.

Hardy, Kevin. "Even Unto Death." *Chattanooga Times Free Press,* February 2, 2014. http://projects.timesfreepress.com/2014/02/02/serpents/index.html.

Hood, Ralph W. "Contemporary Serpent Handling Sects of Appalachia." October 16, 2012. Virginia Commonwealth University archive. http://www.has.vcu .edu/wrs/profiles/SerpentHandlers.htm.

Hood, Ralph W., and W. Paul Williamson. *Them That Believe: The Power and Meaning of the Christian Serpent-Handling Tradition.* Berkeley: University of California Press, 2008.

Izbicki, Ashley. "Building Owner Evicts Snake-Handling LaFollete Pastor." WBIR-TV, Knoxville, June 19, 2014. http://www.wbir.com/story/news/local /2014/06/19/building-owner-evicts-snake-handling-lafollette-pastor/11000287/.

"Jolo Journal: When the Faithful Tempt the Serpent." *New York Times,* September 11, 1992. http://www.nytimes.com/1992/09/11/us/jolo-journal-when-the -faithful-tempt-the-serpent.html.

"Knoxville Zoo Caring for Snakes Seized from LaFollette Church." WBIR-TV, Knoxville, November 7, 2013. http://www.wbir.com/story/news/local/scott -campbell-morgan/2013/11/07/twra-cites-snake-handling-pastor-seizes-snakes /3466283/.

Kuruvilla, Carol. "'Snake Salvation' Pastor's Collection of 53 Venomous Snakes Seized by Wildlife Agents." *New York Daily News,* November 8, 2013. http:// www.nydailynews.com/news/national/53-poisonous-snakes-seized-snake -salvation-pastor-article-1.1511099#ixzz2k6DoWvYb.

"LaFollette Snake-Handling Pastor Arrested on Traffic Charges." WJHL-TV, Johnson City, TN, March 15, 2015. http://www.wjhl.com/story/24549418/ pastor-andrew-hamblin-arrested.

McNeal, Jill. "LaFollette Pastor Wants to Reverse Snake-Handling Ban." WATE-TV, Knoxville, July 9, 2012. http://www.wate.com/story/18985975 /lafollette-pastor-wants-to-reverse-snake-handling-ban.

Morrow, Jimmy, and Ralph W. Hood. *Handling Serpents: Pastor Jimmy Morrow's Narrative History of His Appalachian Jesus' Name Tradition.* Macon, GA: Mercer University Press, 2005.

Odom, Michael. "Dennis Covington's *Salvation on Sand Mountain:* Descent and Vision in the Southern Memoir." *Southern Literary Journal* 46, no. 1 (Fall 2013): 96–109.

Pond, Lauren. "Why I Watched a Snake-Handling Pastor Die for His Faith," *Washington Post,* May 31, 2012, C1. Also available online at https://www .washingtonpost.com/lifestyle/style/why-i-watched-a-snake-handling-pastor -die-for-his-faith/2012/05/31/gJQA3fRP5U_story.html.

Smietana, Bob. "Serpent Handler TV Star Has a New Cause: Religious Liberty." Religion News Service, November 12, 2013. http://www.religionnews.com/2013 /11/12/serpent-handler-tv-star-new-cause- religious-liberty/.

———. "Snake-Handling Believers Find Joy in Test of Faith." *Tennessean,* June 3, 2012, A1.

"Snake-Handling Preacher Turns Himself in to Campbell County Deputies, Ordered Held on $200K Bond," WATE-TV, Knoxville, March 15, 2015. http://wate.com /2015/03/15/snake-handling-preacher-under-investigation-in-campbell-co/.

"Wife, Friend, Testify Against Campbell County Snake-Handling Preacher on Assault, Reckless Endangerment Charges." WATE-TV, Knoxville, March 19, 2015. http://wate.com/2015/03/19/wife-friend-testify-against-campbell-county -snake-handling-preacher-on-assault-reckless-endangerment-charges/.

Williamson, Seth. "Awesome Music Trumps Serpent Handling at West Virginia Church." *Roanoke.com,* September 21, 2011. http://blogs.roanoke.com/cutnscratch /2011/09/awesome-music-trumps-serpent- handling-at-west-virginia-church/.

INDEX